The Gift Giver

*From the Brink of Hell to the
Hands of Healing*

By Richard Francis Xavier Bingold with
Nathaniel Worman

This Autobiography, written in novelistic form, complies with the
following Subject Index: Nonfiction, Inspirational, Spiritual,
Self-help, Religious, and Memoir.

First Edition: April, 2003

ISBN: 09740177-0-1 (soft cover 60# alkaline paper)
Library of Congress Control Number: 2003092955
Copyright: March 5th, 2003.

Cover Design: Anna McCullam, Artist, Braham, MN
and Richard Bingold, Author

Editors: Jacqui Robinson; Johannesburg, SA
James Costa; Elma, NY

Published by: Spirit Publishing
Alburg, VT

Manufactured in the United States of America

For ordering information:
Contact: Richard F.X. Bingold
Email: Pilrosary@vlink.net
Web Site: www.Pilrosary.com
1-800-788-4076

*Declaration: Some names of persons, places and organizations
have been changed to protect the innocent.*

Dedication

To my children;

Richard Dennis
James Edward
Barbara Elizabeth
Catherine Alicia
Patrick William
&
My wife Monique…

And Wayne Connick…
Who risked his life to save mine.

Table of Contents

Foreword

You are about to be inspired. Your heart is about to be touched. For here, Richard Bingold gives us the witness of his life—how God called him out of darkness into great light. It is the intriguing story of a lost soul—bound by alcohol, pride, self-ishness and sin—now free by the amazing power of God's Spirit. It is the story of another prodigal son returning to the loving arms of his Father and into the heart of the saving Son.

About to drown after an horrific boating accident in Florida, Richard became the object of God's grace when God sent a young boy to Richard's heroic rescue. In a hospital bed with multiple fractures and serious head injries, he had time to rethink his beleaguered life.

Inspired to go to Medjugorje in April 1993, Richard experienced a deeper miracle and was given a ministry to bring others to Jesus through Mary. Richard's life is truly amazing, often inspiring. He now is Mary's troubadour of faith and love, bringing her message of conversion, faith, hope, love, repentance and prayer to many, not only here in the United States, but to Ireland, England, Medjugorje and other lands as well.

Richard once ran with Eddie Egan of *The French Connection* fame. Now he follows Jesus to bring the good news of peace and holiness, love and mercy, kindness and sacrifice to a world badly in need of such graces.

To those who look upon him now and wonder,

"Is he for real?" he can answer,

"I know where you are coming from. Been there. Done that. But now no longer. I've got a life, a new life that only Christ can give. For that, I want to thank His mother for claiming me as one of her own."

Like St. Augustine before him, one can say of Richard, "Thou hast made us for Thyself, O Lord. And our hearts are restless until they rest in Thee."

As the familiar song goes, "I once was lost but now am found; was blind, but now I see."

I have known Richard for years now, and can attest that he is for real, really real; as authentic, humble, and honest as can be. I've watched him share his witness and seen hearts opened and touched. I've seen him pray over hundreds with his large, special hand-made rosary (from rocks from Medjugorje) and witnessed people being healed.

I feel so humble to know this wonderful servant of the Lord who is willing to go to one person or a hundred. It would take at least ten book to give a full of account of how Jesus and Mary have entered into his life. He is truly a troubadour of faith and love, a gentle giant who always remains a humble servant.

Two bishops, Bishop Jame Moynihan of Syracuse, New York, and Bishop Kenneth Angell of Burlington, Vermont, have endorsed his ministry. I endorse it as well.

O the depth of the riches and wisdom and knowledge of God!

How unsearchable are his judgements and how inscrutable his ways!

…From him and through him and to him are all things.

To him be glory forever. Amen. (Rom 11:33, 36).

> Father Bill McCarthy, MSA
> Co-Director
> *My Father's House*

Preface

This book speaks about a pilgrim, Richard Francis Xavier Bingold, who came to Medjugorje for existential reasons: to take steps as important as life itself: Thirsty, he came to drink; hungry he came to eat, and sick, he came to be healed.

In his journey, we are reminded of the voice of one crying out in the desert to make strait the way of the Lord God who chooses real life and blood people and concrete times to communicate His word. As God in the time Jesus chose Bethany across the Jordan to speak, so God in our time chooses where and when His mission is to continue.

For this reason, a new Bethany and a new Jerusalem will keep coming and never cease speaking to our hearts. God's disciples will never cease being called. Those people who received the Word, and those places where it happened, are called to speak in our time. The Spirit of God has consecrated them. For this reason, the testimony of this book is an echo of the bibical word of God spoken in our time.

Richard has been prepared and molded long enough to hear the Word. God never removed His presence. On the contrary, these pages show how many ways he has manifested Himself. God's work is real and obvious, but only at His places, at His times and in His ways. When a pilgrim is ready for it, God puts a seal of sacrament to it.

Richard grew up with the life of America—with the life of technical breakthroughs as well as those political, economic, and cultural events which affected his life and the life of his family from the very beginning. The major events of the Twentieth Century in the Western Hemisphere, influenced, built, and often destroyed lives. Richard and his family were caught up in this maelstrom.

This book, then, is the story of a life lived in our time, where unforeseen and uncontrollable events were often greater than human strength, and therefore created decisions and led to steps that influenced the thoughts of his family and himself, and its surroundings.

This book speaks about the miraculously gentle way of God where at every moment His hand was present, even at the most tragic times. This is the story of how events of the world, where for such a long time God took a backseat or even appeared to be totally absent, affected the life of an ordinary man.

However, in every page in some mysterious way it is being confirmed that there was not one single moment where God was not present. Already now, Richard with his pilgrimage and testimony, has reached and touched the lives and future of his family as well as the lives of thousands of people who have heard him speak and with whom he has prayed.

Those who read these pages will be reminded of bibical events happening in our times.

Father Svetozar Kraljevic
Medjugorge
July 9, 2001

Acknowledgements

Before and during the writing of this book, the thought that provoked me constantly was, "This book must be truthful testimony, because readers will ask themselves this very question. It has to be accurate throughout, even though certain names and events have had to be altered for personal reasons."

When I approached Nathaniel Worman about writing this book, he asked me why I wanted to. My answer then as now is simple and direct: If my journey through the heartache and joy, addiction and recovery, anger and foregiveness, of my life will help one person see himself or herself in a different light, then the toil and pain of writing this book and opening old wounds will have been worth it.

I have tried to be honest, even to the point of feeling again the pain of the events that took me astray. Not only did I have to deal with my own conscience, I was being queried—often cross-examined—by a professional journalist, Nat, who needed the truth in order to put everything into perspective.

He painstakingly sought out all the evidence he could lay his hands on—personal background, names and dates and events and failures—in order to piece together the puzzle of my life. At times, he looked at me and wondered: Who is this man? Is he being completely honest? A lie here, a deliberate side-stepping of the truth there, would have contaminated the whole effort. I knew he had to examine every detail in order to make a path through my life that the reader could follow and come away believing.

Readers will draw their own conclusions, perhaps different from ours. Nat had to exercise imagination to get through the maze of information I gave him during the hundred or more interviews and conversations we had over a two-year period. In addition, he read my journals and listened to tapes in which I spoke of the spiritual crisis and climaxes of my life. He spoke to family members and friends. He attended my prayer meetings and watched as I settled the Pilgrim Rosary on the shoulders of one suffering person after another.

We have worked diligently to present the reader a work that can stand on its own, the true testimony of a life that had gone astray, of a man who had caused his family and friends untold pain. The true testimony to the Lord's Divine Mercy and how, no matter how ill we behave, He stands ready to forgive, heal, and use us, if only we surrender our will to His.

Every event in this book is true. Other events, that caused others great pain and suffering, had to go unwritten in order to protect the innocent, a decision arrived at after long discernment and much love.

Heartfelt thanks are in order for many people.

To Nat Worman for his patience, his work ethic, his insight, and above all his friendship. He has my unending admiration. I enjoyed working with him to the end. His ability to catch my emotions and thoughts and put them and my life into words overwhelms me.

To Jim Costa, the retired teacher of Elma, New York. His patient attention to every word, sentence, paragraph and chapter, and his brilliant critiques, gave the book the virtues it possesses.

To the Reverend Father William (Bill) McCarthy, MSA, co-founder of My Father's House, a retreat center in Moodus, Connecticut, for his Christ-like manner in always being "there" for me, as priest and friend, advisor and guide.

To the Reverend Father Svetozar Kraljevic, OFM, Franciscan priest in Bosnia-Herzegovina, my deepest thanks for his guidance and his friendship; his willingness to listen to me and trust in me and for graciously calling me "The Rosary Man."

To my children and my wife Monique for standing by me through the pain and the suffering.

To Richard, James, Barbara, Catherine, and Patrick, my children: I love you all more than life itself.

Finally, a extra measure of gratitude to Wayne Connick, Pomano Beach, Florida, whose courage, quick-thinking, tenacity, amazing strength, and calm confidence at the moment of crisis, saved me from drowning and to whom I owe my life and the opportunity to find myself. I believe the Lord gave him all he needed to accomplish an impossible task, an unbelievable rescue.

Greater love hath no man than this, that a man lay down his life for his friends. John 15:13

Thank you, Wayne.

Chapter One

Storm Warnings

When I hustled across the dark parking lot that stretched along the marina to Bootleggers Bar, I could see that this was no night for a boat ride and it was a boat ride the guy I was supposed to meet had in mind. The boats and docks jerked against their moorings and the palm tree fronds flapped and I could see the Hillsboro Inlet lighthouse blinking its gloomy warnings.

But one more risk in my life as a private investigator was the least of my worries. Though I had been working with two famous New York cops and watched how they operated, all you really needed in this business was common sense and the right instincts. I had both. What really worried me was the mess my life was becoming and, because of it, what had happened in the last four hours.

Ahead of me, a woman's heels crunched the gravel, her form outlined by the overhead lights that drenched the broad padded door of the bar in a dull red. Two men, one from each side, closed in on her and I started forward. But when they reached her elbows, she turned to one and then to the other and the night air carried her laughter as all in one smooth motion the men picked her up, all three laughing now and the woman crying out,

"Oh, you two devils," her tiny feet treading air then touching earth, the padded door opening for their passage into the blue smoke and clinking glasses, the roar and ripple of men's and women's voices intertwined.

I stopped in mid-stride. Put *her* out of your mind. Put the last four hours aside. Focus on your job—on Peter Short, the guy the agent sent you here to watch. And I hurried on ahead, but when I reached the padded door instead of turning the knob, I turned away, took several steps into a shadow, stopped again, and peered into the dark. Watery chains clinked beneath the misty light of the marina and the lighthouse blinked its warnings. I smelled salt and thought of seaweed and its tangle of coils, loops, and knots, and felt suffocated and angry. I broke out a cigar. Two couples followed each other into the bar. I took a several draws and thought, How had those last four hours gone? What had I been doing…

…Not in any hurry, a good cigar between my teeth, I had held to the fast lane when I drove down here from Joe McLaughlin's party where I had gone from the airport. Monique, my second wife, was flying back home to Montreal to stay with her family for a few weeks. To think things over.

"Must you take all these chances?" she had asked one more time. "Egan, ugh. So a movie, whatever it was, told the story of his life. And then, there's your friend, Bob Danner. Both of them with pictures in the paper. For what? You keep telling me, but I can't understand it, like you'd rather be them than you."

"The *French Connection*.The movie was called *The French Connection*," I said, cheerful, patient, trying to smile.

"No, Dick, I *know* the movie. I *know* Gene Hackman was the guy named Popeye and that he was supposed to be Egan. But what…"

"Women are supposed to be thrilled by movies and actors …"

"Dick."

"What did Egan do in real life? Why was his name on TV and in the newspapers? He did what he did in the movie. He…

I've told you all of this. Are you listening?"

Monique was barely listening, wanting to be gone. I was reciting a kind of mantra; we'd both heard it before and now it had meaning only to me, but I muddled on. "Egan was a detective for the New York City police and made the biggest drug-bust in the city's history. And Danner, a chief of detectives, recovered the Star of India sapphire stolen from a museum."

"So?"

"So it doesn't hurt being in business with two famous cops."

Then suddenly, she was paying attention. Her lovely face changed color. She was angry. Her eyes filled with tears. "And of course you're safe being in business with two famous cops." She bit her lip and said, "You've got a wife, Dick," and I brushed on by and said,

"It helps working with guys who know what they're doing," worried, that I had not heard something she'd said.

She looked away, then down, and picked up her bag before I could do it for her.

"Does drinking help?" she asked, and, without kissing me goodbye, turned and went down the ramp until she faded into the crowd. I waited, and looked for her, but when she didn't reappear, I turned away, and headed for Joe's party.

On my way, I blasted my horn at an old biddy in a red Cadillac the length of a football field and remembered the words I hadn't taken in, "You've got a wife, Dick," and turned fullface and glared at the old woman and slammed the accelerator to the floor and looked up in time to swerve by an ambulance going full speed with its siren screaming. I was glad to get to Joe McLaughlin's party, an open house to celebrate his new real estate office, and have a few minutes with Joe before the crowd arrived.

"Why the gloom?" he had asked me when I ambled in and I told him I'd had a bad night, then went on about a bartender our agency had been hired to watch and how with match sticks he kept track of what he had pocketed and had to account for at the end of the night. Joe began several times to tell me about himself, but I interrupted and went on about Dick Bingold and finally on our third or fourth drink he said irritably, "What's stuck in your craw, Bingold?"

"It's amazing," I went on, "how these bartenders fool themselves and think they're getting away with it and their lives get more and more complicated when all they need to do is tell the truth. The truth simplifies your life."

I stared into my Scotch and water and saw a bubble trapped at the bottom of the glass and made sure it worked its way to the surface then finished off my drink. Behind us, the party was gathering steam, glasses clinked and the voices of women chimed.

"Joe, darling."

"Louise," Joe said, standing up, his eyes going from her to me and back. "Meet my old buddy, Dick Bingold." And I got up, sure she would be friendly, but she turned away, saying, "Take care of old buddies, then."

"Yeah," I said, thinking suddenly of something I'd forgotten, that I was supposed to have picked up my nine-year-old daughter, Catherine, for a movie, and I went on, telling Joe about a priest I had known who said what often happens to us is that we betray our own natures and that we keep on betraying our own true selves until we hit bottom and wake up.

"Thanks," I said to Joe, hearing him at last. "Straight Scotch would be fine," and the drink appeared and Joe said:

"Y'know you don't deserve her, don't you? A beautiful woman like Monique and an ugly guy like you."

I smiled, pretending for the moment that I didn't know what he was talking about, hoping he'd feel stupid bringing up my wife when we were just two buddies shooting the breeze. I finished off the new drink and my beeper went off.

We stood up and Joe frowned and I said, "Like all women she's afraid—afraid that one of these days I'll be found face down in the Atlantic and then there's the old alcohol question and the question of—that I'm a work-alcoholic." I stopped, then said, "She's a good girl," and Joe nodded, about to turn away, then lifted his face toward the hallway where the phone was and we drifted there and stood for a moment in the shadow.

"The truth is," he said, "guys don't know when they have it good. Like me. Not that there is a thing wrong—look, Monique's got looks *and* a brain. I mean, what's up with you, Bingold? Do you get me?"

I smiled and felt lousy and Joe said, "Well, at least you're smiling," turned to go, then came back, saying, "Who says you drink a lot? We have good times, that's all. Sure you drink. We're not alcoholics. We're not druggies. We're right there Monday morning, back at work, digging and scratching out a living. We never let our families down."

"Smiling?" I asked, swallowing hard, thinking of *my* family, then putting the thought aside.

"What's that your attorney calls you. What's his name?"

"Hennekam. Dick Hennekam. He says that most of my schemes are pie-in-the-sky. He calls me the Blue Sky Man."

"Blue Sky Man. I like it. Gotta go. You know what my ex said? Don't get a swelled head. Don't get sore. She said she felt good around you—not too safe, but good. 'He's fun. I love his stories,' she said. But you know my ex—has her own thoughts. 'Dick seems cut loose from any moorings,' she said. 'Is he Catholic?' she asked me and answered her own question. 'I don't think he's Catholic.'"

"What did you tell her?"

"I said you were a good Catholic and she asked me where was the evidence?"

"No wonder you two broke up," I said, staring at the phone booth.

"Seems it doesn't help being Catholic."

"It's worse," I said, and my beeper went off a second time.

"Worse?"

"Demanding. Our faith is a demanding faith and the annulment is a good example because, you see, it recognizes the truth, it…"

"Who's talking about annulment?

"…recognizes the truth that a marriage from the beginning had the seeds of its own death and when you dig down to those seeds you got to face the pain and the question, 'Is something wrong with *me*. Am I *entitled* to an annulment?' And when you try to answer that question, you got to look straight into the mirror and face Dick Bingold."

"Hey, there, Joe. Joe, old man. I'm Robby. Robby Waring."

Joe turned, shook his hand, said, "I'll be right with you Robby," and turned back to me.

"Look, Dick, I know you take these things seriously, but you went ahead and married Monique without an annulment. You just went ahead and you married outside the church, without an annulment and did hitting that rock break you up? All I'm saying, is that things are fine. You worry about the wrong things."

"Who, me? Worry? Like Ali, I float."

"Yeah, you float, you oaf. You're affable, but you don't float."

We laughed and I felt beat up and excited and went out into the booth and dialed the number and on the other end of the line was an agent of the Organized Crime Bureau, telling me that one of the prime suspects in a drug-smuggling business, Peter Short, was at Bootleggers. Would I see what he was up to? We knew him as a partner in Continental Seafoods and were now almost certain that inside the bellies of its fish were tiny packets of cocaine. He knew me as a mortgage broker dickering with a bank to obtain a mortgage for him so that he could buy a $450,000 seafront estate...

I stood a few minutes longer in the shadow by the padded door, listening to the boats and docks jerking at their moorings and feeling the wind blow my cigar's smoke away and some of my guilt with it. Joe was right. The annulment would take care of itself. Monique and I would be just fine. In my mind's eye I saw the woman's tiny feet treading air and I seemed to hear in the tangle of seaweed Monique's voice, saying, "You've got..." But I sauntered out of the shadow into the red light and turned the knob on the padded door and went inside.

Chapter Two

Lost and Alone

Through the blue haze of cigarette and cigar smoke, I picked out the regulars, from Sammy, one of the powerful underworld bosses, to a quiet table of men and women of Ft. Lauderdale's wealthy and exclusive class, to loud tables of new money, to guys like me, tanned, middle-aged, and on the prowl. Single women, burned everywhere by the sun, lounged and laughed.

"Dick, buddy. My old buddy," Sammy called out.

"Yeah, Sammy?"

"How come you never ask me for anything?"

"Because I don't need anything," I said, and went on up the bar where I had spotted Peter Short, while behind me I heard Sammy saying above the chuckling of his cronies, "That's our boy, Dicky Bingold. Affable. Gutsy. A cool dude. Had a forty-five stuck into his gut and the trigger pulled. Know what? Misfire." Loud guffaws.

Then Peter Short's voice came clear.

"She does seventy in any sea, up one side of a swell, down the other," he was saying to a woman in red and two young guys, carpenters, who had worked for me before I became a private eye full time.

"Why, Mr. Bingold, here you are," Peter Short said, putting a sarcastic twist on "mister." "Hey, there, bartender, the drinks are on yours truly, Peter Short."

"The usual?" the bartender asked and I said "the usual" and

a short glass with ice and Johnny Walker Black Scotch whiskey and very little water slid my way and I lit a cigar and blew the smoke toward the ceiling and winked and wished Peter good health and he put his shoulder to me and glanced up, searching my face for a split second, then said,

"Hey, man, you look like John Wayne. Anybody ever tell you you look like John Wayne? You walk like John Wayne?"

"Seventy-miles-per-hour, Peter?"

"What, say?" Peter asked, then shot a glance over my shoulder when to the sound of breaking glass a gust of wind blew a door shut, his eyes dancing nervously back to intercept my gaze then frowning and then making his lips smile. "You know, my racer. I've invited you take a ride and tonight's the night. A Scarab Wellcraft. One slick sea-going racer. Know what I'm beginning to think? Know what I think you think? You think I'm not good for it. You're an affable guy, but you think," he said, turning to face me and reaching a finger out to tap me on the collar of my flowered shirt, "that…"

"Banks are slow, banks are careful, Peter," I said, drawing back, trying to stay cool and focused, irritated by his irritation and noticing once again that he was a bully at heart.

His head bobbed. He drank. He smiled. He looked at and around me and back at me, barely listening, planning something, and when I downed my drink, he winked at the bartender and another Scotch and water sat there and his face sat there, an inch from mine, a look in the fractured blue of his eyes that carried a warning.

"Paperwork, Peter," I said, leaning away. I wanted to keep him in focus, keep a step ahead of him.

"Oh, sure, paperwork. Who hasn't heard that line before? Where I come from all you need is a handshake. Understand? Know what I mean?" His bad breath and aftershave were a deadly mixture. "Because if you don't…Look. That racer cost a cool… Hey, come see," and he pushed away from the bar, then came back and sat down. "Look, Dick, that racer cost me sixty-eight thousand. If I'm good for sixty-eight thousand how come your bank…"

"Not *my* bank, Peter."

"*Well? Well*, are you a hotshot broker or not?"

His eyes slits, his nose diving on each "*well*," he was suddenly truculent. "*Well*, y'must know that Peter Short knows other brokers. Has other *contacts*."

He steadied himself, reached a hand to his left , snapped his fingers, and brought the hand with a drink in it back to his lips. I knew the bartender. I knew that he would have gladly broken Peter's jaw for that bit of insolence. I would have helped him. I knew Peter's kind. A small, fine-boned man, an axe-shaped head on a muscular neck, he bullied with sudden darting lunges then laughed when his bluff failed.

Now he did just that, banged out a laugh and waved a hand at me and yelled to the bartender for another round of the same and we launched into real drinking, talked lies and nonsense and chewed handfuls of peanuts and let our glances turn to long stares that fitted into answering stares of eyes above bare shoulders and the sunny weight of scantily-sheathed bodies.

"No, he was killed," I heard one of the carpenters say.

"I know a simpler recipe for lasagna than that," I was saying to a pair of eyes.

"Who was killed?" his buddy asked.

In a glass, ice rattled. A door banged shut. "Never knew his name. Battered silly. Beyond recognition. Crashed into a jetty."

"Crazy," I heard Peter say. "The Hillsboro Inlet jetty?"

"Tell me," the pair of eyes said. "I like things simple."

"Oh, hell no. Down the coast. A racing boat at night."

"Stupid," Peter yelled, then snorted, pushed away from the bar, and stood up.

The pair of eyes looked at me. I looked at Peter and blew smoke from my cigar and then clenched it between my teeth.

"Well! Enough! Enough! I know you, Dick. You think Short means short. Short of cash." He cocked his head toward the patio and marina. "So just let Peter Short teach you a lesson."

I turned and smiled and said goodbye and we made our way through the crowd and blue smoke, out of the bar, across the parking lot to the marina and down some steps and on to docks and among boats jerking at their moorings. And riding there in the dusky moons of dancing lights was that beautiful sea-going racer. A wave rolling under the floating dock made Peter do the two-step. One of the carpenters knelt and ran his hand over the trim. My eye ran along the red stripe around the racer's sleek deep-V white hull, light and fragile and ready for speed. Ever since I flew along streets on my bike a kid of eight delivering dry cleaning, nothing pleased me more than speed, being fast and first.

Peter squinted at me through the bobbing lights and I heard over the rising wind, "Here's a thought. Freeport. The Grand Bahamas. Seventy miles out there in the dark and we'll be there in an hour. How about it?"

I looked down at him. His eyes glinted. His voice was sharp, like a scream held in. In the past two hours I had matched him drink for drink, a dozen, maybe more. He had disappeared from the bar several times. Now I wondered: Has this guy been sniffing cocaine too?

Leaving Ft. Lauderdale behind and heading north, we skimmed by Lauderdale-by-the-Sea, Sea Ranch Lakes, Pompano Beach, and Lighthouse Point where before my divorce I had lived with my children and my first wife, Beth, in a house worth two-hundred thousand dollars.

We sped through the Intracoastal Waterway, and by a marina where, after my divorce and broke, I lived on my boat, the only thing the divorce decree let me keep. We stopped at the Cove Restaurant for a couple of six-packs of beer, then drove through the gathering gloom toward Hillsboro Inlet, the jetty exit and the open sea.

"Different fuel for different engines!" Peter shouted, holding the beer aloft.

The wind had picked up. You could see in the dark the whitecaps of larger waves. Peter's eyes gleamed. We approached the place where the arms of the jetty, one from the north, the other from the south, almost meet and leave a narrow opening.

"Let's see what this baby will do!" Peter shouted over the roar of wind and engines. "Let's see if we can make Freeport in *less* than an hour."

"Yeah," I shouted back, thinking two things at once. How I'd feel out there, free, on the open sea, in the dark, in a high speed racer, the foam flying. And, I thought, maybe now he'll show his hand. At that, Peter ducked and the Scarab picked up speed.

"She's got more power than that!" Peter shouted, drawing back from the throttle and turning to me. Now I could see in the light of the orangish dash lights his face in the dark wind and from the corner of my eye, the carpenters, beers in their hands, smiles on their faces, sitting by the huge engines.

Peter stared for a moment at a spot below my chin, then reached his forefinger toward me and touched my medal of the Sacred Heart that lay against my chest in the "V" of my flowered shirt.

"For good luck," he said, suddenly solemn. "You always wear that?"

"I always wear that," I repeated, feeling like my private space had been invaded. Feeling like I had been accused. Angry that he had touched what once had belonged to my dad.

"You don't seem the type. Reckless. Full of life and all that," he said, sinking to sentimentality. "An old girl friend of mine, now, was always praying to the Virgin Mary. Always calling on the Virgin. Always going to…What you Catholics call it? Mass?'

He drew sideways, toward the controls.

"Mass."

"You go to Mass all the time, you Catholics. Every Sunday. Do you go every Sunday?"

"Every Sunday," I lied.

"And confess?"

"And confess," I lied a second time and told myself I wasn't lying.

The boat flew. It was strange. It seemed we stood in a hollow, protected from the dark wind, from the night and the waves. Then Peter Short did it: he lurched sideways and down and I heard the throttle slam forward into its last notch.

"Well, *mother!*" he shouted.

And I saw what he saw and we knew it was all over. To our right a gleam showed us the open sea. To our left there were nothing but waves jumping up and falling back, like jaws with white caps for teeth chomping on the rocks. Instead of the sea opening out the wet rocks of the jetty closed in.

Gagging and spitting blood and salt water, I woke in the dark to find that the boat had collapsed on me like an accordian, pinning me between the engines and the windshield. The only lights were the dismal city-glow far up in the sky and the shimmering orange of waves rolling over my shoulders.

I heard a voice, Short's, calling, and saw his hand reaching toward me. Outraged at his stupidity, I worked loose my one good fist and swung. He ducked and yelled, "To hell with you!" and backed off, turned about, and clambered out on all fours, his boney fanny outlined against the black night.

And I was alone. The waves washed and hissed. The boat lurched, dropped deeper, and held. I gagged on the colored water, convinced it was my blood. I remember thinking, thinking madly, I'm here, I'm here and I can't move. Thinking furiously, This is it. This is it. And then: No, No. Oh, no, it can't be! And then I said weakly, speaking to the boat and the orange smear of sunken panel lights, "Hold on!" And that perfectly useless remark forced on me the knowledge that I was seconds away from death and I had not even called on God for help and foregiveness because the most devastating thought in the world had driven God out of my mind: I was in a state of perdition and headed for Hell and I could say nothing to save myself.

Hammered by waves, the hull wrenched and released me and I sank to my neck. I gagged and spat and put my head back and opened my mouth and yelled,

"Help."

One arm lifeless, I reached out with the other and grabbed a rod as the waves lifted me up and let me down. Outlined against the sky-glow of city lights, I thought I saw several shadowy forms and a bobbing boat. It was no such thing. A wave larger than all the others, pushed me aside and broke my grip. The forms were a mere dream. A dream of the past, of my life, of those things I had done and left undone, a misty shimmering path carrying me through time, back to childhood, back to my beginnings.

Chapter Three

Hair-Burning & the Blessed Smile

"Little *sister*," my brother said, tormenting me, pouring something sticky and smelly on my head.

"Uncle Bill," I called out. "Where are you, Uncle Bill?"

"Gone. Gone. Uncle Bill's gone," John sang, pushing me into the corner. I smelled the dust and the sticky stuff and guessed that here again I was somebody in one of John's plays—and I let out a wail.

"Cry baby, cry baby," he taunted, rubbing the sticky stuff into my curls. "Shirley, Shirley, Shirley. Shirley Temple curls," he whispered, rubbing.

"Mom," I cried. "Mom."

"Mom's gone Christmas shopping, but not for you. Only for me. They found you in a garbage can and who could like anyone found in a garbage can?"

John had me cornered, between the sofa and the wall. "My friends say you're my little sister. We'll see about that. We'll see about those curls," he whispered, pushing me down and leaving me snuffling, his voice coming from the kitchen where there was the sound of opening and closing cupboards and drawers, shouting, "I found the matches!"

I ducked and thought of Dad running his hand through my curls and how he chuckled. I knew he liked them. Mother called them Shirley Temple curls. Why didn't she protect me from John? She didn't say a word to him when he threw the prickly flowers into my face.

There were big stones with marks. "Greens, my family, are buried here," Mom said. "I was already doing housework when I was your age, John. I took care of six brothers and sisters when I was sixteen."

John ran and shouted. Dad put his arm around me.

"Your great grandfather Karl's buried here," he said, running his hand through my curls. He chuckled. "He was a baron from Bavaria. Baron von Bingold. A beautiful door. He packed it like a Christmas present." John was quiet, listening. "When hoodlums jumped him one night, he threw one of them through the door. Smashed that beautiful door to smithereens."

"Killed him," John whispered.

"John," mother said.

Dad talked in his story-telling voice. "Your great grandfather raised carriage horses on the north end of the Island. Manhattan Island. He was a giant and made money wrestling then bought the land. Then he invested the money in businesses."

"Bars," John said. "Four bars."

"Oh, John," Mom said.

Then the flowers hit me and I cried.

John came running from the kitchen, shaking the box of matches.

"You're Joan of Arc," John whispered happily, the match lit, held close to my curls and the greasy stuff now, his hand pushing my face between the sofa and the wall.

I wailed and wailed, hoping the lady next door would hear. She made me feel like mothers make you feel. One time she hugged me and kissed my neck. Some day I would write her a letter and tell her how much I liked her. One, two, three, maybe four letters. She wouldn't push me off her lap like my mother did. I ran and jumped and bang! I hit the floor.

John pushed harder, one hand gripping my curls, the other holding the lit match. Mom wore the Lord dangling from her neck and once when she was in her bed, I saw the Lord resting on one of her softnesses. I heard her whisper with her eyes closed, "Blessedvirginmary." And now when I repeated that word, John laughed and laughed and put the match to my curls and they burst into flame, darting into my eyes and mouth and stinging my ears..

"Here! Here!"

It was Uncle Bill Hayde's voice and I was coughing and spitting and sinking into the dark when he whipped off his jacket to smother the flames and then sat me down in a chair and I wailed and through my tears I saw John run away.

"There, there," Uncle Bill said. "What a stink. My god, what a stink. John? John where are you? What the devil's been going on here? John!"

John appeared, Uncle Bill turned and jerked forward and grabbed him by the shoulders, picked him up, shook him once, and set him down, saying, "Don't let me catch you *ever* pulling a trick like that again. Hear me?"

When Mom came back breathing hard and carrying big bags that rustled, she puffed into the apartment and looked about and the minute I saw her I burst out crying

"What's that odor, Bill?" she asked my uncle, and I felt her hand on my head and heard her say quietly to herself, "Your curls, son." She sniffed. "Burned." She was very quiet and I heard her say goodbye to Uncle Bill quietly and then I heard her say without raising her voice, "John."

I heard the door to the cupboard open and close and I heard the cat-o-nine-tails' stinging the back of John's legs and I heard John scream and Mom sat me down in a hot tub and scrubbed me all over and dressed me and sat me down to hot stew.

"Cry baby," John said.

"Eat, young man," she said, turning to John. "And don't hold your finger up. That's *girlish.*"

Snug in bed behind my eyes, it was black, but when a hand scratched my head through my curls, I knew it was Dad's.

"They do smell," he said very quietly. "Did John put that grease in your curls?"

I moved my head.

"I thought so."

His hand squeezed my shoulder and when he leaned down and kissed me goodnight I knew he didn't blame me and I knew he wasn't mad at me.

I heard him stand up and way up there in the dark I heard him say, "What d'ya think, Son? Time to cut them off? You're a big boy now. What d'ya think?"

I heard a sigh and woke to the sun coming up.

Sun through the sacistry window lit up Father Nolan's glasses and then his naked wrinkled elbow and then his glasses again and now his mouth when he said, "Tell me, Dick, what was going on out there?" He hung his vestment on the top peg, above mine. Mass was over and he was angry.

When I opened my mouth and began, "Father," the sun seemed to burn brighter on his white, very white vestment and my white prayer book and my white shoes and my white pants and white jacket and the open air rushing and Dad beside me driving my cousin's convertible all came back to me.

"Hold your head up and stand straight," Mother said to me as she saw us out the door. "And behave this time." She wouldn't let me forget my first confession when, upon hearing the priest's voice through the grill, I had dropped from my seat to the floor and, on

all fours, had crawled beneath the confessional door, across an aisle and up toward the altar under three rows of pews. There I popped up and sat at innocent attention until a nun grabbed my shoulder painfully and marched me back to the waiting priest.

"Yes, Mom," I said.

She was staying home to cook and get the house ready for family and guests for my first communion celebration. She was staying home to care for the intruder, our new family member, my little sister, Irene.

Dad, driving that convertible, was taking me to St. Nicholas Tolentine Church where I would join my St. Nicholas Tolentine Grade School classmates. Dad gripped my hand as we drove steadily through the sun and I pictured last night in his basement workshop where I put the finishing touches on my model airplane and he had said, "Son, I'll be changing jobs." I had looked up. "The Germans sank the boat that carried all the cars I had ordered." Steady as a rock, he looked at me. I looked back at him and I was short of breath. I loved him.

"S-s-sankthem?"

"Sank them. A German sub torpedoed the ship."

From the seat of the car I saw the cloud of Communion white my classmates made, wearing their white jackets and holding their white prayer books, and I joined the cloud and we trod through the solemn half-light toward our pews, reserved for us up front. Perfumes and soap filled the air and proud faces of fathers looked on from all sides. The mothers looked on with worried faces, afraid of mistakes.

"Well, Richard?" Father Nolan said, adjusting his black jacket and the crucifix. When I just stood and looked at him, he leaned forward and said, "And why, tell me, didn't you ring the bell on time? You looked dazed." He tapped the side his head.

"Dazed?" I asked, gaining time. I was afraid. I didn't want to admit that I had been in a daze, that I hadn't heard him whisper, "Richard, the bell" the first time, and I only came awake on the repeat.

The heat of his fault-finding burned my face and brought to mind how Mom made me feel when spotting an error on my homework her hand lashed out and hit me night afternight with such force I felt sick and dizzy. Red marks were left on the back of my legs from her cat-o-nine-tails and blisters on my fingers when she held them over the gas stove flame. I would go to bed sick at heart only to be waked by her smile the next morning with the news that she was taking John and me on a shopping tour to buy new clothes. Bacon and eggs and hot buttered toast would be on the table for breakfast and at noon we would be treated at Woolworth's Five & Dime with ice cream sodas while Mom spooned up her hot custard.

"Richard? Richard, do you hear me? Are you in a daze again? Answer me. Answer me now. I require an explanation."

Father Nolan's nose was a foot from my nose and his voice so sharp and dark his words hit me like hot stones. I flinched, then coughed to cover up my fear.

"Yes, Father," I began, stopped, looked over his shoulder at the sacistry window where the sun had been but that was now a black hole of cloud and then back into the room where I located Father Nolan's face again and blurted, "She smiled at me, Father. She smiled."

"Who smiled?" Father Nolan came back at me, jumping on the word "smiled."

He looked at me. I looked back at him. "You're girl friend?" he asked, interested, irritated.

"No, Father," I said straight out, "the Blessed Virgin Mary smiled at me. She…"

"Well," Father Nolan snorted. "Don't let it happen again."

Chapter Four

Mother and Son

"Where's John these days?"

Did Coach Lapp ask that question to torment me? Whenever I ran into him, he would frown, then ask me that question and I came to the conclusion that he didn't like me because he didn't like my brother. I was breathing hard. I had just run from my last class.

"The City," I said, and thought, *"If I'm not home in time for supper, I'll catch it from Mom."*

"Oh, the City, is it," Coach Lapp said, looking first at a yellow pad on a clip board then down at a stopwatch and then away.

In a distant field a wood bat hit a baseball hard. Pale air smelled like Mother's clean laundry. The sun spread all over the field and lit up two tiny figures, a girl who stood at the brick corner of the high school building and a runner at the farthest thin arc of the cinder track.

"That's Bobby Lippmeir," Coach Lapp said. "He'll go far. Goes to Georgetown next year." He turned back to me, "What's he doing in the city?"

"Wall Street," I lied. I didn't want to say, "Actor," because that could mean only one thing to Coach Lapp. I knew why. On my way to the old man's apartment (I hated going there, he was so skinny and weak), I met John by chance at a busy corner, the light changing, yellow taxis rushing at me, people hurrying by me.

"*Hi, Dick,*" *he had shouted, then said aside to his friend,* "*My brother, Dick.*"

And the man had replied, "*Oh, dear, your brother.*"

For hours afterward, I didn't know why, my face burned with shame and embarrassment, even as I stood in the airless fourth-floor walk-up on 23rd St. where the old man, James Lynch, a distant relative of Mom's, was living out his days. I smiled. He frowned, and said,

"*Why you in such an all-fired hurry, boy?*"

I was there to pick up the container of the meal Mom had me deliver the day before.

"*So I don't waste any time getting back to you with a hot meal,*" *I said, smiling.*

"*You're a smart alec, I believe,*" *the old man said.* "*A fast tongue. Well, get along. Success makes a failure of your kind. With me, your smile will get you exactly nowhere. The only hope I hold out for you is that your mother came from Connemara.*"

"*Yessir,*" *I said and left and on the subway, heading home, I realized why I felt ashamed. Why Mom and Dad seldom talked about John: He had shamed them. He was queer. A fairy. A smile from a man's powdery face came at me across the row of subway seats and it was all I could do to keep from throwing up. But I made it home and went to bed early.*

Bobby Lippmeir appeared life-size to our left, his neat track shoes flickering sun and snapping cinders. Coach Lapp pushed down on his watch, looked at it, then looked up and yelled, "Four minutes, six, Bobby! Cool off." But Lippmeir didn't break stride when he called out, "One more lap, Coach."

And I took out after him, my heart pumping with excitement. Bobby Lippmeir widened the gap between us and when I ran faster, he made it still wider. I poured it on for several more laps and when I crossed the finish line, Bobby Lippmeir was standing by Coach Lapp who was talking to Bobby but looking at me.

"Good going, Bobby ," Coach Lapp was saying as I trotted up to them. Then he drew Bobby aside, put his arm around him, and spoke to him quietly, out of earshot. My face was red with the run and embarrassment. What was I trying to prove? I looked through the sunlight and saw the girl. Bobby Lippmeir went one way and I went the other. But before I had taken a half dozen steps, I got the surprise of my life: Coach Lapp had called my name. When I ambled up to him, he was looking at his watch and holding the stub of a pencil against the yellow pad and clipboard.

"Bingold," he said, not looking up, "you did pretty well in gymnastics—as I recall." He looked back and forth between the pencil and his watch.

"Yessir," I said. "I scored all 'tens.'"

"Yes, of course, perfect 'tens.' And they tell me you box, and…"

"Yeah," I jumped in. "Dad taught me to box. Knocked me out once. He fought Tunney to a three-round draw and…"

"…but I didn't know you could run," he went on, not listening. "Your brother was certainly no runner."

And, not sure at all whether I was telling the truth, I blurted out, "I can do a mile in four minutes flat."

"Can you now? You just showed me what might have been a six-minute mile. You? A four-minute mile?"

"I was wearing old sneakers," I said, and he laughed and I managed a laugh and broke into a sweat. The girl was still standing by the corner of the building.

"Well, how about it?" Coach Lapp asked.

His voice was suddenly kind. He put out an arm, hesitated, then put the arm around my shoulders. "Join the cross country *and* track team, Dick. Be good for you. I can see you need the training. How about it? I'll see you tomorrow afternoon," he said, hesitated again, then said, "You'll go far, Bingold. *If* you'll just be sensible. *If* you'll just be disciplined." And he walked off, his clip-board and yellow pad clutched in his hand and swinging back and forth with each long stride.

But then he stopped and turned around and called after me, "Incidentally, Dick, you just did a mile in four minutes, seventeen seconds. Not bad. Not bad at all."

"It really hurt him to say that," I told Carman, who had been waiting for me by the building. I looked at my watch and took her books and strode around the building and to the street.

"I'm so proud of you," she said, catching up. But I could tell she was irritated. "Just once," she said. "Just once." I had known Carman since my junior year and she knew my mother well. "She won't bite your head off," she said, working her hand and arm in between my arm and side. "Just once be late for supper." I hurried on, a smile on my face, feeling proud. I looked down at Carman racing along by my side. "You've got a smudge on your cheek," I said. She jerked away. "Oh, Dick," she said. "Oh, Dick." And she pulled her books out from under my arm, and darted off, down a side street where I saw a mailman running up a short flight of steps.

"Bye," Carman called, but wrapped in Coach Lapp's words, I hurried on, too important to answer. Too intoxicated. All the painful mail-order exercises I had done—first from Dr. Scholl to cure my flat feet and then from Charles Atlas to build up my muscles—were paying off. I would be a great athlete.

Two blocks from home, I stopped by the ashes of the con-struction shed where our gang hung out before we burned it to the ground. Cross country *and* track, I was thinking. I couldn't believe it. But something was the matter. Someone had called. I came to and stopped. There, from the street to my left, came two of my pals, Fred Drew and Frank Liotta.

"You sure got your head up and locked," Frank called.

"Must be Carman," Fred said.

"You can't trust girls," I said, suddenly irritated. My pals stared at me and then all three of us were staring down at the ashes.

"You put that last stick on, Bingold," Frank said. "Three days after the Yanks put the wood to the Dodgers."

"Those were the good old days, weren't they?" Fred said.

"Yeah," I said. "I wanted to see how hot I could get that pot-bellied stove."

"Like the time you almost broke your neck climbing high as you could in that pine tree on Lake George."

"That was some camping trip," Frank said.

We stood there, the sun setting. We were held by a feeling that would not complete itself, as if something was waiting to begin.

"We talked a lot," I said. "About girls. About everything. Gotta go."

"How come your smiling so much, Dick?" George asked me, leaned down, picked up a stone, and threw it hard, against a nearby oak. "You have any idea what a jerk Bingham is?"

"Get another job, Georgie," Frank said. "Hey, Dick. Maybe he can work in the City for your dad."

"Gotta get home." I tried to smile. "Sure, if he won't call my dad a jerk."

"*You're* dad a jerk? Whatta y'do there on the weekends anyhow?"

"Simonize and sweep up and now and again drive a customer around."

They both looked at me.

"You don't lie, do you, Dickie? Frank asked.

"Never," I said. "See you guys."

"See you," Fred said.

They turned and went their way and I turned and went mine and when I opened the front door, I was greeted by the noise of a scraping chair and the sound of Mom's voice.

"*Richard?*"

I started forward over the polished parquet, saying as I went, "Good news, Mom. Coach Lapp…"

But before I had taken three steps, Mom filled the frame of the kitchen door, then came at me, Irene peeking over her shoulder.

"I've told you and told you," she said, propelling each word with a fresh burst of fury, her heels striking the floor faster and faster. But when she saw me back up, she stopped, lifted her foot and took off her shoe.

"You are late! You are late!" she shrieked, her face discolored and bloated, her hand drawn back ready to hurl the shoe.

But when I stopped, she started forward again, lifting the shoe higher as she came. I was panting from my run home. Even my nose stung with the exertion. Mom came on and I felt small. Shamed. Coach Lapp and Carman and my buddies towered over me. Then I felt my body straighten and my hands go up, my palms facing each other.

In a final lurch, Mom stopped.

"You raise your hands to me?" she shrieked. "You raise your hands to me?"

The shriek reached the pitch of a scream—then stopped. Her mouth dropped open. Irene's face dropped from sight. Mom's hand, still holding the shoe, was still raised. She was trembling now, her eyes darting right and left, as if she was looking for an escape.

I kept staring at her, my hands up, trembling, and then I knew my whole body was trembling. Mom's face looked flat and white, as if she had forgotten the shoe. Had I hurt her? Our eyes met and our hands dropped. Standing steadily on one foot and with a steady hand, she put her shoe back on.

"Sit down and eat," she snapped, then turned away. Her words were small, as if she had forced each one through a narrow opening.

I eased into the kitchen, avoiding Irene's eyes. I sat down. I heard Mom behind me and a plate appeared. It didn't make any difference that I didn't feel like eating. I ate.

And Mom said, "Wait until your father comes home and hears about this," her voice sounding as if it had worked its way up from the pit of her stomach.

She sat down. The only sound in the kitchen was a fork or knife striking china, then silence, and the three of us glanced at each other. The front door had opened.

"You're home early," Mom said in that same trapped voice.

Dad greeted us each in turn, then looked at us each in turn again. He saw Mom positioned by the stove and knew the lay of the land immediately. He stood by the door where he had stopped after greeting us—and waited.

"Dick raised his hands to me, Ferdi," she said in that strange voice.

And, with both Irene and me listening, she told him everything, just as it had happened. That I was late. That I hadn't apologized. And that all I had done was hustled through the door talking about school and sports. That the meal had gotten cold.

Dad looked at me. He didn't have to ask if what Mom had said was true. But I knew he was waiting for me to make the next move. And I did.

"I'm sorry, Mom."

Then he turned to my mother and said, "I think he's reached an age when he must defend himself, Irene."

Then he turned to me and I knew it was time for me to go upstairs to my room. But when I got to the bottom of the steps, he called me back.

"What about sports?" he asked with a glance at Mom.

I stared at the floor. "Coach Lapp asked me to join both teams."

"Both teams?"

I looked up. "Cross country *and* track. He thinks I can become a gre…A really fast runner."

"If anyone can, you can," Dad said, and I went.

And as I climbed the stairs, the house was silent, not a sound from the kitchen. When I got to my room and began to undress, I realized how hard Mom was trying and I decided to try harder myself.

Chapter Five

Anxious Hours

We liked the silence of the lake when we woke in the morning and looked across at the quiet houses and we were full of fun and noise and talk as we crossed the water rippling away to the north and landed to the sound of church bells, knowing very well there was nobody who would force us to go to Mass.

We were at the Lake George dock to pull up our three canoes, to drive into town to buy beer and supplies and go back across the lake to camp for another night.

I called home to tell Mom and Dad I was fine and that the weather was perfect and that there was supposed to be a storm tonight but that we would be in our tents and safe. Then we went back across the lake, Frank Liotta, Fred Drew, Bill Paone, Jerry Skaee, Ronnie Drew, and me, paddling our canoes and seeing the clouds gathering in the southwest.

The trip had come about on the spur of the moment. At lunch at Forest Hill High, Frank had told us that his dad had given him a new Studebaker convertible for his birthday, and in the next five minutes, we had cooked up a three-hundred-mile round trip to Lake George.

We let the wind blow in our faces and closed our eyes to the hot sun and at a hamburger drive-in, we bantered with a carload of girls, and when we ran down to the beach to rent our three canoes, we spoke with two or three girls we knew and several we didn't, then pushed off across the lake, tents and supplies all aboard. I looked back at the beach and saw the glisten of water on tan legs as a girl ran through the water, calling to a friend.

"Yeah, there," I shouted in the direction of the beach.

"Down boy," Ronnie said. "This is a *bachelor's* club—The Bachelors' Protective Association."

I turned away and thought of what one of the girls at the drive-in had shouted at me, "Hey, skin and bones."

We let the canoe drift in the wind.

"What do girls really want?" Bill Paone asked, pausing with his paddle across his lap and staring at a low rim of dark clouds to the south.

"Money and a good time," Fred said.

"They want to make fun of you so you got to love them," I said.

"Now there's a deep one," Frank said. "What's that supposed to mean?"

"They tease you for the power of it, don't you see that, Dick?" Jerry said.

"My aunt said all girls want are babies," Jerry said, dipping his paddle in and giving the canoe a shot forward.

"That's what I mean," I said. "You can't trust them."

"What ever happened to you and Mivela?" He was talking about one of my best friends in grade school.

"Who knows?"

"Trust? Who's talking about trust? What you do with girls is have fun," Fred Drew said. "You have fun. We were meant to have fun." He passed around a beer he had opened.

The wind rose as the sun set, the opposite of what usually happens, and we poked up our fire and the sparks flew off into the dark and the first rain drops whirled down. Bill's buddy was in Korea and we talked about how U.S. planes had bombed North Korean dams to flood the rice fields and when we would be snagged by the draft. I said I was planning to volunteer and get my stint over with and something Fred said made me anxious: That there was a cut-off date by which you had to join up to be eligible for the GI Bill to pay for college.

"There's no question you need a college education to make a good living," I told the guys, their faces shining out of the dark of the towering pines and black night.

"You got your job testing ignition equipment at Bethlehem Electric with nothing but the promise of a high school diploma," Jerry Skaee said.

"Dead end," I said. I didn't tell them that Dad knew the manager. "Without an education, it's a dead end."

"I see where Stalin died," Frank said.

"Russians are making as big a fuss over that as we would if something happened to Joe DiMaggio—or Bobby Lippmier," Jerry said. "A year ahead of us and almost a national track star."

"Yeah, at Georgetown," I muttered, and whacked a stick against an outcrop of rock.

We ate our fried hamburgers and drank coffee with grounds floating in it and strong enough to lift you off your feet. We had another bottle of beer each, hugging our knees and watching the sparks fly off into the night. Maybe it was just hard to talk over the wind, but we got quiet, like we were waiting. It was then something solid and sudden passed through the air and I wondered if the guys had heard it, but I didn't dare ask. I felt stupid. Two of them were already talking about making a trip up here next weekend and I told them I wouldn't be able to make it, and when one of them asked why, I said I had told Father Nolan I would serve eleven o'clock Mass.

"You still do that?" Fred asked, turning his head only slightly in my direction.

"As a favor," I lied. "And anyhow, Dad's shorthanded and wants me work for him next weekend—at Brewster Motors."

Then the storm hit and we retreated to our tents. The rain struck the tent hard and the rising wind shook the canvas and I thought, *It's time you grew up, Dick.* I dropped off to sleep and a bolt of lightning and a crack of thunder brought me full awake. I broke out of my sleeping bag and out of the tent into the storm and found the beer and drank a whole bottle and in the next five minutes I had everybody awake and undressing and in seconds we were down to our underwear and I dared them to follow me and we ran to the shore and dove into the cold water and the flashing of the lightning and the roll of thunder.

"You cudda gotten us all killed, Bingold," Fred Drew shouted above the wind of Frank Liotta's Studebaker convertible.

When we stopped at the drive-in about four in the afternoon, there wasn't a single car there. We ordered, and then four girls, two in front and two in back, drove in and we heard them ask for Cokes. I stared across at them and their eyes seemed darker and their skin looked hot enough to burn your finger. I held one girl's stare for a long long time and when we drove off, I thought, *Maybe she liked me. Elvis can make a girl shriek just by pointing his finger at her.*

When we drove up to the front door of our house in Kew Garden Hills, Mom was surprised; we were home a day early. But when I unloaded my soaked clothes and sleeping bag, she knew why. Within the next two hours, she had everything washed and dried and put away in my dresser and my closet.

"Haven't you had enough for one weekend?" she said when I hung up the phone and told her it was Frank and Fred, wanting to know if I'd like to see John Wayne's latest movie and she just looked at me and didn't say a word when I hurried out the door. The movie was great and made even better because of what we had done just before we bought our tickets—from Fred's brother John's silver flask, we each had had a swig of whiskey.

On a day in 1954 I stood in the bright sun that made the concrete sidewalks blindingly hot and wondered what I had done. It felt good to get it over with; to have made up my mind, but I wished I had put it off and had given it more thought. I adjusted my tie and turned a single button of my first camel's hair jacket through its buttonhole, and hustled away from the Army Recruitment Center, talking to myself. I had already signed on the dotted line when the officer in charge told me I was just a week too late to be eligible for the GI Bill.

Though I made enough money at Bethlehem Electric testing ignition equipment to buy my first camel's hair jacket, I had been worrying about getting a real job and making real money. And I knew I lacked the education. Not only that, my high school grades were average. Now I was stuck. It would be two years before I could get back home, find a good job, and get my college degree at night. And I would have to pay for it myself. I would be playing catch-up all the way.

All this went through my mind as I sat in Fred Drew's four-year-old convertible Ford, smelling the odor that overheated leather seats give off, the sun heavy and bright and hanging low in the sky. There was no undoing what I had done. I pushed the key into the keyhole, pressed on the starter, and eased into the traffic. I had borrowed Fred's car for the trip to the Army Recuiting Office, and was supposed to have it back by six.

When I reached the Veligh Place shopping area, I slowed, cruised into the parking space, and stopped beneath a stand of shade trees. It was then I saw her, walking out of a store, evidently heading toward her apartment. Mivela Johnson. She carried a small red package under her arm. Her step was like her, bright and quick.

I sat up straight and felt the skin of my face stretch tight against the bones and when I drove up beside her, she stopped, put her hand up as if to touch her forehead, and smiled—just as crazily as I was. She adjusted the red package, almost lost it, laughed out loud, and got in beside me. I turned the radio up to *Three Coins in the Fountain* and swung out of the parking lot and into the street.

When we drove up to the curb by the sidewalk that ran by the door to her family's apartment building, I reached down and turned the key and when the sound of the engine and of the music died, all the jumbled humming of a big blue day jumped out at us and we turned to each other and burst out laughing. I had known her from the time she was the smartest, prettiest girl at St. Nicholas of Tolentine Elementary School.

"I had a secret crush on you," I told her now.

"Oh, Dick," she said, "you never told me. Why?"

And we began to talk, our voices the least sound of a summer afternoon, the droning dome of traffic, the strike of a woman's heels on concrete, the merge and separation of male and females voices. We followed a stream of walkers to the corner, then sauntered back down, licking chocolate ice cream cones, smilng with each lick, and feeling, when we sat back down that we had done something important.

"Wait," Mivela whispered, and disappeared into the pile of bricks and windows and the car clock labored away at making five minutes go by and she was back beside me, the pupils of her eyes dark pools, her smile gentle and lovely. And as twilight turned street lights on, she moved a hairsbreadth and I slipped my arm around her shoulders and she twisted and turned full toward me and I brought her to me and we kissed—and sat back—and talked some more.

"When are you leaving?"

"For?"

"For the Army?"

"Oh, the Army. In two weeks."

"What kind of things do you do—in the Army?"

"Police," I said, a little too loudly, then laughed. "Control. I like control. Maybe I'll be in the military police—an MP."

"You? Police? Tell me something." She looked down. "I never knew…I heard that you were…That you were asked to leave St. Francis Xavier. I *loved* that uniform you wore."

It was a time for confession—the warmth of summer twilight, the hour. "I put fists up when a teacher threatened me with a Latin grammar. He thought I was going to hit him."

"Were you?"

"Yes," I said—and felt a screw of anger. But I smiled. "I was glad, because I was back with my pals—and was able to graduate with them from Forest Hills High."

I picked up her hand and held it in mine and when I put both my hands back on the wheel, I felt sad, the hundreds of windows of the brick building staring down on us, waiting. I couldn't tell her I'd never felt like this for anybody before, because I hadn't, and that tied my tongue.

When I drove away, two falling stars took a long long journey through the hazy dark and a click made me look down. The convertible clock showed one o'clock in the morning. The summer dew as I drove was one long stream of dim and twisting wet, behind me, with me, ahead of me, flowing…I knew Fred Drew would wonder where I was. I was supposed to have returned his car by six that evening. Mom would be waiting up for me and she would be mad too.

And when I finally got undressed and put my head to the pillow and stared at the ceiling, I found that I was angry too, even while sitting there next to Mivela. At her? At what? Was it something when I was a kid? In the morning, I would do my Charles Atlas tension exercises and eat a big breakfast, but I would still be a skinny kid. Join the Army? A kid like me?

Chapter Six

Breaking Out

Father Benson, his Army chaplain's uniform neatly pressed, his head on the side, his hands folded on the clean surface of the wood desk, waited for my answer. I sat by an open window in a low stuffed armchair, he in a wood chair, without arm rests. He had asked me, "How do you know that girl, Dick?"

I stared back at him, pushing aside a new idea: Hadn't I had enough of priests? All the same, I was relieved. Was that all he wanted to know? We had crossed the street yesterday, holding hands when Father Benson's car drew alongside the opposite curb. He wound down the window and called to me and when we stood by the car, he looked at me, then at the girl, then back at me and said quietly, "I'd like to see you in my office tomorrow morning, or afternoon. It's up to you."

I choose late afternoon because a drink wouldn't be far off and now here I sat and I knew enough not to hem and haw because he had already told me I had a fast mouth. So I lied.

"I met her at a market, behind a stall, with her parents."

Father Benson passed air through his nostrils and slumped, ever so slightly. It was clear he didn't believe me.

"Is that so? Well, Dick. Fine. That's fine, Dick."

Then he filled out his uniform again and moved his folded hands forward on his clean wood desk.

"Yes," I went on. "She's a fine girl. We went to a movie. I saw her home. I…"

But Father Benson raised his head. He wasn't listening.

"Let me see if I'm able to put this forward in a logical, reasonable way, Dick. You and your friend, Walter Reilly, have been most loyal and dutiful, for which I thank you. You have served Mass, you have attended church, you have gone to confession…"

I listened. There was something wrong that I tried to make right. I wanted to tell Father Benson, Yes, that's right. But it's all wrong. Then he did it himself.

"Eighteen months ago you sat in that very chair and cried from homesickness and the next night you were—I regret the need to be blunt—you were so drunk you did not know me. Didn't know me? You didn't see me. And when you and Walter dropped me off in Munich on your way to the wedding…"

"Wedding? Yes, of course. To see Grace Kelley marry…"

"I appreciated it but did you know that…Tell me, Dick. What is the first rule of confession?"

My mind was a blank.

"To tell the whole truth and nothing but the truth, to put it in a secular fashion. I have suspected…What a terrible word. I'm not a policeman, Dick."

I could see he was confused and ashamed and I was confused and ashamed and I waited and sweated and wondered about the girl.

"My first impulse when you picked me up to drop me off in Munich, was tell you to turn around and return to barracks. Question you more closely. Assure…But…"

The hands slid forward and his chin dipped.

"…but, I thought, 'Dick and Walt are good soldiers. They work hard. Let it go—for now.' But now I've got to tell you, I know the GI…"

And I fell through the chair and found myself sitting, staring, Father Benson's face blotted out by a stone wall gleaming in the dark.

There is the stink of urine and the sound of gutter water running. We amble on the light side of the street. A wet stone wall gleams on the dark side, where a door opens and licks light into the street. The door closes and light licks back to dark. The stones gleam. The GI we call "One On" whispers stinking breath into my ear, "Disgustin' animal." All four of us have halted and peer at the disjointed spider of a man swimming his way up the street, along the gleaming stones He is whistling. Piercing the night with a sound to melt your heart. I wish I could sing a reply. A check. I step aside and stand alone until One On whispers, "Now." And all four of us— our skin saturated with alcohol, our sweat stinking of alcohol— cross from light to dark, in the crazy gallop of a single loose-ligatured animal. We engulf the whistler, crushing him in the twine of our dirty arms, legs, feet to the pavement. A hand slips into his back pocket, yanks flat leather out…

****

"I expect…" Father Benson began.

"The wallet was empty," I blurted. "There was no money in that wallet."

"I expect," Father Benson pushed on, "that Dick Bingold… What, Dick? What did you say?"

I sat frozen, watching Father Benson's chin rise then staring down at his folded hands on the surface of the plain wood desk.

"That was another wallet I was talking about," I lied again. "Another one. I didn't do that."

"What wallet? How did you know…Dick. Dick. It *was* you."

My heart beat in my mouth and in one desparate move, I reached forward and folded my hands on the desk, exactly like Father Benson.

" As I was about to say. I expect…Dick Bingold, on his own,

after serious reflection, serious discernment—at another place—at a sacred place—to make a full and complete confession."

I pushed forward again, ready to say anything, do anything to be thought well of by Father Benson again. But with only a slight raising of his folded hands, he went on,

"Not here. Not now. I expect you once again to take your religion seriously. To get out of the dark wood you are in. You can't go back to the Dick Bingold you were eighteen months ago. But you can do penance, seek forgiveness, seek Our Lord's grace. Because if you don't...Do you understand, Dick?"

"Yes, Father," I said, struggling to stand, barely opening my lips.

As if a heavy stone were on my shoulders I trudged heavily to the door, thinking I was through, but found I wasn't through yet because Father Benson called me back to him and without asking me to sit down said in a clear voice without hesitating on a single word,

"Let me tell you something about yourself, Dick. Of all the young men I've known over here, you're among the few with great promise. You've got a loving nature—a loving nature that you are going to betray—and keep on betraying until some day you get taught—until in some fashion of his own choosing, God teaches you a lesson."

I stared back across the room at Father Benson. He did not give me an encouraging smile but instead, looked at me coldly and said,

"Dick, about the young woman. She is well known in the district. She is a common prostitute."

I made my hands into fists.

"Need I say more?"

"No, father," I said.

Under my feet, the floor moved. I did a two-step and

caught myself and walked out into the overcast of a moment that wasn't afternoon or evening but a faint imitation. And then I hurried on, remembering that Walter and I had agreed to meet for a beer but when I got to the PX Walter wasn't there and the place was empty, except for a skinny man and an old lady who was wiping a table clean with a white cloth. She didn't look up and neither did the man in a white apron leaning on a counter, the pencil he held in his left hand moving over the pages of a ledger.

I hurried away and caught a bus to town and when Walter and I finally hooked up, I was already on my tenth or fifteenth beer and when I saw her looking across the bar at me I got up and sat down beside her and said, "You know what they say about you?" And when she didn't answer, I whispered, "They say you're beautiful." Walter disappeared. When I saw him at the post at a late breakfast the next morning, he asked,

"What are you smiling about?"

"Did I dream it or wasn't there Mass this morning? Powdered eggs aren't eggs at all—they're phony."

From a narrow opening in the messhall wall came steam, voices, and trays slamming.

"Sunday? On Sunday? You were in fine form when I left you."

"How come you didn't wake me? I was waiting for you to wake me but then I realized—I mean, I dreamed—there wasn't Mass this morning, that is, I dreamed it was Monday."

A single tray slammed and hard heels hit the varnished floor when two GIs walked by, one saying to the other,

"Expert smart aleck, friend," and they shoved on up between the tables and out the door.

"What's that all about?" Walter asked.

We got up and took our trays to the opening where the

steam billowed out over a metal counter and put our trays down and meandered out into the company street where the day was bright and empty.

"That's Lipsky," I said. "He doesn't like me. He doesn't like the fact, me, of all people, got one of these," I said, tapping my Expert Infantry Badge. I had worked hard for it.

"Never saw such big hands that Lipsky's got," Walt said. "How you know each other?"

"In my squad," I said nonchalantly, remembering the times I had given him an order and he had given me the finger.

We were sauntering on, feeling the big sky of a Sunday morning and the swelling peacefulness of the warm sun and seeing way down the street two figures the size of matchsticks, waiting.

"Need help?" Walter Reilly asked me.

"Might as well be now," I said. "No, guess not," and he turned off and when I reached Bill Lipsky, his pal faded, and we were walking alone into a field bordered by sycamore and a dense green hedge. My neck and face were hot and my heart was hammering and in my mind I was crouched and ready, looking for exactly the right spot to hit him but I was having a tough time getting mad. Walter was right: he had huge hands that now made huge fists.

I made my voice steady and said, "Seems a crazy thing to do on a Sunday morning."

We had reached the hedge and an outcropping of stone.

"Y'know, Bingold, that's what gets me—you're not only smart aleck, but you're smart ass. Hear me? Smart ass. You can't leave well enough alone. You pick, pick, pick. I don't get it—a skinny beanpole like you being smart ass."

He had squared around, his back to the hedge and the stone, those huge fists hanging limp against his belly, his thick shoulders rounded, his face heavy and dark, the slit between his lips wafer-thin. It's all in the timing, Dad whispered. Lipsky glanced over my shoulder and I dropped into a crouch, my left up, my right protecting my chin. He looked down at me.

"You ain't forgetting something are you, smart ass?"

I straightened, he dropped his fists and turned and we walked through the hedge, stumbling over a pile of stones, and when we came out on the other side, out of sight of any witnesses, he swung. The roundhouse made an arc of dark in which all at the same time his chin appeared and my crouch uncoiled with a terrific pain in my left hand.

On my tenth beer, I settled a plastic bag of ice over that left hand and bragged to Walter Reilly, "He went down like a sack of grain and I didn't wait to see him get up." And when Walter said, "He'll report you, for sure," I said I didn't think so and in the street, on our way to another bar, I saw a car that I recognized and when it went by eyes behind the glass took me in and then looked away and I watched the car shrink then turn left and disappear. It was Father Benson.

By a window at an open-air restaurant Walt and I sat opposite each other, the fingers of my right hand around a beer that sat on top of a plain wood table. I could smell the horseradish that covered the beef sandwich Walt was finishing off.

"First time ever, Dick, I see you without your mouth full," Walt said.

I moved my beer and inch forward and looked down at it, then picked it up, and finished it off. The bag of ice dropped to the floor and I drew in my left hand.

"A helluva Sunday," I said. "It's the hand. Feels like a nail's straight through it. Two nails. How about it, you want to make that trip to Paris and see those girls? Here's the plan." I was feeling afraid, cocky, and angry, all in that order, or all at once. And I thought, *Who or what are you resenting, Dick?*

I straightened up and smiled and pulled the empty bottle back to me across the clean wood. "I'll get Joan to write to me pretending she's my cousin and we'll spend Thanksgiving with Joan and her friend. How about it?"

Walter Reilly wiped his mouth with a paper napkin.

"I promised Father Benson I'd serve Mass that weekend."

And I said, "That's just the point. We'll be in Paris."

Richard's mother, 1907

Richard's Mom (top row, 2nd from left)
Thirteen children in the Green family

Richard's Mom, Irene (far right)
Rockaway Beach, 1922

Richard, age 3

Brother John, age 7

Richard, age 3

Richard, age 11

Richard, age 13

Richard's mother, 1957

Richard with his father, Ferdi, 1972

The gang downs some beer, 1953

B.P.A. guys on Lake George.
(Richard to right of tree)

Camping out at Bear Mountain
(Richard second from left, 1948)

Richard dodging traffic
(Paris, 1956)

"Cloudy Haven" 1949
(Kiki) Frank, Fred and Richard

Fred Drew and Frank Liotta
w/pot belly stove for
"Cloudy Haven" Clubhouse

Mivela Johnson with
Richard at a dance
"a sweetheart of a girl"

*Richard on the German border during the
Hungarian invasion by Russia, 1956*

*A foxhole called home-
German border, 1956*

Chapter Seven

Flirting With Death

Far above me, voices and bodies moved in the dark. I strained to see up, out of the hole. No, I decided, try to climb out. Don't puke. Mom said goodbye and Dad said goodbye but all I saw of them were their shoulders the color and shape of carboard cut-outs. A match would have set them alfame.

"Any permanent…" one voice began.

"Hold on," said another, and a nose and silver eyes came near. "Round," the voice went on. Then it came clear: "He's coming around. No, no permanent damage."

But the hole sucked me back down inside it. Someone said, "Father Benson?" He had put a stethoscope next to my heart. I tried to smile, as a way of thanking him.

"No, Doctor McCormack—I'm Doc McCormack. Pulse?"

"Father Benson, the Catholic chaplain. Normal," a woman's voice said

"Your rank, soldier?"

Now I woke up; they were talking about me.

"Specialist Third Class."

"Your name?"

"Bingold. Specialist Third Class Dick Bingold. Is it raining, sir?"

"Touch your nose. No, your nose. Fine," the same voice said, nearer this time. "You're doing just fine. No, the thunderstorm's gone through—like Kansas."

I opened my eyes to spectacles with silver rims and flooding through me came a wave of warm thankfulness. Doc McCormack had been with our outfit when we trained in Kansas.

"The sleet and hail of Kansas," I said. My left temple didn't feel my forefinger and I managed to say, "It feels numb, sir."

"You've got four stitches there, soldier. You're lucky you're alive. Your eyesight. We're worried about your eyesight. You may see double for a couple of days. Like two people. We'll know fairly soon whether there's any permanent damage. You want me to call Father Benson?"

"I'm gonna be sick."

"Here, here," a woman's voice said, a warm hand rubbing carefully under my Johnny and across my bare shoulders and raising me up. "There, there, love. There's a sweetheart."

"Thank you."

"Thank you? Aren't we polite. What our mothers teach us stays with us all our lives. Permanently. Like faith."

But instead of puking, I burped and slid awake and made something like a chuckle and felt the warm hand slip across the skin of my ribcage and I closed my eyes and when I opened my eyes it was early morning and it was raining still, a dull steady misty rain that must have been falling all over Germany. I tried to see through the mist to what had happened and all I could see was a building made of stone.

My head ached and where there should have been one windowframe, there were two. I closed my eyes and worried and waited for words or pictures to come to mind to tell me what had happened to me. But instead, I thought of stubs of milk cartons fitted together like an eggcrate into which Dad packed Mom's cupcakes that he sent to me every month. I swallowed and fought back tears. Then it came to me that inside the big empty building of stone was the gymnasium where voices echoed through the stink of Absorbine Junior and sweat.

"Darlin' boy."

Nurse cleared her throat and, pressing close to me, adjusted my pillow and stung my temple with Iodine. I flinched and said,

"Still raining?"

And then I remembered what had happened to me.

"Still raining, dearie," she said and touched my shoulder and said through the frog in her throat, "It's a joke, but you'd make any mama swell with pride." A cart went by outside the door, thick soles squeaking.

"I'm going to puke," I said and her shoulder dropped, metal hit wood, and she came back up with the pan in my lap and her warm hand on my forehead.

"That helps," I muttered.

"Did your mother hold your head that way when you were going to be sick?"

"No," I said and belched and we each clucked a laugh. At the end of the bed, she made a note to a paper on a clipboard.

"Concussions cause all sorts of mischief," she said, but bit her lower lip and glanced diagonally up over the rim of her spectacles. "You young men," she said and was gone and I felt sick again but slid down and turned on my side and stared into the stony fall of rain and my brain lurched like a paralyzed limb to reach for something but couldn't get it and I closed my eyes and saw her on the bed by the high window. Father Benson cleared his throat and I woke up and instead of Father Benson, Walter Reilly was sitting there, a brown paper bag—or was it two?—held tight to his side. And when I saw it was one we each downed two long swigs of whiskey before the nurse came in for lights out.

"That eye looks awful," Walter said. "You look different. You don't look like yourself at all."

"Yeah," I said. "I see one too many of you."

"My double," Walter said.

"You see mine?"

"All the time," he said to a jerk of his head.

"I said lights out, boys," the nurse said, looking at me as if she was seeing me for the first time.

Then she frowned and left and Walter stood up and looked down at me and said, "What happened to you anyhow?"

And I told him as much as I could, that I had been playing pool and that I was on my fourth or fifth beer, when a couple of black guys started yelling and I went to see what was going on.

Walter Reilly shifted to the other foot. The nurse looked in, frowning.

"You don't trust me," Walter Reilly said brightly. "I'm leaving. I'm leaving. I'm leaving for certain this time."

"Death and taxes," she said, trying not to laugh. "What else is certain? God has a plan for all of us but I'm never certain which one is mine."

I strained forward, hoping she'd keep talking, but she said, "A buddy of yours here says he must see you. Five minutes. No more than five minutes, or you get even *me* in trouble."

In the doorway stood a GI I'd seen in a dream. Or was he real? His white teeth shined against his dark skin through a sheepish grin. His khakis gleamed with starch and cleanliness.

"How're you, man? Come by to see how you're doing."

"Doing fine," I said and with an effort I looked at Walter then back at the GI and he caught on.

"Fullard," he said. "Thought you'd know me. Couldn't forget me. Your head was in the way of that iron dumbbell. I'm sorry."

He lit up with a firey outline and when I blinked he stood there in hospital light, the smell of adhesive tape and rubbing alcohol and a trace of whiskey in the still air.

"You're not Lipsky," I said and we each tried to laugh.

"Lights out, *now*," the nurse said. She said "now" through a frog in her throat.

"Oh," I said, trying to make a single image out of him. "You're the guy…"

"Yeah," he said, then repeated, "I'm sorry," then waited. And when Walt and I looked at each other again, Fullard said, "Do me a favor. If you report me, I'm outta here, back to the States."

"Who says I'm going to report you?"

"Thanks, man," he said, his face lighting up. "Thanks. If ever you need a favor, just ask for Fullard. Private First Class Donnie Fullard. Quartermaster Corps, headquarters company. And look, man, thanks for stepping in. That Harlem kid would've murdered my brother. They say, what they say is, he lasted a round once with Sugar Ray."

The nurse cleared her throat, "O.K. Enough. Vamoose. You GI's are no proof of it, but there are rules, y'know. There's right and wrong. You boys may not believe it, but God knows you. He knew you in the womb."

Fullard and Walter Reilly looked at her and went and she arranged my sheets.

"You must be Catholic," she said.

I frowned, I don't know why.

"Oh, I'm sorry. You asked for Father Benson. Isn't he the Catholic chaplain?"

"Yes, yes. Mom had prayer groups to the house. I'm Catholic. Do you think there's permanent damage?"

"When I married, I drifted away from the faith," she said, and paused. "I volunteered for service in Germany and seem to drift even further away. No. You were hit hard but you're young. Young and healthy. You'll see clearly in a couple of days. Doctors are always over-cautious."

She stood halfway between the bed and the door, in a lonely place. I was suddenly very very tired. I pulled my hands out from beneath the sheets, saw two of her, stretched—and then yawned. She lifted her chin, turned, and walked out the door.

I tried not to think of what she had done just before she had lifted her chin. She had flinched. Why were women so complicated? So hard to understand? Why couldn't we understand them?

I turned to the wall and the springs of the bed squeaked mournfully. I drifted to sleep and woke with a start, hearing the words, "…he's paralyzed, for life—I'm guessing."

Just outside my door, two nurses were talking, almost whispering. I moved both my hands and said loud enough to be heard,

"Nurse?"

"Yes?"

"Paralyzed? Who's paralyzed?"

"Settle down, now. Settle down. An accident on the Autobahn. Now you just settle down. You'll be fine."

Chapter Eight

Interlude

Joan wore a crew-neck shetland sweater and a plaid skirt and knee socks and loafers and her clothes fit every inch of her exactly. I said that was a fine letter she had written me, posing as my cousin, to show my company commander, and that on the strength of it, he had given me a seventy-two hour pass to spend Thanksgiving with her. In the back seat Walter and Joan's friend, Pat, laughed. We had fooled everybody, and here we were having the time of our lives in Paris. The girls were American students at the Sorbonne and Joan's dad was a commander in the Navy.

As I drove, I told Joan and Pat about the iron weight that had fractured my temple and made me see double and Joan trailed her forefinger over the bumps where the stitches had been and we laughed and I pressed down on the accelerator of the Mercedes and we pulled up in front of their tiny hotel where they went in and came back down with a basket. We rolled through Paris and out into the country by a river where we sat on the blanket they furnished and chewed bread and cheese and finished off one bottle of wine and started on another and babbled on about the last time we had seen them.

"Oh, that lipstick you bought at the PX, pretending we were your wives," Joan said.

"Like gold," Pat said. "Heavens! She won't let me touch it."

Walt said nothing; he let me to do most of the talking. He watched Pat as she watched Joan and then I got up and took Joan by the hand and we walked a very fine line along the river, just barely getting our feet wet, me doing the talking, telling of my giant of a great grandfather, Baron von Bingold of Bavaria, and the prize door with the initials, "VB," etched into the frosted glass. He had shipped the door to America where he picked it up on his arrival. We walked hand-in-hand and I told the story.

When Great Grandfather Karl, carrying a leather satchel, set sail from his West Side brownstone into New York evenings of the 1870s, he disapppeared in seconds, and when he returned five hours later, the satchel chinking with change, he might be at his choice door before his daughter, Josephine, peering through the frosted glass, caught sight of him, for he always dressed his six-foot-eight-inch, three-hundred-pound body in black. At each of his four bars, his huge hand wrapped about the stub of a pencil, he did the arithmetic of the day's action that, coin-by-coin, and bill-by-bill, he deposited in the satchel, then returned home. Only once was his habit of years broken.

Hearing his footsteps and seeing through the glass his shadow fall and rise as he bent down to blow out the gas lamp, Josephine reached to pull open the door—and drew back in horror. Out of the dark and across the haze of a nearby streetlamp, three dark forms tended to one point from different directions. In the next second, they all diverged, one flying through the door, the second down the steps, and the third into the bushes from whence he pelted off into the night.

When the police arrived, they found one man dead and a second bleeding and senseless in a bed of glass. On the top step, his bowler hat on his knee, sat Great Grandfather Karl, tears trickling down his face. Assured by the police that the hoodlums didn't deserve his grief, he shook his head back and forth, back and forth, saying, "Ach! Mine door. Mine beautiful door."

When Joan laughed, a man in a floppy white hat stared at her and I did too and then looked a long distance back up the river where Pat and Walter were supposed to be but were nowhere in sight. As we made our way back, not walking near the water this time, I squeezed Joan's hand and felt a kind of sickness. Where we had picnicked, the blanket and basket were gone and the grass pressed down.

"Goodness," Joan sighed. "Isn't it awful how time flies?" A big white bird flapped its wing and made a laughing sound, and we laughed, and Joan said,

"You seem so quiet."

"Yeah," I said. "Thinking. Got to be in Rome next week and I ship home in another two days after that."

"Rome?"

"Rome." I hoped the bird wouldn't laugh again. This time it flapped its wings and splashed off shore into the deep part of the river. Joan was looking at me, smiling, waiting for me to go on, the smile not taking me quite seriously enough. "Got an appointment to see Father Best. Father Best at the American School—the American School of Theology," I plunged on. Still she waited and then I said, "I'm thinking of applying for admission and then train—train for the priesthod."

This time it was Joan who laughed. The bird glided on the water, lowering and lifting its head, the "S" of its neck and drop of its beak awkward and graceful all at the same time.

"*You?*" she said. "An affable love like you?"

And I burst out laughing, took a step toward her, put my hand at the small of her back and pulled her close and kissed her softly.

"Hey, you two."

It was Pat's voice and we turned and in a few minutes we were back in the car, heading for Paris. Later, after Walt and I had showered and shaved, we picked up Joan and Pat at their apartment and headed for dinner and dancing at *The Whiskey-A Go-Go,* just off the av de Champs Elysees. Joan wore a white blouse and black skirt and laughed when I told jokes, one about an Irishman and a priest, and we passed the wine and then danced and in the dark of early morning we drove through the misty sunrise with the windows down and stopped beneath the leafy branches of trailing trees and slept in each others arms and when we found Pat and Walt again, they were crossing a street in the full sunlight and at noon we stood opposite each other at the side of the car, its windows wide open and Walter and I got into the car, me driving, and put our hands out the windows and waved and we last saw Pat and Joan waving and very small in the distance.

On the S.S. Washington, heading home, the days of the past two weeks were like cards in a deck, shuffling through my memory, first one way and then another. I wasn't sure when I had been to Mass or Confession but I was sure that I stood in St. Peter's Square and before that in a phone booth, talking to Joan

"*Did you see that Father Best? "she wanted to know.*
And I said, "Yes."
"*What did he say?"*
"*He said," I said into a phone on the edge of St. Peter's Square, barely hearing Joan's voice above the towering murmur of the gathering pilgrims.*
"*Yes? I can barely hear you," she said, laughter edging each word.*
"*I said he said—Father Best said—and I said of course he was right because it's not a decision to be made lightly, that I should sleep on it, go…"*

"But what did he say?" *Joan asked, then laughed.*

"He said I should wait a year—go home and think about it and then write him."

"Dick?"

"Yes?"

The rising murmur of the pilgrims hid what she said, and I said into the phone, "What?" And then she made her voice clear.

"I'm glad," *she said and I looked from the booth and saw above the thousands of pilgrims gathered in St. Peter's Square the high bright sky.*

"Write," *she said.*

"I will," *I said.* "I will," *and said goodbye and hung up and stepped out of the booth and was carried on into the Square by the movement of the crowd.*

I looked up and over thousands of heads, and at a great distance I saw a tiny figure of a man appear on a balcony and even from where I stood I could see him raise his hand. It was Pope Pius XII making the sign of the cross on all our foreheads. People around me held up objects to be blessed, here a boy with a shining trumpet and there a woman with a newly-knit sweater. And at the farthest reach of their mother's or father's hands, babies held their faces to the sun and to the blessing, and I put my face up into the sun of his blessing too.

At dusk, to the sound of cars gearing up and down and the mumur of hundreds milling about the Square, I kneel in an empty pew and run quickly through the prayer, "O my God, I am heartily sorry for having offended thee, and I detest of all my sins, because I dread the loss of Heaven and the pains of Hell. But most of all…" And I stop, and rush to the words, "O my God, give me grace to know wherein I have offended thee…" And I stop again and get up and hurry out of the church. I am very hungry.

We exchange stares during my first plate of spaghetti and I

*ask her to join me for my second and she helps me finish the third
bottle of wine and when we are walking, the starlings are moving in
the trees, and whistling, and dropping on us specks of bark and dirt
that she brushes from my shoulder with a very small hand. A car
goes by and I know the face set in the frame of the window. It is a
Catholic chaplain from another outfit. I wave to him and he waves
back and I take the girl's hand and we walk on.*

On the deck of the *S.S. Washington,* a familiar voice
addressed me.

"That you, Dick Bingold?"

It was Father Benson and I thought, *Is Father Benson the
only Catholic priest in the U.S. Army?*

"Heading home at last," he said, turning to look over the
railing.

"At last," I repeated, knowing he wanted to chat. But instead
of turning with him and placing my elbows on the rail—imitat-
ing his motions as I often did on the trip out—I scooted on by.

"Movie, Father," I said.

"Right," he called after me. "A good one. I saw it. *Man of ...*"

I stopped.

"Excuse me, sir?"

"I said *A Man of a Thousand Faces,* with James Cagney."

"Oh," I said, and hurried on.

But when I had put my hand on the door to the rec room,
I stopped, turned, and hustled back up the deck.

"Forgive me, Father. I didn't mean to be rude," I said,
putting my elbow on the railing beside his. "Wanted to tell you I
saw Father Best and His Holiness and he said he thought I ought
to wait a year."

"Wait a year," he repeated, thinking, looking straight
through me.

"Yes, Father. To make an application to the School of Theology."

"His Holiness said you ought to wait?"

We each gave a short laugh. Several GIs scuffed along the deck behind us. *Would the beer hold out?* I wondered, and Father Benson said, clearing his throat,

"Will you be glad to get back home?"

"Wait, because I'd thought—am thinking about—the priesthood. Home?"

The sea was perfectly calm and had no marks on it at all. How did anybody know one direction from another?

"Did you ever hear the riddle?—One man left home and another man came back home. How many men were there?"

Someone had stopped behind us, off to my left. I had an idea who it was, but Father Benson had said,

"Do you know in what way the Eighth Commandment is linked to lying?"

I took a deep breath and tried to think of something clever to say for I knew he was only talking, exploring a point—a point of theology. And he went on,

"Bearing false witness against your neighbor—that's lying, isn't it? Thus, the Eighth Commandment includes, wouldn't you say, every kind of falsehood?

Father Benson turned to me for an answer and when all I did was nod, he said,

"From my own experience, when things seem out of whack there's a falsehood sneaking about somewhere—in the heart, perhaps."

"Dick?"

It was Walter Reilly's quiet voice. Father Benson turned.

"Well, old home week," he said, and pushed away from the rail. "Hello, Walter." He took us both in, then looked at me. "We'll talk later, Dick. It's simply a matter of what is fitting. I heard of a man who trained for the priesthood because there was just one thing in his life that he could not bring himself to confess. Interesting concept?"

Silence. And then he said, "You'll both do me a favor if you serve Mass in the morning," and eased off down the deck and Walt Reilly and I went the other way.

"Just great," I whispered. "Why us?"

Walter walked along beside me and I was saying,

"Serving Mass was O.K., before I left home, I mean, it was what I did. And now—I don't know. That was a long time ago."

"What the devil was he talking about—the Commandments—right out in broad daylight?" Walt Reilly asked.

We laughed. "I haven't the slightest," I said, and thought, *I'm sick of priests,* and said, "Bright man, Father Benson. He's educated, knows Aquinas by..."

"Who?"

"Aquinas—Saint Thomas Aquinas—by heart."

"My sister fell for a priest once.

We stopped by the door of the rec room.

"He was an old man—must have been thirty. She was fourteen. We told her priests don't marry."

"What did she do then?"

"She cried."

We laughed and I said, "Women don't waste their time on priests. They're nuts about policemen, for their uniforms, and undercover agents for what they know."

"Then," said Walter Reilly, fixing the idea in his brain and smiling up at me, "A guy should be a cop in the day and a private eye at night."

We pulled open the door to the odor of an over-heated radiator and shape of heads and shoulders and people moving and talking across a black and white screen.

"Hey, Walt," I whispered. "You're a joker. I didn't know you were a real joker."

We found seats.

"That's because Dick Bingold thinks he's the only real joker around."

It took me a long while to get interested in the movie. Afterward, we bumped into one of my friends from California who winked, opened, then closed, the door to brooms and the smell of cleaning fluid, pulled on an overhead light, and pulled out a silver hip flask. It's dented surface showed finely-etched initials.

"M'gung ho louie won't miss it," he said, pushing the flask into my face.

I grabbed it and swallowed a half dozen times and handed it to Walter who took a swig, then handed it back to the guy who had stolen it. He almost finished it off when he handed it back to me and then I did finish it off.

"Whtta y'say, another swig?" The guy's breath stank.

Walter didn't move and I reached into my pocket and handed the guy a five dollar bill.

"For both of us."

On the outside of the door we watched him slide away, his right shoulder close to the metal wall I was leaning against. The wind was up in the dark and I felt the wall shiver.

"Storm," I muttered.

"You wouldn't have a habit, would you, Bingold?"

"What's eatin' you, Walt?"

"What's eatin' me is that what I've discovered is that you're so smooth nothin' catches on to you and you don't catch on to nothin'," Walter Reilly said and hastened off, hugging the wall, passing into and out of shafts of light from the portholes—shafts of light that tried to pierce the night but that barely lit up Walter Reilly.

It was great to see the Statue of Liberty and I only caught sight of my best Army friend from a distance when he raised a hand to wave. That was the last I ever saw of him.

Chapter Nine

On a Dark Road

"Gloomy," my father-in-law, Ted said.

"There, you two men," said my mother-in-law, Catherine, standing back up from the pastrami sandwiches she had adroitly placed in a small space without touching a pile of LP records. When she drew back, I saw her eyes coast over Ted's face sadly.

She made her voice louder, "And here are two ice-cold drinks, my dears." She walked toward the basement steps, then called out over her shoulder, "Thanks for getting *all* the storm windows on in one afternoon." I heard what she said, but Ted didn't seem to hear. He was staring at one of his thirteen stereo speakers he had designed, installed, and wired himself. We were surrounded by hundreds of his unnumbered LP collection.

"Thanks, Mom," I called back to the sound of her heels on the steps. "You're welcome."

"Gloomy," he repeated. "Dylan's a gloomy cuss. I've got all his recordings, but he's a gloomy cuss. You'd think here in nineteen sixty-four with the whole world coming down around our ears you wouldn't be so gloomy."

I took a long drink and a large bite of pastrami and swallowed more drink and said,

"How about, '*Oh, Pretty Woman?*'"

Ted chewed his sandwich silently and then drank down half his bottle of beer. He held his mouth shut and burped. Beth and Catherine said he was a handsome man, and I guess he was. His hair was thinning, but still, he had a youthful look, and had no pouch.

"What say, Dick? The first time ever I put those storms on in one afternoon. If your only child is a girl, then where's the help? Imagine a little thing like Beth carrying a ladder. They say this is going to be a cold and stormy fall." He leaned forward and picked up the other half of his sandwich, held it an inch from his mouth, and said, "Gratitude? Dick, let me give you a piece of advice. Turn Dylan off, will you please? He's too gloomy. How about *"I Feel Fine?"* Where the old folks came from, everybody knew everybody else. Where did you live in Kew Gardens?"

"Seventy-sixth Road."

"That anywhere near the stabbing? How is it that all those neighbors could listen to that Kitty Genovese scream and do nothing about it? That's wrong, to do nothing, isn't it? You think of a sin as doing *something.*"

Ted put the rest of the sandwich into his mouth and chewed it thoughtfully and seemed to listen to the music.

"Luke, Chapter Ten," I said grinning. "The Samaritan, because he acted in accord with the Commandment, Love thy neighbor as thyself."

Ted looked across the table at me. "You and your dad are close, eh? He's proud of you—proud of you for graduating from St. John's University, I suppose? Theology. I often thought I might take up theology."

Ted's lids were heavy with early Saturday-afternoon drowsiness, the way my mother would drop off for a catnap from which she might awake, find a mistake on my homework and slap me hard.

I finished my drink and sandwich and got up and put on 'Oh, Pretty Woman," and sat back down and said,

"Yes, for a while I thought about studying theology, but—" I yawned, and thought, *When did I last go to confession?* I licked my lips and tasted the last of the pastrami and wondered, *What's the matter with Ted, anyhow?* Two years ago, when I first knew him, he looked like nothing could stop him and it was great to shake his hand and feel the same, that nothing could stop either one of us. I had just met Beth, their only child.

I see her face, her mouth when she laughed: her lips when I gazed at her across the dancefloor. I see her running, the water of Jones Beach splashing around her ankles.

I see her, lovely, petite, walking beside me into St. Patrick's Cathedral through the immense hollow sounds of muffled voices, a distant door closing, the strike of a heel on varnished hardwood. I see the rows of votive candles and the statue of the Blessed Virgin Mary. And I see us kneel at Our Lady's Altar where I close my palm on a box in my pocket, withdraw it, and turn my palm up. Beth breathes in. I press a tiny knob with my thumb and the lid pops up to reveal the engagement ring. Afterward, hiding our grins, we sit opposite each other at Stauffer's Restaurant. Before desert, and after a bottle of wine, I tell her there is a spot of grease on her right cheek, by her lip. She hurries off to the restroom. I don't know why she's upset.

But when we reach her house to share our excitement with her parents, we've made up, and plan a boat trip up the Hudson to. When I reach home, Mom is still up, Dad in bed, asleep. Mom frowns and fixes me a late-night snack.

"Marriage is expensive, Dick," Mom says, looking at me as if I've made just one more mistake.

"That's good, Dick. That's a good thing. Beth knows what she's about," Dad says when I catch him before he leaves for work. I bolt outside, the sun is warm and the air bright and clear. A perfect day for a trip on a river. I drive over to Jackson Hights to pick up Beth. She and her parents are standing in the hallway.

"Don't be late now, Beth," her mother says
Her father looked at me steadily, then says
"What kind of bosses they have there at J.J. Newbury?"
"Now, Dad," Beth says.. "Don't let Dick get going about Mr.
Ewen."
"Yeah?" her dad said.
"Yessir, I…"
"Don't need to sir me. Just call me Ted."
"He's the best boss a man ever had—Ted."
"Is that right."
"Now let them go, Ted. I want Beth home early."
"Beth takes care of herself," Ted said. "The best executive
secretary Johns Mansville company ever had takes care of herself.
What makes this Ewen so—outstanding?"
"The first day I met him…"
"Please, Dick," Beth said quietly.
"…he was wearing a tie and vest and jacket and he came
right around his desk and shook my hand he made me feel as if I'd
known him all my life and there's not one time I've ever heard him
raise his voice. One afternoon…"
"Dick."
I noticed Ted was smiling at me—or was he laughing—and I
shut up and felt like a skinny kid on his first day of school.
"You got your whole life before you, Dick," Ted said. "With a
boss like that, who can stop you?"
Was he joking? He looked serious, but a light played about his
eyes.
On our way out of Jackson Heights to the piers, I told Beth
about standing in St. Peter's Square and watching the Pope make
the Sign of the Cross over thousands of pilgrims. I wanted to tell her
about other people I'd met and other things I'd done but when it
came clear to me who those people were and what those things were

I had done, I closed my mouth. Before we got to the piers, we stopped for a drink, and when one led to another, we decided to have a meal then go to a movie.

Ted woke with a start, looked about, and said, "Hey, there, Dick. Sorry."

I stood up.

"We're having people in for cocktails and dinner, so I'd better get on out to Hicksville," I said, looking about me for my jacket.

Ted raised his eybrows and held his eyes wide, and right on me, then got up himself, turned, opened a small closet, and removed a bottle of Teachers Scotch. We took a snort each.

"We were talking about gratitude," he said, picking up one of his albums and staring down at it. "I just learned today. Well, just what did I learn today? Keep moving, Dick. I know you'll keep moving. Until you're stopped."

When I said goodbye to Catherine, she saw the expression on my face, and whispered as I put on my jacket, "You can't keep a...," she began, stopped, and bit her lip. "You can't keep a good man down," she finished, and turned her head away. I waited, trying to guess. But when she didn't go on, I kissed her on the cheek, then gave her a long hug.

On the way, I stopped to see a friend, a bartender, and we shot the breeze for a couple of hours, about how Cassius Clay would get his comeuppance one of these days and the design of the new Verrazano Narrows Bridge and the race riots in Harlem and Philadelphia. We had a few drinks, and then I was on my way—home to Hicksville, Long Island, but it was late, and our guests were to arrive in an hour. Beth would be angry, Richard and James would be horsing around, and Barbara would need a change of diapers. Diapers, diapers, diapers...their smell, their feel, makes me want to forget—and yet—to remember.

Diapers…In his office, I'm standing before Mr Ewen, my arm extended ceremoniously, in my hand a cigar. His eyes play on me with a perfectly even delight. On the shoulder of his dark pinstripe suit there's a grayish spot. He stands up, puts out his hand, and says in his quiet way, "Congratulations, Dick. Fine. Fine. You'll make a fine dad." As I go out the door, Ann, his secretary, goes up on tiptoes and kisses me on the cheek, and I say in confusion, "Fine. Fine." And Richard Ewen's mellow voice floats across the room, saying, "Kindly drop by for a chat before you go. Y'know, Dick, the word that fits you is 'affable.'"

On the wall, the clock says nine-fifteen, the calander, July 12, 1960.

Out in the office there is loud laughter and back-slapping as I hand out more cigars. I'm greeted by grins, winks, and sparkly eyes. The heartiest good wishes come from Wyn Smart, who hates my guts and ,we all agree, is Mr. Ewen's favorite. Work has come to a dead halt. I've waited a long time to be the center of attention for this reason, for I have slapped many of my co-workers on the back when I have taken their cigars and they have announced the arrival of their sons and daughters. Now it's my turn.

I take a puff of a cigar and think,"My son, Richard." You don't think "dynasty" in America, you think, My son. Or my daughter—and that's as far as it goes—and that's why it's so deadly important.. Mr. Ewen has "III" after his name, but that's Richard Ewen, Yale and all.

The office settles into routine; I'm on the phone, planning a trip to set up fixtures for a store opening in Ft. Lauderdale. I slide in a call to order flowers for Beth. We've been married a year.

"Mr. Bingold?"

I hang up the phone, having ordered the flowers.

"Yes, Ann?"

"You have every right to daydream. Mr. Ewen will see you now."

I make my walk deliberate and steady and when I enter, Mr. Ewen stands up, and comes around his desk, his hand stretched toward me in quiet ceremony. I look on the shoulder of his pinstripe jacket for the spot. It's gone. He has seen my glance and shakes my hand.

"Excellent choice of cigar, Richard. Fine. Fine." I see that he has placed it where we both can see it, on his green blotter that is surrounded by knickknacks of all sorts, including a silver sailboat and a photo of a woman in a silver frame.

He sneezes,"Tiff!" withdraws a folded white handkerchief from his rear pants pocket, pats his nose, then refolds and puts the handerchief back, all in one deft, hardly-noticeable motion. But he says nothing about a cold. He doesn't say I look like the cat who has swallowed the canary, or make a single personal remark.

"I'm proud of you, Dick. You're affable. You add to our staff. You've taken hold. Fine. Fine work. You'll make a fine father. Patricia and I will celebrate our thirty-fifth this year. Dropped by to see our grandchild this morning. Feverish. Colic. Little fellow left his signature on my shoulder," Richard Ewen says, dusting with the fingers of his right hand the shoulder where the gray spot used to be.

I look at his jacket, wondering if my clothes are too loud.

"I won't keep you. My best to Elizabeth. Kindly tell her for me, please, your trips won't last forever. I spent too many nights away from my wife and children. Too many drinks. Too many nights away. Until I found others to…Found men like you to do the job. But then it all came to an end and here I am. Well, enough musing. Such is fate."

I'm not used to letting other people do all the talking, I feel dumb, and want to say something, so I say,

"You mean such is God's plan?"

Mr. Ewen looks at me, smiling. "Well, that's one way to put it." In the throb of seconds, I'm glad: he's miffed, and has shown it. He smiles wider.

When I get to the door, his mellow voice makes a warm path across the room to me, "Oh, yes, I meant to tell you. You'll see a mark of your added responsibilties in your pay check next week. A start. A start. Fine. Fine job, you do. But don't…"

I am standing in the doorway and somebody calls me and instead of listening to Mr. Ewen, I turn away, and by the time I turn back, he has turned, and is sitting at his desk, the fingers of his right hand touching his forehead as he gazes down at a sheet of paper.

The lights of an oncoming car are on high beam and I put mine on high beam and blast my horn at him as he zooms by in a blinding scatter of hard-diamond light. Will I be early enough to help Beth get ready for the party? She would be able to tell me what was eating her dad, why her mom looked at him so sadly. I put my beams on low. The only car on that dark Long Island road was far off, its lights dim and small. Something told me that I knew what was up with him and for some reason what Mr. Ewen said to me in 1960 floated into my mind. In fact—and I was almost afraid of the fact—I could quote it word for word.

"There's an end to every climb. We each find our own level at last."

I stepped on the gas and the distant lights came closer. I was glad of the half dozen drinks under my belt—they made me more alert and more competent. The car whipped by and I pulled into a shabby bar, one of the letters in its name missing. I wondered if I ought to buy one more bottle of Johnny Walker Black for the party. I knew the bartender; I decided I'd have a shot or two and then ask him to slip me a bottle for a price. I was right. We had a meeting of the minds and I was on my way, angry.

Too many drinks? Richard Ewen is a good boss, but he most likely has no idea how to drink and enjoy it and clearly he's wrong when he says there is an end to every climb and that we each find our own level at last.

The road ahead was black an unlit, wet, and narrow. I put the speedometer at sixty. Diapers. I can almost smell them. Feel them. Most likely Mr. Ewen never changed a diaper in his life. I put the speedometer up to sixty-five and thought of another Richard. My son, Richard.

****

For the first six months of Richard's life, I help change his diapers, bathe him, dress him. Beth is too ill to lift and care for him all the time.. Our one-bedroom apartment is small, close, and hot. Richard is crying. I throw a towel over my shoulder, place him in the palms of my hands, and put his bobbing head on my shoulder—and hustle back and forth in the narrow room. I've just come in from a class at St. Johns University having flown in from Ft. Lauderdale. I tap Richard's back to get a burp. And he cries louder. And then—I take him off my shoulder, yank him around to my eyes, and staring straight into his little puckered face, I yell in a rage, at the top of my lungs, "Stop crying!" He jerks his tiny head back—stops breathing— catches his breath—and cries louder.

When I drove up the driveway to our house in Hicksville, Long Island, the tears dry on my cheeks, the first thing I saw was that Beth had not turned on the front door light and when I hustled into the front hall, the house perfectly still and she standing there, in the act of putting out fingerfood, I told her about the light.

She was pretty and slender and she took a long long look at me, said, "Beautiful," and walked away, into the kitchen. I followed her, carrying a brown paper bag.

"Want me to change Barbara's diapers?" I asked, trying to swallow my sadness away, trying to make up without admitting a thing.

"Barbara's asleep, hours ago."

"I'll say hello to Rich and James."

"James is asleep and Richard is almost asleep. They were waiting for you and they finally went off to bed. They got tired waiting for you. There's one thing you can do."

"Yeah?"

"Put out the booze."

I felt better and longed to go to Rich, take him in my arms and ask him for foregiveness. But I reached down into the brown paper bag and pulled out the extra bottle of Johnny Walker Black.

"I'll get the ice ready," I said. "I got an extra bottle of Johnny Walker Black. Hey, that dish. What is it? It smells great. Did Fred and Cathy say they could come?"

"They did."

I put my arms around her, and she turned away, and I said,

"What's wrong with your dad?" and she turned back, and looked up at me.

"What do you mean, what's wrong with Dad? He was told his company was sold. Do you know what it feels like to be without a job? Please, Dick, either get out the liquor or go upstairs and shower."

Chapter Ten

Riding High

I put the tray with Beth's coffee and slice of toast on the bed beside her. Her dainty right hand rested on her large stomach as with her left she put down the phone receiver. All I saw of Barbara was her small hand on top of Beth's. I saw rumpled sheets. My side of the bed.

"How old is Barbara?" I whispered to Beth and what I was looking for happened: Barbara's small hand spread out four fingers.

"No," I whispered. "You weren't born in fourteen ninety-two."

And Barbara scrambled away from the opposite side of the bed, ran over the foot, and jumped into my arms, saying loudly, "Nine sixty-four!"

"Nine*teen*sixty-four," I corrected her, and she frowned, wiggled away from me, slid down my leg, and ran from the room, calling, "Teen, teen, teen."

"No, no, no," another voice shouted.

"Nuthead!" came a third.

And James and Richard flew into the room, rounding the end of the bed so fast, James fell, and slid against the wall. Richard beat him to Beth's side, and James came up panting and dry-eyed.

"Rich said I fell asleep and didn't see them beat the…

"Who beat Oakland. Who? Who? Who?"

James wasn't about to cry.

"The Packers?" I asked.

"The Packers!" James yelled.

"See, see, James said…"

"Enough, both of you," I snapped, irritated. "Green Bay beat Oakland thirty-three to fourteen. In January. Super Bowl Two. I was there, remember?"

"Oh, Dad," Rich moaned, and

…"told y'so," James taunted.

And they were both out of the room and pounding down the steps.

"Does it really make any difference?" Beth asked.

"Does what make any difference? Who was that on the phone?"

On the summery air of the room there was the fragrance of Beth's favorite perfume. I tapped the morning's newspaper nervously against my leg.

"Who was that?"

"On the phone," I insisted.

"Dad."

"How's he feeling?"

"Must you always ask how he's feeling? I mean does it really make any difference whether Barbara leaves out 'teen?' Why tell Barbara she's wrong before you tell her she's right?"

I saw Beth's hand jump. She looked down, and smiled and we exchanged a brief smile.

"Right, right," I said. "I've got to get going—to Chicago—a funny kind of inventory problem out there. The guy there's going to make trouble. It's just that, your dad isn't his old self."

"That's *your* view. He's fine. He's fine. Why are you always suggesting…You know, everyone says you are so…Optimistic. If they only knew you…That happened four years ago. The business of Dad being passed over…"

I felt the need of a shower and a shave. I tapped the newspaper faster.

"I'll fry them some bacon and eggs," I said.

"Barbara likes Post Toasties. When will you be back?"

"How're you feeling?"

"Dick," she breathed out impatiently. "I'm feeling just fine. I'm feeling just fine. Look at me. I'm feeling just dandy. Nine months is a long time." Her fingers moved so quickly it was hard to take in that her tears had welled up and had been wiped away. "You'll be how many nights in St. Louis?"

"Chicago," I corrected her.

We stared into each others' eyes, looking for a disclosure, a confession—then instantly gave up. A shrouded figure stood out in my mind, her face barely visible, what she held in her arms, hardly recognizable.

"Today's Monday. Should be...I'll be on the afternoon flight on Thursday." I sniffed. "Rich must be starting the bacon." I could smell Beth's perfume and rubbed my fingers on my stubble. The curtains billowed white with summer breeze. On the side of my wife's head, a curl lifted up and fell back.

"Look after the children first, before you shave, will you? And ask Rich not to play that record one more time. I'll be down in a moment."

I went out and came back.

"What record?"

"The Yellow Submarine. It drives me wild."

And the song, "Both Sides Now" swayed through my head as I headed down stairs, thoughts tumbling through my brain, *Would I be in Vietnam if I didn't have kids? What would I have done in My Lai? Could I have stopped those killers of King and Kennedy? Our country is being taken over by foreigners and college kids. Why do I smell incense?*

And when I reached the bottom step, I knew I was too late. Rich had already fried the bacon and eggs and put them on two plates, one for him and one for his brother. He had even reached down the Post Toasties for Barbara. I watched their tight small bodies bent over their food from a distance, loving them. But when they pretended not to see me, the love was swept away by anger. I took a step toward them—to read them the riot act, about keeping the house neat and looking after their mother. But I turned on my heel, and ran up the stairs to get a shower. I knew I would miss my plane if I didn't keep moving.

A shower and a shave behind me, smelling of *Aqua Velva*, I stood at my dresser, sorting out and cleaning up my wallet. I wanted only the papers I needed for the trip. I threw some out, but kept the business card from some IBM guy. I turned it over and there was her phone number with the area code that included St. Louis. I licked my tongue. I had reduced my alcohol intake: Last night, I had cut my drinks by fifty percent, to five before dinner. And we drank only one bottle of wine, of a label and vintage I hadn't had since my last trip to Ft. Lauderdale. And I went on about Ft. Lauderdale as if I headed up its Chamber of Commerce: the sand, the sun, the water, the fishing, the number of first-rate bars. When I said it would be a great place to live, Beth frowned.

I glanced at the headline in the morning paper, *Police Crack Down on Rioters at Democratic Convention,* and threw it aside and thought, *We're all out of control,* turned, tied my tie, and corrected myself, *The U.S. is out of control.* Brisk and ready, I folded the newspaper and on the fold a headline and photo caught my eye, of a New York cop who got back a sapphire or something. I snugged the newspaper under my arm and hustled out of the room.

Beth was downstairs and dressed and the kids were watching *Captain Kangaroo* when I came down. My heart was pumping. I had a job to do and would get it done and Richard Ewen would have to give me another raise. Beth looked neat and pretty and ready for any challenge. She went up on her toes and gave me the brush of a kiss. And when I had taken a half dozen steps down the walk and turned to wave goodbye, the doorframe was empty.

The flight to Chicago lifted off on time. Who was this guy I had to face? A veteran J. J. Newbury employee. Why would a veteran J.J. Newbury employee jeopardise his pension and retirement with some underhanded scheme? Beth seemed so *little* sitting there in bed. Would she be O.K. when the baby was born? I glanced at the morning paper again, and there that photo and headline was again: *Star of India Sapphire Recovered* and the name of...

"What would we like this morning?"

"Is it ten o'clock yet?." I smiled up at her pretty Scadinavian face. She was a blonde with a minimum of make-up. She gave me a smile with something extra.

"Ten-ten," she said.

"Then, yes," I said. "I'll have a Johnny Walker Black. I make it a rule never to drink before ten."

Long Island turned slowly beneath us and I tried to pick out just where our house in Hicksville was and where the apartment in Kew Garden Hills was where I lived until I married Beth. But a veil of clouds made everything obscure. *That's the past,* I thought, *you have to live in the present and the future.*

The engines roared darkly, seeming to drop in speed then pick up in a forward surging. I dozed. And when I came to, the captain was telling us to buckle our seatbelts and I went through that dream of landing we all go through and was walking along a sunny ramp through which flights to places all over the world were being announced, when I saw a man I thought I knew. But I changed my mind, and walked on, and was about to leave the terminal when I saw the man again and this time I knew him, a former J. J. Newbury employee who had been let go because of a drinking problem.

"Coomey," I said. "Coomey Fenimore."

"Migod Dick Bingold."

As usual, he looked neat, trim, prosperous, and wore his usual summer attire, a Brooks Brothers seersucker suit. But when we looked at each other over a cup of coffee and a cream-filled donut, I saw the frayed collar and in his eyes, the look of pain, a tiny black scribble, like the signature on a death warrant.

"What's the matter, Coomey?" I asked, my heart torn.

"You mean it _shows?_"

"It shows."

His hand shook and he spilled coffee on his shirt front as he put the cup to his mouth, and when he put it down, I looked down, away from the tears.

He warmed his palms on the cup. "I dropped the ball on a General Electric contract," he said in a steady, businesslike voice. "We were about to sign." He cleared his throat emphatically, like someone with the world under control. "But there was something I wasn't told." He stopped.

"Coomey."

"Yeah?" He looked up.

"Tell me what's the matter."

And he told me. All through the worst of his drinking years, one thing he had always done was to keep a roof over the heads of his wife and two kids. The kids had graduated from college and he still had the house—for the moment—but the bank had decided to foreclose if he couldn't come up with the three-months-in-arrears mortgage payment. And his wife was dying of cancer.

I was looking down all the while, into my lap, making out a check. Coomey Fenimore stood up. I didn't look up. He walked away. And when I did look up, I was finished.

"Coomey?"

He came back.

I handed him a check for an amount that would flatten my checking account. Maybe I could make it up from our savings, dig into our small savings.

"Good God, Dick. No," he said looking at the check.

He thrust it back at me and our hands collided in midair. The check crumpled, fell to the floor, and as Coomey Fenimore walked off, I retreived it and slipped the check into my pocket. I had done my best and was relieved. But when I stood waiting for a taxi, we met again.

"Goodbye, Coomey," I said, shaking his hand. I lowered my voice. "Once you said…You said…You remember what you said. About…If ever I needed anything…Well, this is when I need something." I pressed the check into his palm, turned away, and got into a cab.

We stood there, Jack (Ace) Reynolds and me, he behind his desk, me in front of it, now covered with sheets of paper, all this way and that, some figures showing, others hidden, so who knew what was where? I had just said,

"Show me, Ace. Just show me."

"*Show* you," he was now saying, evenly, slowly amazed and domineering. He squinted his pale blue eyes, as much as to say, "Who the hell d'ya think you are?" And then he said, "All you need, Bingold" head down searching among papers and coming up with a yellow sheet "is this."

He handed me the the yellow sheet and I held it like a dunce, almost ready to take it and get away. Could I be wrong? A secretary in an outer room had stopped typing. Even he air conditioner had stopped. Ace Reynolds smiled.

"Service isn't what it used to be." He walked to the window, picked up a small wrench, tapped metal, turned a knob, then returned to his desk, the wrench in hand. The air conditioner hummed. I was still holding the yellow sheet.

"Give my very best to Mr. Ewen."

He put out his hand to shake the hand that held the yellow sheet. And I pulled back the hand and said,

"I think I'll take a walk, Mr. Reynolds, and take a look," and I turned and walked away. I knew the door from the office into the warehouse, a wood door with smudges about a large dented brass knob.

The secretary, a large woman who, I was suddenly sure, liked to eating as much as I did, began her typing again, looking sideways at scribbled note.

Jack Reynolds moved quietly to my side.. I had no idea what I would see, how I would identify a single item, or what I would do if I could. It was all one foolhardy risk, to insult a veteran J. J. Newbury employee, bring down Richard Ewen's disapproval on my head, and, worst of all, show such poor judgement. Was I a team player? Did I know people well enough to know when to insist, when to give way? I wanted to take over Richard Ewen's job some day; be among the top brass. Was I throwing it all away in one toss of the dice—and for nothing?

"Well, Bingold?"

Reynold's voice was phlegmy but cool, his manner a mirror of Richard Ewen. I looked down. I was still holding the piece of yellow paper. I glanced at it, saw a row of numbers, committed them to memory, and stepped aside.

"After you," I said.

I stood holding the door open. Reynolds walked through. I closed the door, followed him to a row of fixtures, a tag fixed to each one. Birds twittered at the very top of the arched ceiling. Chicago traffic moaned and roared. I heard a distant siren and close at hand, across a narrow space between the warehouse and an open window, a radio or record playing, *Mrs. Robinson*.

"Well?"

I looked down at the yellow sheet, up into the pale blue eyes, and hesitated. He was, after all, a likable guy, about Richard Ewen's age. What *was* I doing? What would I prove, after all? I felt like putting my arm around him and suggest we go for a drink. I was tired of his attitude that he belonged to some club I was shut out of.

But then he said—and at first, I didn't get it, because he said it with such superior finesse, so quietly, with such authority,

"I believe my report of your visit, Dick, will not be favorable."

And I picked up the tag and the numbers matched the inventory number of the fixture he said he had already shipped off to other stores. I showed him the numbers on the yellow sheet and nodded in the direction of the fixture itself.

"Are you satisfied?" he asked quietly, relaxed, his pale blue eyes taking me in.

"Yes, Mr. Reynolds, I am."

Again, I hesitated, and then said bluntly: "On this sheet, you've listed fixtures that you've sent out, to stores in your region." And then I made a sweep with my hand. "The fixtures we're looking at this very minute."

I thought that would make him wilt. But the pale blue eyes held steady, though this time they were looking me up and down, as if to say, "If you only knew what a dunce you are."

I stayed at the Statler that night and went to the bar and sat on a cushioned stool and instead of Johnny Walker Black Label I drank a half dozen or so of Teacher's Scotch on the rocks. Afterward, I ordered steak smoothered in mushrooms and a bottle of red Merlot of exactly the right year. A half hour later, I went to the cashier, popped a peppermint onto my tongue, paid, and was going out the door when a friend of mine, Hank Hyatt, walked in. He was headed for the bar and I joined him.

We recalled old times, when he and I worked for J. J. Newbury, and Al Holzer was our fixture supplier. Hyatt, up-and-coming, bright, willing, though not always for his own good. For him, the first consideration was the organization. We had become good friends after work and had been able get things done at J.J. Newbury which needed doing. Al was deliberate and had a knack for making everything about business finance clear.

By midnight, we had formed a mutual admiration society and by the time I went up to my room, we had decided that, if the opportunity ever arose, we would go into business together. We were to meet for breakfast. I waited, I ate. He never showed.

Chapter Eleven

Nosedive

When I walked back into our New York office that Thursday afternoon, I asked to see Richard Ewen.

"You're smiling," Ann Allerton said, meeting me at his door.

"I am?" I asked her and winked. "Great to see you, Ann."

"Successful trip?"

"Very," I said, and then tried not to say, but said it, "I've made a start on cleaning up that mess out there." Chicago in our New York minds was a blotch on the landscape by a big lake.

She raised her eyebrows and motioned me through the door. Richard Ewen had at that moment put down the phone and when he looked up, a cloud passed over his face. I swallowed.

"Won't you sit down, Richard? I won't take any calls for a few minutes, Mrs. Allerton."

I was trying to smile and at the same time trying to find some other reason for Richard Ewen greeting me with a frown. Then I had it: the phone call was disturbing news for *him*. And my smile ran away with me. He would have a heart-to-heart talk with me and give me another raise. He replied to my smile with a limited smile of his own.

"I want to get right to the point, Dick. But first, let me ask you, how is Mrs. Bingold?"

I felt sick.

"Just fine," I said cheerfully. "The due date is August twenty-first and I think—I believe—I'm sure—than that will be the day."

The way Richard Ewen folded his hands and looked at me reminded me of something, a long time ago, in the Army.

"Perhaps it is my fault, Richard. I may not have made myself clear. However…I thought *you would get the picture.*" A grinding to a halt and silence. I heard something click. Did Richard Ewen have false teeth? "Jack Reynolds is one of our oldest and…He is one of our most trusted employees. Our friendship goes back many years."

I sank in my chair and my cheeks reddened, as if I had been slapped. Had I misread Reynolds and the situation? Made a mountain out of a molehill?

"However." And Richard Ewen seemed to raise up into his suit again, as if he had just found something more cheerful to talk about, as if he had gotten across a bridge that I didn't know was there, from one territory to another, neither of which I had any idea existed. I felt sick. "However," he repeated. "Jack has one fault—if you can call it a fault. He is a worrywart. He has this habit, Richard. We all have these habits. He holds on to inventory for an *emergency.* You will understand, of course, the emergency need not arise to prove the preparation for an emergency wrong. You and I understand that. But…"

I was thinking of the total comfort of the Lost and Found Bar.

"…all these years I've never been able to convince Jack Reynolds of it."

We were standing and I was turning and we were walking—drifting—over the carpet and I saw Ann Allerton in a blur and I was riding the elevator to the ground floor. Never in my life had I been told off with such finesse.

****

I would go straight home because who knew when Beth might go into labor? I stopped, glanced at the light, and walked into the street. Traffic stopped one way and filled the cross street with rubber, metal and speed and blasting horns. Once Toots Shore said to me, "*Bingold, you got presence.*" I hurried on, catching a glimpse of myself in a showcase window of naked mannequins and instantly straightened my back and lengthened my stride. Reynolds and Ewen were wrong. I had done the right thing. A block later, I turned into the twilit murmur of the Lost & Found Bar and Lounge. There was the lonely drinker at the bar's center, a half dozen of the easy regulars at one end, and a big guy who seemed to own the bar leaning forward and talking to the real owner, my old friend, Bob Farley, at the other end.

"Dick," he said, reaching out for my hand, not quite with the speed I expected. "Marvelous to see you. Meet a really old friend of mine, Bob Danner."

"Now there's a shake," Danner said when I squeezed his smallish hand. Because the lids covered the top half of the whites, his eyes seemed to be half open. His lips, before he flashed me a mechanical smile, were turned down at the corners. His jaw seemed large until you saw that he held it in a permanent thrust. And now I realized that I had seen this face before. In the newspaper, on Monday, when I left for Chicago.

"The Dick Bingold special?" Bob Farley asked.

"The Dick Bingold special," I said, knowing he meant a double shot of Johnny Walker Black with ice and suggestion of water. I turned to Danner. "So you're *the* Bob Danner."

This guy in an easy-fitting dark blue serge suit straightened slightly and ticked his chin to the left. "Whatever that means," he said, then flashed me the brief smile. "What are you, six-three?"

I liked the guy in spite of himself.

"Yeah, six-three and overweight at two-forty-five.

"Box?"

"Some. Dad did. Stood Gene Tunney to a three-round

stand-off."

"No," Bob Farley said, unable to restrain his interest. "You never told a whole lot of stories, but never *that* one before."

"You never asked me before," I said, finishing off my drink, thinking, *No., Mr. Richard Ewen. You are wrong.* "At a West Side smoker. I was fourteen—in nineteen forty-eight." I was warming up and Bob put another special in front of me. "Gene shouted at my dad, 'Hey! Here's a lefty that stands righty.'"

"Come on," Danner said. "Come on."

"Swear it," I said, reminded of something. A strange memory: of Dad kneeling before the Eucharist and making the sign of the Cross on his muscular body as he rose from the rail. "He was a swimmer. He and his buddies swam to Cony Island from the Manhattan docks." I caught something in the air and I stopped bragging and decided to chance flattery.

"I followed that Star of India sapphire case," I lied. "The guy that got it back for the museum deserves a lot of credit."

Danner brightened. I liked the guy. He carried himself with authority and power and when he pulled a wallet from his pocket, the twilight of the bar made a golden glow of his badge. He had power. Bob handed me my second or third drink. Every seat at the bar was taken. Now there was the sound of the voices and laughter of women. *Beth,* I thought, *and the kids.*

"Sure, thanks," I said. Bob Farley had said,

"One for the road?"

"I've got to catch that six-twenty for…"

Bob Danner turned to me. "For?"

"For Long Island. Hicksville."

His eyebrows went up but his eyes still seemed half open. He nodded. "Thought so."

We shook. "We'll meet again, I'm sure," he said. "Whatta y'pay for an 'estate' in Hicksville?"

I was standing, still shaking his hand.

"Depends," I said.

"Of course," he said, a little more friendly, then repeated, "We'll meet again, I'm sure. Ever meet the friend of all good people, Eddie Egan?" I was smiling and stepping back, anxious to catch the six-twenty. "You will meet Eddie. We'll have dinner, here, at the Lounge, one of these days."

I glanced at Bob Farley. "Eddie Egan," he explained. "Eddie was the main guy the largest drug-bust in the City's history. They plan to make a movie of his exploits—I hear."

"Oh," I said. "The Lost & Found is the place to be."

They laughed and I was in the street stepping briskly to catch the six-twenty.

Each wheel of a commuter train weighs fifteen tons and all four of them under the bar car were sending redhot shockwaves through the eight-ton, continuous-weld rails that ran through the Long Island countryside. The bar swayed and Leonard behind the bar came toward me and went away and the three other guys I had treated, their felt hats on the back of their heads, swayed with me.

"S'great worl," said the man next to me.

"Great," I said, and meant it.

"Got something for you, Mr. Bingold," Leonard said into my ear. I had been one of his best customers over the years. It was about time he gave me some special recognition.

"One more for the railroad," I called out cheerily.

My buddies laughed. We drank and Hicksville was announced. I turned to Leonard and he handed me a slip of paper. And I knew what his gift was: I glanced at my bill for the month: $149.10, and shoved it into my pocket, and thought, *My commuter ticket for the month is only fifty dollars.*

Beth was waiting in a long line of cars and we edged our way into the early summer evening and onto a long black road that lifted and fell and turned then turned back and we talked about Chicago and when she asked me how it went, I said, "I'll most likely get a raise out of it. I solved a problem with the inventory. Actually, I had to confront a guy, put him in his place, make him fess up."

The hood of the car reflected the sun and I asked her how she felt and she said she felt fine and I asked her how the kids were and I pressed on the horn and a guy on a bike wobbled and almost went into a ditch and I slipped my arm around her and she didn't resist and I drew her closer and only then did she pull back.

"Your dad called," she said in a flat tone.

We got home in time for me to see all the kids and with my success in Chicago we were all in a great mood and I held the phone call from Dad away from me and I sat on the couch and the kids piled on top of me and we wrestled and played until I looked at the clock and sent them off to bed with a warning they had better settle down, fast.

When I went to the phone, I saw that Beth was frowning, and when I passed her, she said, "You needn't be so…So abrupt with them."

I held the phone. "Discipline," I said. "Kids need discipline." I dialed Dad and Mom's number and the phone rang a long time and then Dad answered his voice was dull and he told me Mom wasn't feeling well. Not well at all and would I drop by Friday or Saturday and I said I would.

****

When I walked into the offices of J.J. Newbury on Thursday, August 22, the pocket to my jacket was packed with cigars. Beth had given birth to a healthy baby girl we had named

Catherine, after Beth's mother.

"You look proud and relieved," Ann Allerton said.

"I am," I said and leaned down and kissed her on the cheek. "I am, Ann."

The gang gathered around, including Richard Ewen, who had come out of his office especially to congratulate me. I shook hands all around, giving a heavier, longer shake to the two or three guys who had had babies in the last six months or so. Wyn Smart stood slightly out of the circle, reaching through it to shake my hand. The air filled with cigar smoke and aimless chatter and then we were all back at work and it was then Ann told me Mr. Ewen wanted to see me. I took a deep breath and went in, thinking, *He hasn't forgotten Chicago.*

"Best wishes again, Dick," he said when I sat down. "I've got a favor to ask of a man who is a new father, if you'll forgive me for getting right to the point."

I nodded.

"I need a job done in St. Louis, tomorrow. A store opening has had to be pushed ahead and I need one of you there, now."

I shifted in my seat, and thought, *"One of you? St. Louis. I would be able to see her.* And I waited, suspecting the worst and I leaned forward in my chair and then it came.

"To be quite open with you, I was going to send Wyn, but his daughter's horse show is this weekend and he begged off. Would you be a able to make things right with Mrs. Bingold?"

"Yes," I said lamely. Then brightly, "Yessir, I can do it."

"Fine," Richard Ewen said. "Fine."

He made a cathedral of his fingers and ticked off what he wanted attended to and I was sure I heard him but when I walked back to my desk, I wasn't sure at all. I would depend on my memory and experience of a dozen other store openings.

It was Dad's voice on the phone. The lights of our house cast windowframes on the snow outside and inside the house there was the fragrance of balsam boughs and the twinkling of greens and reds and that scrubbed look children have when they are expecting something. Catherine was in a playpen by the fireplace and Barbara had decided her dad was fair target for a tackle. James and Rich, at peace for a change, were kneeling on a window seat and watching the snowplow go by.

I listened into the phone and tears came to my eyes, briefly, and I heard in my dad's voice a tone I had heard all my life: *When something needs to be done, you are the one to do it. You are my favorite son.* I swallowed. I could feel his loneliness. After forty years of marriage to the only man she had ever loved, my mother was dead. By her side sat the man who had always been faithful to her, my dear dad. For the last thirty-three days, as she lay unconscious in a coma, he had never left her side. Nurses could not forget that day in and day out, often in the middle of the night, he put his lips next to her ear and spoke to her, never believing she could not hear.

"Son," he said into the phone. "I want you here, *now.* I don't want Mother taken from the hospital until you are here."

I said, "Yes, Dad. I'll leave in ten minutes."

He hung up and I stared at the receiver, whispering, "Hail, Mary, full of grace," then replaced the phone on the cradle, and thought, *Mom I can forgive you everything, but I can't forget.*

"Dad?" Rich called to me from a place in the room that was dark.

"Yes, Rich?"

"What's the matter?"

Beth came from the kitchen, drying her hands.

"Dad wants me at the hospital."

"*Now?*" Beth asked.

"Mom has just…" I began, and looked at James turning toward me and Richard now in front of me and Barbara by Beth's side. "Our Lord has just taken Grandmother to Heaven."

"She's dead?" Rich asked.

And he came to me and James was beside me and suddenly we were all by the fireplace, Catherine reaching up to be taken into Beth's arms and I told them Grandmother was dead and Grandfather needed me. I bowed my head and they bowed theirs and I said,

"I am the resurrection and the life, saith the Lord; he that believeth in me, though he were dead, yet shall he live; and whosoever liveth and believeth in me, shall never die. Hail, Mary full of grace, the Lord is with thee." I looked at the bowed heads through a blur, then whispered, "Holy Mary, mother of God, pray for us sinners now and at the hour of our death." I waited in the silence for a sign, then whispered, "Amen."

There were five soft "amens" and the movement of hands and arms as we each made the sign of the Cross over our face and chests. Tears sat in the boys' and Barbara's eyes and Catherine clung unknowing to Beth.

"It's Christmas eve, Dad," James said.

"I know," I said, my tears burning for Dad. "I know."

Rich stared at me then at James.

"Dad has to do what he has to do, James," Rich said, hiding a sudden surge of pride.

And I looked at him and thought, *Rich, you're only eight.* And we drew tight in a circle and hugged and I was in my coat and out the door and on a long snowy road into the night.

As one month faded into another, I kept on the go for J. J. Newbury, to Los Angeles, to St. Louis, to Cincinnati, to Toledo, to Atlanta, and to Ft. Lauderdale. Wherever I went, I was always under the gun, designing fixtures that hadn't been thought of, and re-designing those that didn't fit, so when I was in St. Louis, we never really had time for each other.

All during this time, as far as J.J. Newbury was concerned, I was determined to present the company solutions, not problems. My file began to fill with letters of commendations from store managers, and Richard Ewen gave me one more raise, my fourth, at the same time he gave Wyn Smart his fifth and final.

I had flown in from St. Louis that Friday morning in the Fall of 1970, her voice still mumuring in my brain, saying, *I must start thinking of someone else.* New York looked dirty and dismal. A a stringy mist searched in and out among parked cars and dark alleyways. The tip of the Empire State Building was hidden by cloud and the office of J.J. Newbury was like a morgue. We all avoided each others eyes. They knew something I didn't. The only person who greeted me with any enthusiasm was Wyn Smart. But it was only the start of an exchange when he himself cut it short, as if he had caught himself doing something in bad taste. When Ann Allerton said Richard Ewen wanted to see me, I saw that her eyes were red from crying.

My hurry across the carpet seemed to get me nowhere while it seemed to take Richard Ewen a half hour to rise from his desk, his face crisscrossed with sparks of light and dark, the flesh of his right cheek by the corner of his lips rippling in a tiny tremor. He cleared his throat several times before he said,

"Fine, Richard. Fine, you're here. They say you did a fine job in St. Louis. Won't you sit down?"

Richard Ewen seemed stouter, older, his neck bulging, as if he were swallowing an object far too large. What seemed to be missing was his grace.

I sat, heavily.

"And that growing family of yours is well, I hope," he began dully. He stopped, looked about, and: "I want to say to you what an affable, competent fellow-worker you've always been these past…" He held up his hand when he saw that I was about to tell him. "I know exactly," he went on. "These past fourteen years. And now…" And I interrupted him,

"Fourteen years and two months and six days. Mrs. Bingold is fine."

I said it with a lump in my throat and in as friendly a way as possible because I was sure I would never know a finer man, a better boss, than Richard Ewen. I saw dandruff on the shoulder of his pinstripe jacket. His tie was slightly askew. I noticed that the top of his desk had been wiped clean. A single sheet of paper lay there. It looked like a resume. He began again.

"Richard," and then said it: "J.J. Newbury is being—has been sold and all the jobs in this office terminated." There was a feeling in the room that a jet plane will make when it abruptly loses altitude. I passed a hand across my face as if that would hide my cheeks' sudden flush. "I had heard rumblings," Richard Ewen said. "But only found out…" He turned to the small April, 1971 calendar and pointed to the twenty-first. "The twenty-first," he said.

"It's fine," I said. I didn't want to watch Richard Ewen demean himself by excuses. He had his reasons. I waited. He would tell me that he wanted me to stay with him, to wrap up loose ends, maybe to transfer with him to the new company. It was then that the print on that single piece of paper caught my eye. And I read the name, upside-down and backward: Winslow Smart, seconds before Richard Ewen covered it with his hand.

"…and there was nothing to be done or said until it all became a *fact*. So, Dick, this is what it would be good of you to do. There is a position in the real estate division of the new organization to which you would bring much needed expertise."

Even Richard Ewen had his faults. There was a sudden explosion that rattled the windows, and he stared over my shoulder at Mrs. Allerton.

"A tire blow-out," she announced.

"Not another riot to stop the war in Vietnam?" Richard Ewen said with a certain hardness. Now he looked at me. All that build-up could mean only one thing: a *demotion* with lower pay. And I beat Richard Ewen to the punch.

"Thank you, sir. You mean I have a job but at lower pay." And I said too quickly, "Thanks, Mr. Ewen, but no thanks."

He frowned.

"You always were a sharp man, Dick. Excuse me, an intelligent man." He stared, and added, "And fearless. I've never known anyone so cool under fire."

The words could not cross the barrier between us; they fell through me, jumbled, tangled, my heart pounding to keep me from suffocating. I was drowning. I was sure my face looked like a man with a high fever. But I recovered.

"Will you join me for a drink at the Lost and Found, Mr. Ewen?"

As always, he was ahead of me. "I was hoping you would join all of us for drinks and dinner at the Plaza this evening."

I was standing.

"You've always been a great—a fine—boss. The best I'll ever know," I told Richard Ewen.

He was standing now, his head nodding, those painful shadows and lights passing through the skin of his face.

"Thank you, Dick. Thank you very much for those words. It's not often I hear words like that."

And when I went out the door, Ann Allerton was nowhere in sight. Rich and James and Barbara and Catherine and Beth stared up at me from their photo frames arranged on my desk next to a can of sharp pencils and pens, a thick glass ashtray with the remainder of a cigar, and a silver swordfish with the word *Ft. Lauderdale, Florida* at its base. Someone had hung on the sword a tiny card that read, *Ft. Liquordale.*

Pushing a warm smile into my face, I went about shaking hands, even Wyn Smart's, each of us saying how we had liked working with the other and how we would stay in touch knowing all the while we wouldn't. On my way out I stopped a moment by Mr. Ewen's door.

"May I have a raincheck for tonight?" I asked across the distance of carpet, then lied, "I promised the children and Beth I'd be home early."

Mr. Ewen looked up from his desk. "Certainly, Dick. I'm sorry, but certainly."

And I hustled out the door, to the elevator, the photos and oranaments of fourteen years knocking about in a carboard box pressed hard against my belly. The door sucked open and I stepped inside and pressed the button.

That's the past, I thought, *you have to live in the present and the future.*

As I rode the elevator to the bottom, my cheeks burned.

"Where've you been?"

I turned out the light and got quietly into bed beside Beth. "Company party."

"Company party," she mumbled, then: "Company party?" she asked, sitting straight up in bed.

I reached out of the blanket, turned on the light, and sat up beside her.

"I thought I might drop by the Lost and Found on the way home, but instead I went to the company party at the Plaza."

"The *Plaza*? Since when did J.J. Newbury treat their employees to a company party at the Plaza? You never told me about any company party."

Stretching her arms into the shadow above, Beth took a shivery breath, then settled, crossed her arms across her bosom, and stared into the night.

"This was a special party," I said, stone sober after a dozen or so shots of Johnny Walker Black Label and soda. I felt like a delinquent, playing a game on a football field with goal posts at one end and a black hole at the other, the field flanked by a perfectly silent crowd in hoods,

"How would you like to live in Ft. Lauderdale?

Instead of staring ahead, Beth looked down at her hands, the fingers of both turned in toward the palms, as if to see the nails, her head moving ever so slightly right and left. She had caught on. She took another shivery breath, but this time without stretching.

"The children didn't even *wonder* were you were. We had dinner, I read to Cath, they did their homework and went to bed." Her tongue was dull bronze. "Two o'clock is a new low, even for you."

"You don't like the idea of Ft. Lauderdale?"

"Mom did what Dad told her. It would kill Mom to lose her grandchildren to Florida. You're the breadwinner. I go where you go. When do you want the house and children ready, Mr. Bingold?"

There was a summer night outside and summer trees against the sky and a neat new-painted frame house on a street in Hicksville, Long Island and all of it collapsed around my wife's voice and tongue.

"*Now* tell me what happened."

I told her and I watched from the tail of my eye the big tears roll down her cheeks and I felt her hand reach out, touch me and withdraw. The tears dried immediately. She was small and distant and I saw her in my mind standing in white saying the marriage vow and I heard my voice reply and I expected the clock on the mantle to strike the hour but all I heard was the steady beat of my own heart. The heart of a runner who once did the mile in four minutes, seventeen seconds, and scored a perfect ten in gymnastics. Who tried to be as good a boxer as his dad.

And I was talking.

"I thought at first I would go to the Lost and Found and then I turned around and showed up at the party. By the end— When they'd all gone, I told Mr. Ewen, 'No," I said, 'it was one of those offers in a life—"

"What offer?"

"To stay with him, in the new company—"

"Doing?"

"Doing? He said, 'The specific tasks can be spelled out later.' But I said....What time is it anyhow? There's hardly a breath of air. 'Ft. Lauderdale is opening up,' he said when I asked him about with National Fabrics—a job with them, in Ft. Lauderdale. 'I had no idea you would be willing to re-locate to Ft. Lauderdale, Dick, and my old friend, Dan Winfield, said, well, sure, we can use a man of Dick Bingold's calibre."

The room and the street and the heavy summer leaves were silent.

"So, I'll fly down on Monday for an interview."

Beth got down under the covers and turned on her side, away from me.

"We won't have to spend another cold winter on Long Island," I said, and turned off the light and lay down on my side and stared into the dark.

Chapter Twelve

Fresh Start

I sat at the bar, the vision of my right eye only slightly blurred from the pinch of adhesive tape. I had been in Ft. Lauderdale only ten days and I knew this bartender by name, had found a house for my family, had begun work with National Fabrics, had rolled my car into Alligator Alley's concrete ditch, and had already gone to court with my new friend and attorney, Dick Hennekam, suing the ambulance driver who had crashed while taking me to the hospital, and the hospital itself, whose records showed that I had been released but whose nurse had rolled me aboard a gurney into a distant room and left me there unconscious for half a day.

"Feeling better?" Nick the bartender said. "Auto accidents are murder."

I drank off my Johnny Walker Black Label. "I've only had two others," I said as a woman took her seat to my left, a man to my right. "They *are* murder."

"We've met before," the man said in a tone of voice I'd heard before. He sat on his barstool with an air of ownership, the lids half-covering the whites of his eyes. And I knew right off who it was.

"Bob Danner," I said. "Star of India sapphire."

My drink was at hand and it was gone and Nick put another before me and I said, "One of Mr. Danner's regulars," and Nick nodded and I turned, nodded to the woman, then said to Danner, "Dick Bingold."

And Bob Danner turned to me slowly without enthusiasm, to load me down with his authority, intimidate me, bully me, and I finished off my second drink by the time he had said, "Chief of Detectives Bob Danner," putting out his hand to shake mine.

In the next instant, he let me know by his tone that firing his title at me was a joke but *at the same time* anyone in hearing would be best advised to take him seriously.

I was grinning.

"Bob," I said, "what do you think—a conjecture, of course, but what do you think, Hasn't the cat as good a right to think that it is playing with the man, as the other way around?"

He paused with the drink at his lips and threw me a dark glance that meant he was up to anything I was and was just as fast if not faster.

"Depends on who the cat is," he said, barely moving his lips then tossing off the drink.

We both laughed and I said to the woman,

"I'm Dick Bingold."

And the three of us introduced ourselves.

"I'm Marie," she said and her smile and her voice collided at the tip of my nose with a soft concussion in which I saw in my mind's eye, the spire of a church penetrating misty dark.

"And where are you from, Marge?" Bob Danner asked.

"Marie," I said.

"Montreal," Marie said. "Sapphire is a deep purplish blue. Milky crystals, of a rich, rich blue," she went on dreamily. "I saw a photo of it—the star sapphire. Millions and just millions of years to make it…" She trailed off and stared at her drink.

"Marge, Marie, it's all the same. Did you know Egan's in town, Bingold?"

"You mean in the flesh? I just saw the movie—it came to town last week."

Marie turned her head.

"Movie?" she asked.

"The *French Connection*," Danner said, glancing at Marie as if she interferred.

"Oh, what a good movie," she said, leaning sideways, listening, barely touching my shoulder. Her voice said too softly for the subject matter, "I love Gene Hackman as Popeye Doyle."

Danner pushed on, "Well, Hackman played my friend Eddy's part," across my face at Marie and Marie breathed out,

"Gene Hackman is a darling."

"Nick," I said, "Fill up all three. Who's that?"

"Guy that just walked in?"

"Yeah."

"Peter Short, Continental Seafood. Five or six outlets, selling fresh fish."

Danner glanced that way, then turned back to me. The drinks had arrived. When they were all at our mouths and before he swallowed his, Danner said sideways into my ear, "Fish. Right. Some fish."

I turned to Marie. "January 10, 1962 and October 29, 1964, dates that will live in infamy. Eddie Egan made the biggest drug-bust in history, and your friend and mine, Bob Danner, recovered the largest star sapphire after it was stolen from the Metropolitan Museum of Fine Arts."

"You're full of information, aren't you, Dick Bingold?"

Danner sounded a little friendlier. "Only two facts wrong, and that's not a bad batting average. How in hell you knew the date of Eddie's drug bust, I'll never know. But the date of October 29 was the date the Star of India sapphire was stolen—and it was stolen from the Natural History Museum."

I offered Danner a cigar and we lit up and I said to Marie,

"There are more French-speaking people in Montreal than

any other city of the world except Paris. It's a really great city."

"Oh, I didn't know that," she said. "I'm here, staying with my mother, working at a bank. I just wanted one winter away from the cold."

"You're on my team," Danner said and blew smoke into my face.

Marie stood up from her barstool and, with a whisk of hestitating pressure on the space around her, turned to go. When I stood up, Bob stood up, and laid a hand on my arm—and Marie made the twilit air of the bar fit softly close about her dwindling figure. She went by Peter Short and disappeared.

"Thanks," Danner said. "Thanks. I wanted to ask something of you.

The voice had become friendly and familiar.

"You've met Eddie. You know Bob Danner. We talked it over. We talked about Dick Bingold. We—checked up on him. Family man. In charge of new store openings." He lifted his chin and staring straight into the mirror of the bar where we saw each other, he said "What d'ya say you join us in Eddie Egan Security Limited? You've got the talents we need. We can teach you the rest—on the job training," he finished, happy with the joke.

The bar was suddenly brighter, larger, longer, Nick clearer. I ordered two more drinks and Bob Danner and I began to talk, and though I heard "cash investment" in place of the word "talents," I knew I could handle anything that came my way. I had already talked to the man at National Fabrics about spinning off one of its departments into a business of my own. I even had a name for it—and I kept it all a secret from Beth—Optimum Design. I would show Richard Ewen.

Chapter Thirteen

Death in the Family

Dad flew through the air, cigar in his mouth, the sea calm, far far out and the pool a sparkle of light into which Dad plunged. When he came up for air, four grandchildren stood with slits for eyes and dark holes for mouths, faces drenched with his splashing, heads back in merriment.

"Oh, *Grandpa*," Barbara yelled. She was especially pleased because just last night her grandpa had given her a new pair of flippers, one of many presents from all of us to celebrate her eighth birthday.

"Grandpa, you're a *delinquent*," Rich shouted.

Licking the water from the splash of his favorite person in the world off his lips, James beamed. Catherine lept up and down, clapping her hands and taking small steps toward the pool's edge. Just in time, Beth reached out and pulled her back to safety.

Towels in hand, James and Rich ran to help their grandpa up the ladder, but by the time they got there, Dad was standing, palming water from his chest and thighs.

From my deckchair, I saw it all: How Florida agreed with Beth. How the big pool sparkled and my forty-foot Chris Craft gleamed. How, dreaming in its polished rose, our Lighthouse Point house breathed light, safety and our arrival. Catherine, our lovable three-year-old, screamed in delight. The Birthday Girl disappeared into the house, returned, chortling, "Flippers, Grandpa. Flippers." I saw Beth breathe in. I saw my father take both towels and wipe himself with both towels.

"Not bad for a seventy-two-year-old geezer, eh Dick?"

Dad's voice and my heart met somewhere there in the bright warm sun. I couldn't tell which was his and which mine. Never had been able to.

My teeth clamped on the earpiece of my sunglasses, my cigar between the first and second fingers of my right hand, I thought, *Nobody can take* this *away from me.* I winked at Beth, and she turned away, and looked down at Catherine. The next instant, the scene was covered by a cloud: I had thrust my sunglasses over my eyes. The trio at the end of the pool broke up. Rich dove in, bobbed up, and shouting, "Dad! Watch! The whole length!" began the crawl. James called over his shoulder, "Lemonade for Grandpa!" and vanished into the house. Beth, carrying Catherine, followed. The two towels rubbing slowly back and forth across his neck, my Dad stood alone.

And I whipped off my sunglasses, dropped my cigar into the ashtray, and, my sockless feet in shined loafers tapping the ceramic poolside, I made haste toward him across the deck. But he disappeared—until I blinked away the glare of sun.

"You O.K.?" I asked. "You O.K.?"

When he smiled, we were both smiling.

"Sure, son. Sure. I am certainly fine."

You haven't seen a thing, I told myself. He didn't grab at his chest and I said,

"How about that lunch I promised? I want to show you around and our new business, Optimum. When you come back for a visit, we'll have more time for everything."

On the way into the house, I put my arm on his shoulders lightly. "You might think about it," I said lightly. "Take it easy. Retire," I said so that he had to say,

"What, Dick?"

And I said, "Lunch. We'll have lunch—and look over Optimum—then the airport."

"Here, Grandpa," James said, and thrust a glass of lemonade into Dad's hands. It was brimming over with big icecubes and sugar and lemon. It filled me with thirst. Dad took two or three sips and handed it to me. I all but finished it off.

"*Dad*," James said. "That's Grandpa's. I made it for Grandpa."

I handed the glass, almost empty, to Dad. "I know," I said. "I know," and I saw in the glass, when Dad had upended it, a ray of sunlight warm and full.

Beth and Barbara stood at our side, Barbara twisting wet hair with one hand, holding dripping flippers with the other.

"You won't be here for lunch, Dad?" Beth asked. "I made a pile of sandwiches."

My face went hot with anger. Dad's glance bounced from me to Beth and back again. James dashed at Barbara and they both went larking round about the house.

"…told you I wanted to take Dad to lunch and show him around," I was saying, my voice barely audible in the thickness of my throat. "Show him Optimum, before he catches his plane." I switched my head to the right and growled, "And please don't let those children make a mess."

I saw Dad's back to us, hastening across the carpet to roughhouse with the children. The Florida sunlight played in Beth's hair and illuminated her face. Her eyes were slits whose glare when they slowly opened were blurred with tears she instantly wiped away.

"Dad," she called, turning away. "Is there anything I can do to help you get ready?"

"Dad?"

Dripping, his face dark, Rich stood by my side, looking up.

"I thought you were going to watch me swim the pool."

"No, thank you, Beth."

It was my father's voice.

"Did you hear me, Dad?" my son asked.

And I looked down, told Rich, "There's such a thing as growing up," saw his cheeks flush, and left the room.

＊＊＊＊

Dad looked down, took off his glasses, nodded, straightened, and put his glasses back on. We had just walked into the shed from the front office where I had introduced Dad to Bob Danner and Eddie Egan. And now I was feeling rotten, because the introduction had not gone well.

"We'll be getting along," Bob Danner said, for once in his life aware that someone else was in the room beside himself. "Great to meetcha, Mr. Bingold," he said, and put out his hand. Dad had taken reluctantly.

And Egan had heaved his long solid frame up to be as tall as Dad and said, "I fool you not, *Mister* Bingold, besides being a fast study, our boy, Dick, here, can make *any* business look good."

Then they had walked out.

Dad hadn't smiled and now he was recovering. And so was I: his disapproval of my partners had made the world look strange.

"Fine work, good solution to an old problem," Dad now told Hank Hyatt, an old friend from Long Island I had invited down to take over the production line at Optimum Design, my company that designed, manufacatured, and sold store fixtures.

Under Dad's gaze, Hank Hyatt smiled proudly, but when our eyes met, Hyatt looked away, and when I looked up, Dad held me in a long long gaze...And I looked back into his eyes and we became two separate people, me, the small boy, he, that beloved dad, both of us—recalling a movie I'd seen—far far up in the castle battlement of our magic workshop, the machinery quiet, waiting to drill, screw, and polish into life the handiwork of his love. …I hurried out of the shop and opened and closed the washroom door and bathed my face and eyes in cold water and then we were on the way to the airport.

"Count on your hands, Son," Dad said as we drove. "Count on your *hands.*"

I felt sick. We sat side by side, the big day drawn about the shadow of our bodies in the moving car.

"I'm proud of you, son. Those fixtures you make are a better bet—a much better bet, you see what I mean?"

"I'll handle them, Dad. Believe me, Dad, I can handle Danner and Egan."

Dad nodded.

The door held open by the attendant who kept shifting on her feet in the high wind, I yelled to Dad,

"Phone tonight when you get home, will you?"

He nodded, holding his hat to his head, his other hand holding his simple small bag. I felt the wind in my hair and a strand of the attendant's hair blew across my lips and I saw Dad grow smaller, mount the steps, and walk through the door and disappear.

"Your dad?" the attendant asked.

"My dad," I said, and hurried to a vantage point by a chain-link fence where I could see his plane taxi along the backdrop of the Atlantic Ocean. *Godspeed,* I whispered, *Godspeed.* I waited and watched and saw the wheels clutch the belly of the frail craft and I waited and saw it lift and go smaller then go smaller again and again until the dot it became, became itself the empty sky.

Cathy Drew and I walked along the sandy beach of Andros

Island, miles away from anything in the sun of the Caribbean and the sand sifting between our toes. Just off shore, on a *Sailfish*, the small figures of Fred Drew and Beth made their way in after a good sail. When we met, we were all laughing, our tongues showing, our bodies glittering in young gold.

"That's what the old man told me," I yelled, ducking down and covering Fred's head with water from my cupped hands. My old loyal friend, Fred Drew, who had been my best friend through boyhood and best man at my wedding. And I went on, "The old fellow said, 'Don't tell anyone I told you so, but you four look like young gold.'"

We howled with laughter and ran another mile and stopped on a wide reach of sand between the sea and our cottage. The night before, our first night here, the moon had been warmly alive in the sky and roll of the sea and over the radio came *American Pie* and *Take Me Home, Country Roads.* It was hard to tell the difference between sleep and dream.

Before bed, over brandy, the women talked about their chldren, friends, and kitchens, and Fred and I drew in and blew out smoke from our cigars and talked business.

"How is it, Dick, you, of all people—a soft-hearted romantic—if ever there was one—if you can be honest—how can you run a business and be a private detective all in the same week?"

In the women's talk, there was sudden break and silence and through the shadow, I saw them look at each other, then, over the sea's wash and knitted musk of air, their soft talk went on. I finished off my brandy and Fred finished off his and I remembered all the movies I had seen John Wayne in the last scene, walk out of a door, alone.

"It reminds me of the story of the two Irishmen, Pat and—
"

Fred snorted loudly and Beth laughed quietly, as if to herself. Cathy continued to say something which had been interrupted.

"Romantic?" I said.

"Beth told me about you singing tenor with that professional singer, going out the door and she called you back and—Beth said—you became—"

"Good friends," I said. "Good friends, is all."

"I like it," Fred Drew said. "Good friends."

So we had gone to bed earlier than expected, our bedrooms separated by nothing but the thin walls of the cottage.

Now the four of us, after our time along the beach, stood on the wide reach of sand dotted right and left by dunes which you sit upon and lose yourself in the warm afternoon sun. And when Fred suggested that he and Beth go back to the cottage, fix drinks, and bring them and an umbrella back, we all agreed. Then, I said, we could go into to town to a crazy little restaurant Cathy had read about in the guide book.

"Great," Fred and Beth said, almost in unison.

"It must have been difficult for Beth, losing both parents so close together," Cathy said.

We sat.

"They were very close," I said. "Like my mom and dad, totally loyal—devoted to each other. Catherine died in late nineteen seventy and Ted about eighteen months later. Totally loyal. They were like…Like one person."

A very young man and women came running by, hands linked, putting us in shadow then sun again. I heard their laughter fade and Cathy's sigh and lap of waves run through each other. She pulled up her knees and hugged them and looked sideways, after the retreating forms.

"You're doing well, Dick, aren't you? I'm so happy for you."

"We've been friends a long time," I said and we laughed and I thought of Dad and she said,

"How's your dad?" and I said,

"Migosh, Cath. I was just thinking of Dad."

And I saw a movement in her throat when she turned to me and I said, "Dad's got me worried. He doesn't like the phone, so there's no way to get him to talk. He—I'm worried about his heart."

"You and your dad are close, aren't you? We all love him. I always thought of you and your dad being close."

The sun went behind a cloud and we both felt at the same moment the long shadow of a chill in the air.

"I love this island," Cathy said. "This was a great idea Beth and Fred had for us to take this trip together. We've all got friendships that go back years and years. Friendships and loyalties…" Her voice trailed off.

Seagulls screamed far out over the ocean's swell. I looked back, toward the cottage and I saw how young and burned Fred looked, toting the umbrella and how youthful and effecient Beth seeme, carrying a small wicker basket. From another direction, came a young woman.

"Mr. Bingold?" she asked, looking at me.

"Yes, I'm Mr. Bingold." I recognized her—a young woman from Florida connected to the inn.

"A phone call," she said. "Your brother called. He said—" she hesitated, then said, "He said it was urgent."

Urgent.

Her narrow face expanded and her eyes burned black with the word and my heart stopped.

Dad.

Neither my friends or my wife seemed to be in the right place or shape and I most of all seemed to be out of place, an animal of ancient and distant origin, bristling with hair and very hot.

Cathy's voice, warm with concern, sounded in my ear: "Dick?"

"What's wrong?" Beth asked, scared—for the children.

And I ran barefoot through the sand, across a boardwalk, and to a telephone in a corner room that looked out on the sea. John could have called from only one place—Dad's—because that's where he had lived for the past two years.

I dialed, got a voice that said I had dialed a wrong number, tried again, got the operator, and gave her Dad's number but she said I could dial direct and I told her to put the call through herself.

I heard one ring and then John's voice, at a distance.

"Darn," he said, then: "There. These phones should be designed to tell one end from the other. Dick? That you? I can hear your voice as if you were next—"

"What, John?"

Stoked for eternity, the sun sat blistering the horizon, burning my cheeks.

"Dick," he said in a rounded actor's tone, "I want you to prepare—"

The sun was now half as large, blurred.

"John, I've called."

"Your father....Our father," he said into a terrific silence, "is dead."

I brought the bucket of ice from the motel hallway and as I fixed drinks I said to Beth, "That is like John. If ever there was anything like John, that was it."

We were all in Pasaic for the funeral. Beth put her hand on my wrist and I made two drinks and handed her one. I sat down heavily and Beth perched on the bed, a yard away.

"It's beautiful," Beth said.

She had seen my fingering the Medal of the Sacred Heart that I now wore around my neck. It had belonged to Dad; he had worn it for years, even before I knew what it was. Tears streamed down my face. I was broken and sad and angry. As I stood above the beach on Andros Island, I could hear Johns' voice over the phone.

****

Dad's body is in the morgue, he was telling me. The morgue in the Bronx.. Someone must claim his body my brother was telling me. Dad, I thought, Dad. He wouldn't let my mother's body be taken from the hospital until I arrived. And now I must go and claim his body. I hated the word claim. Dear Mary Mother of God, I must go and comfort this of my Dad from which his soul is departed.

And they had told me, This way. And we went in silence. And I said, Yes, that is my father, Ferdinand Bingold. That is his suit and tie. At the desk, the brisk officer on duty stared back up at me, shrugging his shoulders. No, he knew nothing of the subject's personal belongings—a sacred medal, his wallet, his gray fedora, his jewelry—a large ring on his left hand, his rosary with its sterlng silver crucifix.

"You know nothing," I said, beating back rising anger.

"There was nothing," the officer said, checking a form with a pencil.

"He was found dead in his car and he had no personal belongings?"

"Nossir."

"May I use your phone?"

"There's a public phone outside."

And I called Bob Danner and when he came on the phone and

I had told him what happened, he said, "Dick, wait there. I've got two phone calls to make. You wait there."

And I waited a half hour and was called to the phone. It was, telling me he had phoned the police station of the precinct in which Dad had been found. "And Dick," he said. "Don't ask questions." Forty-five minutes later, an officer showed up with a brown envelope and Dad's belongings, including his fedora and wallet and rosary and ring. I never said another word and went away.

"Dick," Beth said. "I'm sorry. I'm very sorry. Your dad was a good man. A very good man."

I had made all the funeral arrangements, with the funeral parlor and the priest. Because Dad had always taken his citizenship seriously and had served several weeks in the Army during World War One, I asked to have an American flag cover his coffin. I had arranged for a dinner at a local restaurant for all the members of the family. Dad would have wanted it that way.

So distant from each other that a hug might snap anyone's hold on sanity, Beth got down from the bed, came to my side, and hugged me hard and I hugged her and she went to the bed and put her back up against the headboard and sat quietly.

"Would you have dinner with the children?" I asked Beth.

"Yes," she said.

And I went out and drove to the funeral parlor and went in and walked down the carpeted hall and sat down by Dad and prayed the rosary—his rosary—bead by bead. And then, just as I had prayed over my mother, I whispered,

"I am the resurrection and the life, saith the Lord; he that believeth in me, though he were dead, yet shall he live; and whosoever liveth and believeth in me, shall never die. Hail, Mary full of grace, the Lord is with thee. Holy Mary, mother of God, pray for us sinners now and at the hour of our death." I waited in the silence for a sign, then whispered, "Amen."

I walked back along the hard narrow sidewalk toward the hotel, thinking of our children, Rich and James and Barbara and Catherine, and how when I told James grandpa had died, the afternoon light gleamed in the stream of tears running down his face…

We sat in the front row, Beth with Cathy and Fred, to my left. So close, you could have touched it, lay the American flag shaped by the coffin beneath it. Across the row from me, sat my brother John. When the priest began, I saw out of the tail of my eye a small hand and a white handkerchief and before either had reached his face, I saw a distant cousin of mine wipe her eyes.

"Dear Mother," I whispered to myself, feeling her presence, feeling that I had returned home, thinking, *Dad, what a life we've all lived and now here we are in our Church together, the Eucharist before us, the votive candles flickering.*

And then I heard John breathing hard, his shoulders moving first to one side and then to the other. I held my handkerchief in a tight ball. John moved again, and then was still. The priest was looking my way. Then John moved quickly.

The faces of your family, looking up at you, waiting for you to speak, have a peculiar effect on you. The eyes, the mouths, the fresh skin of the very young, the skin marked by the experience of age, all make you want to become a good person. To speak well of each other. To be a witness to a gathering in, when nobody is lost or alone. Now, John having done what he had done and having failed to show up for the meal, I had to say something, for everyone there, now looking up at me at the restaurant, their plates loaded with potatoes and steak and green peas, had seen John bolt from his seat, grab the flag from the coffin and cry out,

"He doesn't deserve the flag. He didn't serve it," and run down the aisle of the church, out the door, and into the street.

Now I faced my family and relatives, trying to say the right thing, hoping we all together could forget.

"Our Lord and the Mother of Our Lord and Our God," I said, smiling, "make us all one, in hope for life eternal. God shall wipe away all tears from their eyes and death shall be no more." I saw restlessness around the table. "I like to think of Dad as among the just who shall shine as the sun in their Father's kingdom. I like to think of him among the glorified bodies of the blessed, who sown in the natural body shall rise a spiritual body and the just shall shine and shall run to and fro like sparks among the reeds."

"Now in Dad's memory, enjoy," I said, and sat down.

There was wine and beer at the table and voices were suddenly loud in argument. Two of my aunts wept, and an uncle said harsh things and left the building. I lost Beth and Cathy in the rising dark, then saw them again at another table and felt reassured. And abruptly, all the places were empty and when I went to pay the bill, a form appeared, a young woman walking toward me out of the shadows of the coat racks, a light like a candle suspended above her hand.

"Thank you, Mr. Bingold," the cashier said into my ear.

Still the young woman came on wordlessly and I saw that the light was a yellow rose on a single stem and I glanced right, thinking she was heading toward someone else. But when I glanced back, the rose and face were all one, the rose now in my hand, and in my ear the slightest whisper, "Your second cousin, Marilyn. Mom and dad loved him."

"Please, Dick, we must go."

I looked down. It was Beth.

"Fine," I said, holding the rose, feeling foolish and touched.

And when I looked up, all I saw was the entrance door closing and in among the coats the memory of a shy smile.

It was dark when our plane took off for Ft. Lauderdale. Beth and I were exhausted. And when we rose so far above the earth that the separate lamps and windows of Manhattan had become a single mushroom of light, and the Allegheny Mountain swelled up in endless tiers of dark, I ordered drink and then a third and then a fourth. Dad was gone. The current of faith and hope that had run through him to me and from me to him when he was *alive* now seemed to have snapped. Beth turned against me in her sleep and I smoothed down her hair and she lay back on her seat, a foot of space between us. Surrounded by all these people, Beth next to me, I felt lost and alone.

I put back my head and slept and when I woke, I saw the lights of Ft. Lauderdale, and thought, *That order for Chicago. I've got to get that order for Chicago out.*

Chapter Fourteen

Ground Zero

"Sit down," my wife said, her jaw clenched.

I stood and looked down at her, prim neat and doll-like, sitting on the far end of the far too-expensive sofa she had lost her heart to in the showroom. I put my empty glass down on the table.

"What are you going to do? Hit me?"

"When did I ever hit you?"

"You've *meant* to lots of time. You've spanked the children harder than they deserve."

Anger set the skin of her face into an electric glow. Her eyes looked big enough for tears, but none came. And I said before I could stop,

"You deserve—" I began.

"*Deserve*," she interrupted. "*Deserve?*" Her voice rose a pitch. And she was off her seat and beating me on the chest.

"Look at you. Look at you," she shrieked. Deep in the house a child cried.

I caught hold of her thin wrists.

"Imagine it," she shrieked again. "Look at you. Smiling. The calm John Wayne all women swoon over. Well, let me tell you, here's one woman who doesn't. A private investigator. What do you know about being a one, a huge big oaf like you?"

She was breathing hard and moving her wrists back and forth in my loose grip.

"You spend your money—you spend *our* money. You—"

"I *make* money. You—"

"You *inherited* money. Dad and Mom's money. Your parent's money. Do you—"

"I've invested that money. I've made money on that money, whether you be—"

"You say so but what do *I* know. You…Keep everything secret. Secret agent. Oh, migod, that fits you to a 'T.' Your children are afraid of you. *I'm* afraid of you. You're a bully, Dick. A bully. Do you hear me? You are one big cheat."

Breathing hard, she stared up at me, the fireworks in her eyes burning my cheeks, the word "cheat" inflaming every muscle of my body.

"You're wrong." I was shouting now. *"You are just wrong,"* I said, marking each word as if that would make her wrong and Dick Bingold right.

I was thristy and glanced down at my empty glass, sitting there by itself, the sign of something that had happened long ago. The overhanging cliff of my forehead forced my face down and Beth flinched, and I saw what I most hated about her: Her fear of me.

I swallowed and stepped back, leaned down, picked up the glass, and walked over to the bar, my hand shaking. The ice clinked and I said through my thickened my throat,

"Like a drink?"

Dead silence.

"I said," my forehead still heavy, my throat now a sickening fuzz, *"would you like a drink?"*

"Would I like a drink?" she imitated me, and I suddenly weighed twice my two-hundred-fifty pounds, every extra pore smoldering and I saw in my mind's eye my Dad and Mom facing each other and a bar and next to me a woman lifting her hand and patting my cheek and I knew in flush of sadness that Dad

had never ever laid a hand on Mom. And I stood there, my back to my wife of fourteen years, trembling, the tears flowing down my face. I held, cleared my throat, and stopped trembling, and wiped both eyes dry.

"I said, Would you like a drink? The regular," the last two words bringing back an old, long-gone intimacy. And when I turned away from the bar, the big expensive couch greeted me, a depression in the cushion where Beth had sat. The big room in our two-hundred-thousand-dollar house on Lighthouse Point overlooking Hillsboro Inlet and the Atlantic Ocean, was empty.

The bar was clean, our glasses put away, the lights turned out, and a voice came out of the shadow.

"Dad? I was having a bad dream, Dad."

It was Barb by the door, her hand pulling at a curl, her eyes blinking. And I was across the room and she was in my arms and I had given her a kiss when she said,

"Rich says he means to run away. Will Rich run away?"

"Of course not," I whispered, smiling. "No, Rich likes to tease."

"Is Mom O.K.? She heard me crying and she was crying."

"Mom's fine," I said, the mysterious weight of a little girl— my daughter—sending me an unfathomable message. "Everything will be fine," I whispered to her, walking into the shadows of her room, the outlines of teddybears and dolls filling me with the grief of being on the wrong road. Of time passing.

"Goodbye, Dad," she whispered when I had put her down into her bed, on her back, her eyes glinting in the shadow, a doll hugged to her side.

"Don't say goodbye," I whispered.

"Sure," she said, smiling. "You're going out the door."

"Yes," I said, catching on but saying anyhow, "No, I'm

heading for bed."

I leaned down and kissed her and we exchanged a look and I went out her door and then out our front door and I was behind the wheel, driving fast, and trying to see beyond the reach of the headlights. In the gloom, a flash of light along a damp stretch of highway and a mist in which ghostly trees waited, I saw it: The spire of a Catholic church, the mist surrounding it in a smooth twist of virgin white. But in an instant, the flash, gloom, and mist whipped behind me and I drew up into the parking lot of bar that was completely strange to me.

When I walked out again, rain cooled my face and made bright dots all over the surface of my car and I drove home and when I drove up the driveway, I saw the bike. Rich's bike. Out in the rain. An expensive bike which, I, his father, had given him for his birthday. The carelessness. The disorder. The lack of respect and love.

The bike, the rain, the door, Beths form in her bed, all behind me, and Rich's doorknob in my hand, twisting, jerking open the aggravating door and the hump of him, curled unthinking in sleep beneath his blue cover and turned back sheet.

Now his eyes are blinking, his palms turned out to rub the sleep away, a glint above one dirty small finger and that glint is the white of one eye, trying to guess what now? What now?

"Let me ask you now, son, what can you possibly mean after all the times I've told you," I hear my voice reciting in a coolness that would freeze a criminal in the dock, "*not* to leave that bike of yours out in the rain. *Some* day you'll learn the value of money and the value of property and what love means— respect and love—means."

The heat runs up through my legs and chest and cheeks

when I see the fright in Rich's face. For now he has taken his fists away and has scrambled out of his bed to confront me, to call my bluff, and I think I see a streak of red blush his face as the flat of my hand slashes his cheek. I hear the thud of a body against the wall and I look down, way down, and see a small boy pushing his own strong body up, using the wall to support the long slow rise and then in the staggered light of a lost night I see this boy whose name I have forgotten stagger across the room, a ball cap and bat in the corner, the photo of a baseball star on the dresser, toward me, his face red down one side, his whole look saying to me something I can't face, that sends me down the hall and into the night, my brain reeling with, *Mother of God, what have I done?*

His face had said to me, "What are you going to do to me now, Dad?"

Chapter Fifteen

Black Hole

You could tell by the movement of the waitresses that our restaurant, *Lauderdale Connection,* ran like clockwork: Giving their undivided attention to each table, they took care of all customers promptly. The busboy was there with ice water right off. Dirty dishes never remained longer than a few minutes. I had a code and I demanded compliance. With the exception of a black neckpiece, each waitress wore white—not quite white. Ivory.

"I saw by the paper—a very short story—that your old partner, Eddie Egan, has married," said my friend and attorney, Dick Hennekam, toying with the salt and pepper shakers and studying me over the top of his glasses.

"Yes," I said, smiling. "I saw that. We're clear of him, I take it?"

"Clear. You paid off his interest here," he said, making a motion with his hand to indicate the restaurant. His hand jerked forward and spilled the shakers. "Generosity isn't always a virtue," he went on, his voice carrying the inky saw-edge of sarcasm and fault-finding. Beneath it, though, you could detect the gloomy friction of a man who knew he loved his fellowman better than was good for him or them.

"Although you and Danner and Egan built this place, you *never* charged enough for your sweat equity. Not ever. I wish I could say you were a *careful* businessman, and *careful* with money, but I can't say that."

He closed his lips tight on the rim of his glass and took a short quick drink.

"And how's your new man—John Q.—at Eddie Egan Security doing?"

"A good solid cop from New Jersey," I said.

We had driven here from his office where he had tied up the loose ends of legal problems my fifth auto accident had caused. In one of the accident photos, I saw a man standing to the side, under an over-hanging roof, like a man hiding from the light, and when I looked closer, I saw that it was me.

"Five crashes since your arrival here is a pretty darned good record," he had said—and had made a black mark across the paper in front of him that felt like a slap.

Dick Hennekam's sunless office had sunk into a ghostly obscurity since the departure of his capable wife with the black bow at the nape of her neck. He clipped his chin down at the black mark, said, "*There!*" then looked up.

"You know what struck me about what you've told me about your dad?"

I took a breath and the murky light of the office dropped us into a darker sea where all you saw were the outlines of file cases and backs of chairs and a pale light through a large dusty window.

"What struck me was that he was a loyal man, your dad. Never one to chase pie-in-the-sky, nor could you call him a Blue Sky Man, like his son. But loyal. Well."

Dick Hennekam stood up and in several shadowy movements, turned a key, placed his brief case in the center of his desk, and put his thin back to me as he made for the door. And with his back still to me, he said, his voice smooth now,

"Loyality—of course—can be overdone—look at Nixon and his cronies—but what sets Dick Bingold apart is that he is a loyal person." It sounded as if he were talking to himself or as if I had listened in on his thoughts.

And we were out the door, travelling along the shore. The distant horizon was held down by a ranks of black clouds. I wanted to say to Dick Hennekam,

Did you know I slapped my boy across the room?

But we drove on, passing the marina where my forty-foot Chris Craft was tied up, and where I had lived since Beth and I broke up, and thinking, *"Dick was the first to warn me that Beth was thinking of divorce."* Next to my boat, in a sheath of dust, sat my Chevy with the hole in the floorboard. But parked at *The Lauderdale Connection* where we were heading, was the leased Olds, a two-door Toronado with a maroon body and a white top. I had already had two close scrapes with it, but escaped with a scratched fender which insurance covered.

"So—a tentative congratulations—and good health to— *Lauderdale Connection*," Dick Hennekam said now as we sat at a corner table. He saluted me with gin and I gulped whiskey. He put his glass down. "Of course, I thought it was one of your pie-in-the-sky schemes—guessed that the outcome for the Blue Sky Man would be bleak."

I was smiling, never doubting that today's strike out would be tomorrow's home run.

"May I?" Carol, our hostess, said, glancing first at one and then the other empty glass. The ivory dress set her figure off.

"Yes, if you please," Dick Hennekam said instantly.

"Mr. Bingold?"

I had been staring at her, a lovely person and beautiful. We had known each other for a short while, and I respected her honesty and goodness. She had confided in me that she didn't have enough money to go north to visit her mother who was in ill health, and I had written her a check for six hundred dollars for the roundtrip ticket on the spot. She had not asked for it; I couldn't afford it, and as a matter of fact, as we sat, the *The Lauderdale Connection* was about to go under.

I decided not to get personal. "Double Mr. Hennekam's and double mine," I said frowning. Then I smiled and added, "So that we can get on with those juicy steaks smothered in onions and mushrooms." Across the room, I saw two empty tables, a bad sign for Friday.

"A single, please," Dick Hennekam said, and then looked up at me. "You know what my dream is, Dick? To close my office and get in a car and pull a trailer and see America with my wife and two kids. I want to see everything and nobody. Not ever again give advice that nobody will take."

Our drinks came and I drank mine and Dick nursed his and we ordered and the black hole in my brain suddenly glittered with that ritzy bar, *Pier 66*. I would talk Dick into joining me and we would drive down there and do some serious drinking. Our steaks came, blood oozing, streaked in black by burned charcoal. I ordered a bottle of wine and when Dick would only take a glass and a half, I finished it off.

"Dick," I began, haunted by unfinished business, wanting to get in touch with what, I didn't quite know, "the crucifixion connects mankind to glory. To a blaze of glory. To grace and salvation and so begins and ends the Bible's history of salvation." My friend looked at me through a cloud of my cigar smoke. "Our dear Mother reaches toward the Lord and back to us and pulls us together. Do you understand?"

Dick Hennekam said he didn't understand and I suggested we continue the discussion at *Pier 66* but Dick said he was to meet a client early in the morning, and wanted to head home. Full of myself, I said a place like *Pier 66* often paid dividends in information about Ft. Lauderdale's underworld. I talked him into stopping at one more bar, and then we said goodnight.

Out in the dark, under a black sky spitting rain, I climb into my car and drive fast, toward *Pier 66,* just the other side of the steel bridge that spans the Intracostal Waterway and its framework looms up in the black sky and behind me, in my rearview mirror, I glimpse the face of a woman, then her profile as she passes me, then the back of her head as she cuts in front. I jerk the wheel to the left, swerve, and in a shower of stones hurtle into a rock garden above which sits the blank face of a house closed down for the night.

In reverse, I fire the engine to top speed, front wheels spin to the stink of burning rubber, and the car leaps backward, clanking onto to concrete. Shreds of my tires leave the rock garden blackened.

Rims clattering on the steel of the bridge, I head for the *Pier 66.* parking lot, pull in, stop, smooth down my hair in the rearview mirror, get out, and walk away. Eighteen holes of golf every week has given me good wind, strong legs. By two o'clock, I've walked back to my boat. In a booth, I phone the police, give them my address, the Toronado's license plate number and colors, and the name of the leasing company.

"It's been stolen," I lie to the police, and give them my phone number at Optimum Design, and hang up.

"That you, Dick?" my friend Richard Lundstrom asks sleepily from one of the bunks in the Chris Craft cabin.

"It's me."

I undress slowly in the dark and slip beneath the sheet and doze off and watch with a black heart as my brother John crushes the model airplane I've just completed and my cheeks burn as my mother passes by, merely glancing down at me, and I wake up, thinking, *O, Dad, O, Dad.*

"You look *cool* this morning," she said to me when I handed her the quarter for the morning newspaper.

I put my hand to the breast pocket of my white freshly-washed-and ironed shirt to check for the cigar and two of my favorite pens, trying to decide her brand of perfume. The clock crowned her golden hair and said eight-forty, exactly forty minutes later than I was used to arriving at Optimum Design.

No matter what, you must always be there to open the store in the morning, Dad had preached to me time and again, never in his life having been late for work. *A different generation,* I thought, and turned away, glanced at the Time Magazine cover, *Nixon's Shattered Presidency,* and by the time I had pulled into the traffic of Federal Blvd. I decided her perfume was Chanel.

When I drove into the Optimum Design parking lot ten minutes later, Hank Hyatt stood bent over, his back to me, his head under the lid of his trunk. When he backed out, a clutch of papers under his arm, he slammed down the lid and turned my way—and looked at me painfully. I had known Hank since J.J. Newbury days and when out of job he called me on the phone, I invited him down to Ft. Lauderdale to head up production. And though he often stood off by himself, thin and observant, he had been a guy who had a knack for getting orders out and on their way. What he didn't like was the fact that I ran Optimum Design in a breathless state of crisis. And neither did another friend, Al Holzer, who had also joined me. He had his wife had settled in just last month.

"The St. Louis order must be all set."

"Almost," he said, frowning, his face now a smooth tan, his left hand hitching up the papers. He saw me start. "Took some home to pin down—" He stopped. "Pin down costs." One of the papers carried familiar handwriting, mine.

"Fine," I said. "Couldn't tear myself away from the TV and the impeachment," I lied, and added, "Nixon certainly stretches the truth."

"Yeah?" Hyatt said doubtfully, then walked off, and he went one way and I went the other, feeling only a trace of the early morning coolness.

The ocean breeze at sunrise had shown me my Dad and me on that early morning ride to Manhattan when he said looking across the floor of the place he sold cars, 'See that man? Go ask him to sing you a song.' And I did and the man simply lifted his chin, opened his mouth and made the air quaver with fleeting melody. Later dad said, Dick, that was Lauritz Melchior. The great Wagnerian tenor of his age.

When I sauntered into the shop, before going to my office, a knott of men broke apart on my entrance, one of them Hyatt.

"Yeah, Dick?" he asked, crossing between two lathes, then stopping several feet away. He wanted me to raise my voice. Instead, I winked, smiled, then said in a tone that made *him* strain forward,

"See you in the office about the St. Louis order."

"Yep," he snapped awkwardly, then raising his voice: "You bet I'll see you in your office.

At my desk, I asked my secretary, Marilyn, to call the local police department and ask whether they had found my car. I made two other calls myself, to check price on two fixtures I was designing, then settled down to work. Traffic poured by on the highway and machinery hummed behind my office walls. I took the cellophane off my cigar, bit off the end, lit up, blew out the smoke, then put it in the ashtray, and worked away at the design, remembering…

Two years, and I've built this operation to a gross of six figures. There I stood in the spring of 1971 in the head offices of Coit International, having taken a private 310 Cessna owned by a friend of mine in an early-morning flight to Dallas. I faced a natty-looking man in black suit, black tie, and black shoes—Al Cohen. No, he said, pointing his thumb at me over the top of his fist. Then a slender man with a tennis court tan and manner walked in. I knew him, though I had never seen him before: Mr. Coit himself. And I made my move. It caught Cohen completely off guard. I walked straight across the floor and, shaking hands and introducing myself, I presented my case. Mr. Coit stared at me, then over my shoulder at Black Suit, then back at me, and said, "Sure, but don't let me down," and walked out.

Marilyn's voice broke into my daydream. "The police called."

She stood in the doorway, a broad smile on her broad face. "They said the car was found—at someplace called *Pier 66*. The tires had been removed from the rear wheels."

"No," I exclaimed, opening my eyes wide.

"Yes, no joking," she said. "Oh, yes," she went on. "Mr. Cohen from Coit is here."

"He called?" I asked, taken aback, refusing to take it in, seeing in my mind's eye his black hair, suit, tie, and shoes. Mr. Al Cohen, himself, who wanted nothing to do with Dick Bingold that morning two years ago in Dallas.

"No," Marilyn said, "I said, he's here. Gone for a cup of coffee, will be back, he said, at eleven. At eleven."

She wrinkled her nose and tried to smile. I saw that when she blushed she did it in patches. She had been loyal. She knew something was up.

"When did he—" I stopped.

"Yes?" She stood in the doorway again.

"Would you please call Shelf Closures for a quote on these?" I asked as she approached the desk. She was a heavy but goodlooking woman. I handed her a piece of paper. I wanted to ask her more about Cohen. Ask her whether Al Holzer had called in. *Be cool, Bingold. Be cool.* I sat back in my chair and blew several smoke rings into the air and watched them drift toward the ceiling and slowly break apart.

It was then I heard Beth's voice in the outer office, speaking to Marilyn. A door opened and I heard her greet Hank Hyatt.

"Yes, Mr. Holzer," Marilyn now said.

They were all hidden from my view by the half-open door.

"So good to see you, Mr. Cohen." It was Beth's voice.

My cheeks hot, I took one long easy draw on the cigar and then making sure none of the ash broke before it reached the tray, I laid the cigar carefully on the curved rim. Rusted in the bottom was the logo and the name of J. J. Newbury.

"Hello, Dick."

Beth was standing in the door. Over her shoulder, I could see dark forms moving. I threw my wrist up to take a look at my watch: Eleven o'clock exactly. Beth's eyes and my eyes touched memories away in the very center of the room and then she advaced across the carpet, the three men in her trail. It took me hours to rise from my chair behind my desk but I did and we all stood there, as if waiting on a street corner for someone else who would give us an order, a direction. An invisible hand. A locution, perhaps, a movement, in someone's brain, the word over the void and the darkness. The world seemed suddenly emptied of wrath.

"Marilyn?" I called out pleasantly. "Would you bring a light from your office—one of the overhead fluorescents has gone out. And chairs. Hank, chairs."

Hank Hyatt hesitated, glanced at Beth, then walked out

with me, each of us carrying back into my office two metal chairs with worn cushions.

"Thank you, Marilyn," I said, and turned on the standing lamp. I pulled it to my desk so that it lit up its surface and the designs I had been working on. I shifted in my chair and pushed the keys to Optimum Design to the bottom of my pants pocket. Now I was comfortable.

"Good flight?" Al Holzer said to Al Cohen.

"Like clockwork."

"June hot in Dallas, Mr. Cohen?" Beth asked. Her voice went smoothly into me then out like quills pulled the wrong way.

"Hot is not the word."

"I was there once in January—once—and it was hot then," Hank Hyatt hurried in. "The tumbleweeds and all."

"Tumbleweeds?"

"Yes, Mr. Cohen. I saw them from the plane window."

"Hmmm."

I looked to the side. Marilyn was staring stony-faced at the crowd, her right hand trembling. Now I knew that she knew what I knew: these people were out to get me.

"The prices, Marilyn we were talking about, maybe you…" My voice trailed off, and we all watched her—as if she were the the sole reason for our meeting—turn away and close the door, but not so that it fit solidly into its frame.

Then I was staring with a set smile, first at one of the four-some, then another, daring each to begin the attack. Here I was, a private investigator, blindsided in his own den. I felt like a fool. But I was surprised too, for in cases like this, all the cards belonged to the prey: I could buck, or walk peacefully. Because something told me this was it. I was the outsider. I had no role to make perfect, no song to get right. There were no words of a prayer I might stumble over. In one way, I was being betrayed by my friends. In another, my world was being created right in front of me. I felt sad and I wanted to laugh. As always, Beth looked neat and attractive, her perfume like her clothes, exactly right.

Then she looked at Cohen.

"We have been friends for years," he began, hesitated, looked at Beth, then back at me at the same time Holzer and Hyatt looked at him.

Three years, I thought. And wondered if "friends" was the right word.

"And you have been—a bright man—to do business with. Bright. Smart. And I thank your for all your courtesies." The light by my desk made his black suit and tie gleam.

Then I listened to the shifting of scenes and shadows, shutters back and forth across a tiny window on the past, each person shifting in his seat at regular intervals. I heard the words. I had interferred with production (Hank Hyatt shifted in his seat); I had not been able to delegate (Al Holzer leaned forward), and I had not been forthcoming about Optimum Design's cash flow and the fact that I had invested a sum exceeding ten thousand dollars in outside enterprises. (Beth lifted her hands from her lap).

"I discussed it with Fred—"

And she stopped, colored, and looked straight at me.

"We all think it would be best," she went on bravely, and I could see behind her words Cohen's hand: he had taken steps to force me out.

It was easy from then on. And at the end of twenty minutes, I pushed myself up out of my chair, worked my hand down into the depth of my pants pocket, and brought out the keys. Not looking up, I smiled, then placed the keys on the papers on which I had been working The light made the keys sparkle. I turned, and headed for the door, then turned, and looked down at Beth, those memories meeting in midair like glass bullets.

"I planned to swim with the children this afternoon. I won't let them down."

"I know," Beth said.

Then I turned, and never looked back.

On the other side of the door, I blew Marilyn a kiss and tried to reassure her I was O.K, that I understood and thanked her for her loyalty. "That's fine, Marilyn. Thanks. Thanks for everything."

And I was on the road, first to my boat to change, then to pick up my children. Unusual for June, blowing across the bow was a breeze from the ocean that was cool. I ducked into the cabin, shed my Optimum Design clothes—the buttondown shirt, the tie and jacket, the row of pens—and pulled on swim trunks and over them, my wrinkled khakis, and then stuck my bare feet into battered loafers. On deck again, I stared down at the beach, no longer wondering what a friend of mine meant when she said, "You've become a regular beachcomber. You've gone native." And when I climbed into my old Chevy and drove away from the boat and watched the dust whirl up from the hole in the floorboard, I thought, *You're on a slide, but you're O.K. Let John Q. look after Eddie Egan Security.* I could taste salt and feel sand between my toes and hear a woman laugh as she ran along the surf and *Rhinestone Cowboy* blasting from a juke box behind me.

When I arrived at Beth's, I found that the children had already gone to the beach, and by the time I arrived, James, Barbara and Catherine were far down at the edge of the surf, and I ran toward them and they toward me and over the wash of waves I heard Barbara shout,

"You're a cool one, Dad!"

And I stopped and put my face up into the bright sun and

was blinded by the bright sun and in that black hole I heard echoing...

You're real cool, Dad.

Dad?

Yeah?

Whatta y'looking at?

The sun.

Teacher told us not to look straight into the sun, Barbara says. It's bad for your eyes.

She's right, I say. She's right. But next time, tell her the sun won't blind you—won't seem like a black hole—if you look at it through someone else's eyes. And then you'll find there's no black hole there at all.

My little daughters look up at me and I hear the surf and their silences and sweep them up into my arms and we race into the water.

"I came to get it."

Eddie Egan stood there, in the front office of Eddie Egan Security, Ltd., his back to a elephant-size TV. I had driven the children back to Beth's house, then picked up a friend, and on the way to drinks and dinner, we had driven by the agency. That's when I saw the light.

Now as I stood facing Egan, she waited outside. His huge, fish-shaped muscular form towered over the TV.

"I kept my key. You don't take precautions and change the lock? You're a trusting sort."

We stood without moving, about a yard apart. What was it about his eyes? And I didn't like the Napoleon position of his right hand, as if it were reaching for something inside his jacket. I didn't like anything about him. Still in my mind's eye was his fat heavy white leg on the bartop, the .32 calibre revolver that stained his skin gunmetal blue, strapped to his ankle. The woman next to him had got his goat by telling him he had no proof he was *the* Eddie Egan of *French Connection* fame. "Now do you believe me?" he had rumbled, then had taken the ugly leg off the bar.

"Always smiling, eh, Dick?" he said now.

Always smiling. I will have it for the rest of my life, that smile. Never step around it into the light of God's grace.

I took a step forward and the hand inside the jacket moved.

"I wouldn't. All I want is the TV."

I held my teeth a quarter of an inch apart and kept the smile on my face and made my voice steady when I said,

"Thought you were settled down, a married man."

"The wife would like the TV that belongs to me," Egan said. "Besides, I always take what belongs to me."

It seemed I could feel the heat from his swollen neck, his cheekbones, his nose. In his prime, when he had made one of the history's biggest drug-busts, I wouldn't have dared cross him. Now he was over the hill, pathetic.

Let it go, I thought. *What difference does it make?*

But suddenly I was outraged. Here stood my past. Divorce. Lost businesses. Sweat equity I never charged enough for. The wrong roads taken. And I moved sideways, and down, leading with my left shoulder, meaning to do one thing, knock him cold, before he made a move, for it had dawned on me that he only pretended to have a gun inside his jacket. But before I could swing, Eddie Egan backed up against the TV, and both of them crashed to the floor.

I stood over him, breathing heavily. He pushed himself backward, worked his buttocks up the wall, and stood unsteadily, his face at peace. He was smiling.

"Hey, Bingold," he said, syliva dripping from his lips.

"Nobody's come up against me like that for years."

I turned my back, walked from the office, and returned with a wet washrag and towel.

"I'll help you to the car with the TV," I said, looking closely at his face, seeing for the first time, something strange. His eyes.

His eyes had the look of moist stone that drips with the hieroglyphs of a concealed life. He had never broken the code of those chamelon-like markings, never had known just who he was or exactly what he did. I looked away. There was something too familiar about those eyes.

"Thanks, Dick. You're not all bad, Dicky. Like *the* Lucchese tells me that Wednesday—that Wednesday, January ten, nineteen sixty-two, the day I wrapped up *the* drug bust of the Century, 'Eddie, you are a stand-up guy."

I looked back at him. Those cave-like eyes seemed very wide apart. Very wide apart. Behind the cold skin puckered on the bone of his forehead, I saw those hieroglyphs and then a stone rolling into place, shutting out the light and cancelling what might-have-been. Would I end my life the same way?

Chapter Sixteen

Monique

I was drowning. Now I knew I was helpless. The whole world was under water. In a dream of safety, I saw Monique. I was back on land, safe and sound and by a table, about to sit down, she stood before me. Anyone that beautiful, I thought at the time, must be nothing but a passing fancy.

There was a roaring in my head and I could not tell whether in the dark I was rightside up or upside down. I was certainly lost, but even so, Monique was there. I smiled and walked on by and when I turned around, a friend of mine was leaning over, talking to her, and she was pointing toward me, and I looked away.

I tried to open my eyes, but water and blood stung and I began to sink when I heard, "Hold on there. Hold on." I beat at the shadow coming toward me and when it grabbed me, I thrashed more, and thought, *Will I ever see her again?* Then, feeling twice my size and fighting against myself, I sank to the bottom, unable to breathe, but suddenly able to hope. Unable to breathe, I saw us walking together, along a deserted beach. It was night and I could even remember the words I used, "I think something is happening to me. I'm falling in love." Struggling to break away from myself, pushing against a burden on my back, I heard her voice, large, and wide as the night and the beach, saying, "I think I am too."

Then we were moving, this burden on my back, and there was no telling whether we were moving up, down, or sideways.

The darkness was overwhelming, except for that one dim light of hope. It was at that moment, something changed. I would struggle for my life. Maybe I was worth saving. The world, once under water, came out clear to me—for the flash of a second—and I saw the night sky and heard a voice behind me sputter, "Hold on. Hold on." And I turned into someone's arms and when I looked again, dark figures loomed over me and reached down toward me and the scream I heard was mine.

****

"Well," a voice hidden in a white light said, "it looks like you are back with us."

Monique stood at the altar, waiting. I walked down the aisle with my son, Richard, and I glowed in his loyalty and in her beauty. And I was walking back down the aisle, arm-in-arm with Monique.

"You must try to help," a voice behind the white light said to me. I gagged and was drowning again and saw water come at me in the starlight and I was diving into something long ago when she had smiled at me and whispered now, "Blessed Mother, help me."

Monique and I were dancing. The sleek long yacht, the *Isis*, moved through the water and the stars came out, the band music seemed to be far away and coming at us out of the past. Dozens of my friends were here with me, celebrating our marriage and my success. Something swayed in the dark beside us, a pendulum, felt-covered. And then we were dancing again. I had signed on the dotted line, a loan of five thousand dollars to rent this yatch and celebrate our wedding. Outside the Church. And I puzzled on those words when a voice, standing beside the white light said,

"I'm Dr. Joe Grover," and he went down my list of injuries: infected lungs, broken collar bone and scapular; broken left arm;

every rib with a break or a crack; and nine breaks in your upper and lower jaws. Three teeth lost. And part of your tongue chewed off. I heard my own voice asking him to stop the morphine, I was afraid of drugs. And then I slept again and woke and round me stood my family, my former wife, Beth, and our children, Richard, James, Barbara and Catherine. I wanted to sleep but I waited—waited for Monique, for she had flown off to Montreal to stay with her family....Indefinitely. But then she filled the doorway and was beside me, leaning down to kiss me and whisper, "You feeling better now, Baby?" I tried to speak around my swollen tongue, and couldn't, and so I nodded. And then I slept again.

Dr. Joe Grover's calipers measured my head, touching it here and there, and when he was finished, he said a few comforting words to me and left the room. I was alone. Staring at the ceiling, I tried to put two and two together, and at long last recalled the night Peter Short invited me to get aboard his sea racer, the Wellcraft Scarab, and take a trip to Freeport, Grand Bahamas. I open my eyes and heaved a sigh, trying to recall the rest of the story. But all I can grasp is that moment I saw the stones of the Hillsboro Inlet jetty rear up, the waves leaping in the gloom. I think I remember a voice calling, "Hold on." But I'm not sure.

"Wayne Connick?" I asked the young man through gritted teeth.

"That's right," he said, his voice low, hesitant.

He had introduced himself because I had read his name and seen his photo in the newspaper and I had asked to see him so that I could thank him in person for saving my life. But now as I looked up at him, I couldn't say a word. Tears streamed down my face. He cleared his throat.

"Sit down, Wayne," I wrote as best I could on a pad of paper—my cut-up tongue was too sore for me to speak clearly. I saw him looking in wonder at the halo fixed to my head.

He took a chair by my bedside carefully, as if he might break something. He cleared his throat again.

"Thank you, Wayne," I wrote, tried to write something more, then wrote, "Thank you," once again.

He sat up straight and said, "You look fine, Mr. Bingold," then broke into a broad smile.

"How old are you?"

"Seventeen—going on eighteen."

He told me about living with his mother after his father and mother broke up, and how he had joined the Pompono Police Department's class in life-saving and had almost flunked out. We looked into each other eyes for a split second, then each of us chuckled.

"I heard you call," he offered.

"I did?" I managed to ask.

"You did. I heard you call for help."

I strained sideways and looked him up and down and managed to say around my swollen tongue, "How much do you weigh?"

"A hundred, oh, I don't know, maybe fifty. A hundred and fifty pounds."

I was growing tired, very tired of talking and writing, but I pushed ahead no matter.

"You know how much I weigh?" I wrote.

He smiled painfully as if any answer he gave would be embarrassing.

"A hundred seventy-five?" he ventured.

And I wrote, "250."

"Five nine," he said, the smile gone from his face as he took the fact in.

"I'm six three," I wrote, my heart filling with an aching pain of admiration and love. His name and heroic deed was splashed across several newspapers, but here he sat, without the least desire to be a big shot.

He stared back at me, then dropped his eyes, and I found that I was staring at him without shame or embarrassment. Tears started to my eyes again and ran down my face. I looked down at my right hand and out along the cast on my left arm, then back down at my hand.

"Mind telling me about it?" I mumbled.

The chair creaked as he shifted about.

"I expected it to be, jump in the water, grab you, and come right back to the boat and bring you back into the shore. But that's not the way it went."

We chuckled again.

"You can say that again," I said, still staring down at my hand.

I waited and heard a clock tick and a voice echo down the hall of the Pompono Beach Hospital. When I looked up, he was staring at me. I could see that he had to know about the rods and pins and halo around my head.

"That holds my jaw in place," I said through gritted teeth. "Doc Grover measured my head, drilled holes in my skull, screwed in the rods, then drilled two more holes, into the side of each jaw, inserted those rods, and hooked wires to them inside my mouth to hold my jaws in place so they can heal."

"Won't the bone grow to the rods?" he asked, staring at the halo, his eyes dark and wondering, a blush standing out on his cheek.

"That's O.K. Everybody wonders. You're the only one with

the courage to ask. What happened then?"

"We were in Dave Johnson's parents' boat and Tommy Wade was with us and Dave said not to go out to the jetty and I talked him into it. At the bridge, they yelled to us that a boat had crashed into the jetty. I was kind of a little bit excited. It was total blackness and I got Dave to drive the boat out there. We got to within forty feet and that's when we noticed orange panel lights and that's when we saw you towards the back of the boat that was starting to go down."

An aide in a blue smock appeared at the door, a tray in hand. She placed it on my lap, glanced at Wayne and said, "Haven't I seen you before someplace? Oh, yes, the Miami Herald. Oh, my goodness." Wayne blushed and said nothing.

"Maybe I should go," he said, staring at my tray.

"Terrible stuff," I said. "Hospital food. The boat was starting to go down?"

"Yeah, it was rough water and there were no other boats around and the waves were breaking up against the rocks and pushing the boat up into the rocks and the stern was going down a little bit under water. I told Dave I thought it would be a good idea if I jumped in and saved you. Dave suggested that we run back and get help and I said it was more urgent to save you.

"I told them, No, I was going in and get you. And I took my wallet out of my blue jeans and dove in. It was a good swim to the boat that was now under three feet of water. I grabbed you and by the time I turned around to tell them I was on my way back, me and you went under. We were wrestling because you were panicking and I don't blame you.

"It was just one big drop from the time I grabbed you. We went straight to the bottom. It was pitch dark. I lost you and I was feeling around—we were at the bottom bottom—and I felt a few rocks and I grabbed your arm and pulled you closer to me. I was running out of breath and went into a squat position and shot up from the bottom. I kept looking up and looking up, it was so dark and black. I just never did think I was going to get to the top.

"When I finally got to the surface I let you go because I was choking and then I grabbed you back towards me, and turned you around and made sure your face was pointing up and out of the water and I grabbed you around the chest. I swam with one hand and had you with the other hand. I swam about the length of two football fields and didn't think I was going to make it. My friends came back and I had them hold on to you while I could get up in the boat and catch a couple of good breaths of air. Tommy and Dave weren't too strong—probably weighed a hundred pound each."

Wayne stopped, glanced at my tray where the food was going cold. I dismissed it with my right hand and Wayne Connick said, "I got my breath and jumped back into the water and we got you back into the boat which was a struggle and when we pulled and pushed you up into the boat, you…"

I looked down at the ugly heep of food. "Yes," I said through clenched teeth and around my swollen tongue, "I screamed."

Wayne Connick blushed and said, "I don't blame you, Mr. Bingold." He was staring at my food.

"Have a roll at least, Wayne."

"Oh, no thanks, Mr. Bingold," he said, reaching his hand forward and taking it from me. When I saw him devour it I felt filled myself.

"You know something, Wayne?"

The woman in the blue smock appeared.

"Now is that nice, Mr. Bingold?" She took the tray, stared at Wayne, and walked toward the door.

"I'll do better next time," I called after her, and Wayne and I smiled at each other.

Now he stood, staring at the halo, and said, "Thanks for taking the time to talk with me, Mr Bingold. I don't see how you can stand that thing."

The room seemed to brighten—and I flinched.

"No, Wayne, no," I managed to say. "It's for me to say thanks. Thank you from the bottom of my heart."

"Goodnight, Mr. Bingold."

He turned and when his back filled the door, I called after him.

"Wayne?"

He turned, his shoulder to me, his eyes shaped to a question.

"You are a good man, Wayne. A very good man."

Wayne Connick blushed and went and I lay back and stared at the darkened ceiling. All the light had gone out of the room, or had I closed my eyes to the light that still remained?

Monique sat opposite, eating from her basket of Kentucky Fried Chicken. She was working at Sun Bank, and had come by at her noon break.

"Thought you would never wake up," she said.

"Why is it so dark in here?"

"Dark? Seems light to me. Hospitals are so clean and light."

"There is *nothing* darker than a hospital."

She chewed and looked across the room at me.

"Maybe," she said, tapping her lips with a paper napkin, "you hide—maybe you don't *look* at the light."

"Wayne Connick was here." I felt tired. "Yes," I said. "It's possible I don't. I wish you had been here to meet Wayne."

Monique began wrapping up the remains of the chicken

neatly. One of the bones snapped.

"Have you thought, Richard, any more about what we were talking about?" she asked, still wrapping. "Before I flew home?"

"I wanted to write out a check for a thousand dollars on the spot—to show my gratitude. I don't think he understood how grateful I am."

"Oh, Richard. Richard. We're just making ends meet, Richard." She stopped wrapping and held the balled up bag in her hand.

"He could use the money—for college."

Monique placed the bag carefully into the waste basket. I could see her trying to smile, to wish away the tears that now welled up. A bright harsh light flashed across the room, reflected from somewhere. We both looked at each other in surprise.

"I've got to make a living somehow, and it's what I know. What I'm good at. Before the accident, I had built G-Man Investigation to six figures—you know that." Talking was tiring. "What did you mean if only I would *look* at the light?"

She stood up, flicked her head to the side, "Oh, Richard, I don't know. I've got to get back." She shot me a glance. "What do you mean when you tell me God's grace is everywhere? There for the taking?" She was angry. "I've got to go." And she turned and went.

Or I thought she had. But she remained, outlined in the doorway, staring down at me, angry—or at least I thought so.

"I thought you had gone."

"It seems like you don't see me anymore."

"Monique. Monique. Of course, I see you."

She stood in a shadow.

"I know what you mean," I said, talking through gritted teeth. "And it's true, what you said about God's grace being there. Somehow, you're right. But—I'm not living—that is, I'm not sinning. Since I met you, I'm somehow a much better person."

She took a step toward me. "But I've got to make a living somehow and private investigation is what I know."

And she turned and this time she went. Her beauty filled the doorframe one second and was gone the next. But her perfume lingered on in the dark. *We're right there Monday morning, back at work, digging and scratching out a living. We never let our families down.* Joe McLaughlin was right on.

I dozed and dreamed. I saw two men, in a dim room. When a brightness suddenly lit up one of them, the other man stepped aside, back into the dark. Then they disappeared and I set out to find them, wondering who they might be.

I woke to a sting and a nurse saying, "Be careful, sir, you mustn't pull on the IV like that." She was a complete stranger.

"Around here, I thought I knew everyone," I said dully.

She made a grim smile and said, "My ex was like that. Thought he knew everyone and everything."

I waited for her to go on, but she let it go at that, and moved along the bottom of the bed and out the door. And when she disappeared, it came to me: the man in my dream who was all lit up was Wayne Connick and the man who stepped aside, into the dark, was me.

Richard's children (l to r: Richard Dennis, Patrick William, Catherine Alicia, Barbara Elizabeth, James Edward and grandson, James

Catherine
"The egg incident"

Catherine with Dad

Catherine Bingold, 1997

Barbara Bingold (daughter)

James Bingold with his son, Andrew

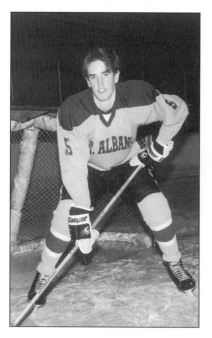

Patrick Bingold-Hockey 1996   *Barbara Bingold, 1994*

Patrick (son) with dad (Richard) 1999

Monique (mom) with Patrick (son) 1999

Richard with Wayne Connick (who
saved Richard's life) a true hero

Rev. Fr. William (Bill) McCarthy
"Another kind of hero"

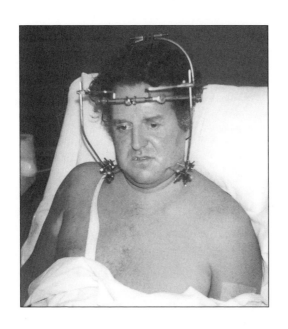

Boat accident - Sept. 1978

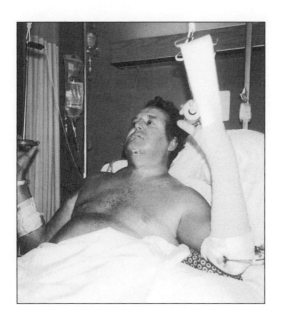

Chapter Seventeen

Deeper Into Shadow

In a straight leap through the Saturday haze of late afternoon, the big car carried me effortlessly southward, sending me at last down a Hollywood side street to a long low building with its shades drawn. Behind one shade, sat a man I had never met, the priest I had driven all this way to see. But why? I turned the engine off. I was fine. Everything was fine. Why did I need a priest? If you asked me whether I was heartily sorry for my misdeeds, I could honestly answer, Yes. What more did the sacrament of penance require?

Just six weeks ago, when I had been out of the hospital only a month, I was back once more. A clot was about to close off the blood to my heart. A man close to our family, Dr. James Casey operated, and saved my life. Afterward, I spoke briefly with his wife, Debbie, just long enough for her to give me the name of Father Dan Doyle, for what reason I wasn't sure. What had I said to her? What had she guessed? I was fine. In passing, maybe, I had said something about the fact that in the several years I had been in Ft. Lauderdale, I had not found a priest to whom I felt close. Just a passing remark. I smiled and she smiled. She was a lovely person. I was fine and my life was back on track.

Under the shadow of Monique's objection, I was beginning to build back my private eye business, under the name of G-Man Investigation. For, with a few minor mishaps I had gotten out of the hospital, and was on my way, becoming a normal healthy business man. And then in late December—it was now the end of February—I endured pain the like of which I had never experienced, before or since. Dr. Joe Grover had unscrewed from my skull the rods that over the four months I wore them, had fused to the bone.

Now as I sat staring at the drawn blinds, a convertible went by, a man at the wheel and a woman beside him. I looked away: I had been taught that some things were right, others wrong: the man was black, the woman white. I was right, they were wrong.

But had I done *anything* right? *Prayed for grace? Examined my conscience? Begged pardon of God? Resolved to renounce my sins?* The sacrament of penance was part of me. But whose sins did penance refer to? What was that! A shadow, like an axehead, flew by me, leaving behind the words, *So that we leave out no sin, we must examine our consciences according to the Ten Commandments.* Yet…what counted were all those Sundays I had loyally attended Mass, not those I had missed. If so, why was I here? Why should I confess to a strange priest, and go over all that ground again?

When I had got from the car into the entranceway, a cloud passed over the sun and when I looked close, the name of Father Dan Doyle in the brass slot was dim, almost rubbed away. But I made it out and went to his door and knocked.

As if it were planned, Father Dan Doyle was just getting up from his desk. But when he came out from behind the desk, he knocked a blue lined tablet to the floor, our hands missing when mine shot out and his went down. He put the tablet back where it belonged—next to a small Bible—and then we shook hands, saying our names at the same time without hearing the other's.

"Haven't we met before?" I asked him, his face looking at the same time familiar and strange.

"Perhaps we haven't met, but perhaps I saw you at _____," and he named a Catholic church in the area I had never attended.

"Sure," I said, wanting his approval. "Yes, of course," I said, for the first time becoming aware of the roughness of the corner of my tongue I had bitten off when the boat crashed. For some reason, my heart sped up. The touch of my tongue to my teeth had made me feel—for a whole long second—like a small boy, learning to talk. I saw the church back home. Father Nolan. And then—but it vanished before I could think what was supposed to be there. It had been replaced by Father Dan Doyle's face. And I I thought, *He is a loyal good man clouded by the mystery of his calling. That the priest is the only person on earth ordained to administer the sacraments...*

"I often think—I often feel like God has given me a second chance," I began, having nowhere else to begin. And I went on to explain the intricate arrangement of steel halo, rods, pins, and wires with which Dr. Joe Grover repaired my broken face and how only now I was beginning to regain the weight and strength I had lost, even though, even now, I was only a shadow of my old self. I stopped, hoping he would disagree with me, that I looked in the pink. But instead, he sat and waited.

"The pain of the accident wasn't nearly as bad as the pain when Doc Grover removed the rods," I said, wanting to take him somewhere mysterious to him, where I held the upper hand. I rose in my chair and chuckled. "It took Dr. Joe sixteen hours to fix the halo to my head and jaws and two hours to take it off, and I was conscious all the while he unscrewed the rods."

Father Dan Doyle leaned forward. "For both? For both, you were awake?"

"No," I said. "Knocked out for the first. But when I went to his office for what I thought was a check-up, Doc decided take the thing off. Two big men were there—to hold me down. I kept yelling, 'Turn left to unscrew! Turn left to unscrew!' And he shouting back, 'I am turning left!' I remembered later the dol, a unit on a scale of the intensity of pain. If ten is death, then what I went through must be eleven, and I thought, 'This is the kind of pain that Christ must have felt on the Cross. And I think now that the very *thought* of Christ pulled me through."

I stopped again and Father Doyle asked,

"A dol?"

"A measure of pain."

"Interesting. I've never heard of that unit before. I would have thought the threshhold of pain differed from—person to person."

"The dol is an attempt to make it objective," I said, aware that we were both talking about something else. "The worst pain," I said, trying to understand what I was getting at, "is the pain you don't feel."

I was sparring because I didn't know what I wanted to say and because now I saw the truth: I was really there to make a full, earnest, and complete confession. To pin down, draw a picture of, the man I had become. Yet I wasn't sure, though sure enough, that Father Doyle was the right priest. If he were behind a screen, in his booth, I might not have thought there was a man listening to me but a priest.

"Interesting concept," he said, mildly, his cheek resting on the thumb of his right fist. "Another way to look at it, would be to think of the pain you can't feel as the pain that you cause others."

I drew back, shocked by the closeness of the remark, trying to think of an answer, and when none came, I said,

"A good Catholic once told me that a lapsed Catholic is no Catholic at all."

"There's really no choice," Father Doyle said without a hitch, looking at me through a great magnifying glass, his eyes twice their size. "You were fed since birth on all seven sacraments of the Church, Richard, and they are part of your body in this life and in your soul through life everlasting." He looked at me with an everyday smile, pulling back from what he had said so that it stood on its own and sank into me deep, like a thorn.

"Of course, you're correct," I said, suddenly contrite, but only in so general a way, my head spun. I knew I was missing something that he saw and would any moment call to my attention. But he only sat, his eyes taking me in, then looking right of me and left, then taking me in again and his silence forced me to accuse myself, lightly. "You're right," I went on, aware he had not said what I was about to say, "I am not prepared for the sacrament of penance."

At that, he looked fully alert. I had been a Catholic since birth and I knew what a priest of his intelligence was thinking. And that made him a man of the world. He wanted to *trust* me and not examine me as if I were a schoolboy. Before coming here I had not come to grips with—hadn't faced up—to the fact that I wanted absolution on the cheap. I had not taken any of the four actions to prepare for confession: prayed for grace; examined my conscience; begged pardon of God, or resolved to renounce my sins.

Now we had come to a standstill. On the air, there was the strong odor of aftershave lotion and clothes that had the clean smell of dry cleaning. I glanced at my dull loafers I wore without socks. Outdoor noises had crept in through the walls, and sat around looking down on us, like so many gargoyles. I was not up to the trust Father Dan Doyle extended me. And I was not up to what he did next. He leaned forward and said,

"Richard—" I liked my full name's ring— "kneel here."

Father Doyle said it with a reluctant authority—and paused. A long pause that seemed to run out the end of the finger that pointed to a rug in front of my chair. A very long pause in which your past begins to surround you, ready to attack. I gathered my strength and my wits and began to kneel. I felt ill, childish. And I thought in a flash, *I'm stronger than this priest.* At the same time I admired and loved him. Once I had wanted to be a priest. Tears brimmed. And then he was speaking.

"I don't want the Church to lose you, Richard. You are no worse than God knows. No more…No more tainted than Christ sees. Not so hardened that Our Mother would turn you…Would not help you in time of need."

The words met inside me in a dark muffled collision, pushing me down on my knees, part of me at a time, like loose clothes in a sack of laundry. At last all two hundred pounds of me were on the floor, my hands folded, holding on for dear life, the yeast of humility swelling my pores and promising peace. But a part of me still peeped out from my darkness, hoping a voice would say, You haven't prepared properly. Tomorrow might be a better time. A dull thud behind layers of plaster and wood, somewhere in the building, a door shut, and I looked up and around. There was the tablet by the Bible, Father Dan Doyle's folded hands, and moving lips. He was saying a silent prayer. He was praying over me. A simple act, praying. I closed my eyes and went dead still.

"Amen," he whispered.

And I let loose: "I confess to Almighty God, to the blessed Mary ever Virgin, to blessed Michael the Archangel, to blessed John the Baptist, to the Holy Apostles, St. Peter, St. Paul, and all the Saints, that I have sinned exceedingly in thought, word, and deed, through my fault, through my fault, through my most grievous fault. Therefore, I beseech the Blessed Mary ever Virgin, blessed Michael the Archangel, blessed John the Baptist, the Holy Apostles, St. Peter, and St. Paul, and all the Saints, to pray to the

Lord our God for me. May the Almighty God have mercy on me, forgive me my sins, and bring me to everlasting life. Amen."

I stopped, held my breath, and added for good measure, "May the Almighty and Merciful Lord give me pardon, absolution, and remission of all my sins. Amen."

Through my closed eyes and sweating body I could feel the force of Father Dan Doyle's forbearance. Since I had not accused myself, he was now accusing me: he knew and I knew—and he knew I knew—I was showing off my good memory, intelligence, and piety. To get even with him, I would make him the most complete confession he had ever heard. I would tell him everything. I would make a confession without omission. And I began.

****

Father Dan Doyle saw me to the door. I wiggled my foot; something was caught in my loafer. "Richard," he said—and I turned to him with a smile—"there is one other matter, a matter it is clear you haven't attended to and seem not inclined to attend to. It is the matter of your—" I smiled at the word, and forgot it instantly.

"The matter of what?" I asked myself as I drove away, my foot heavy on the acclerator, the warm wind whooshing. The important thing was that Father Dan had given me absolution. Two cars braked at the same instant and barely missed each other. And I had confessed without a single omission.

I was feeling good. I was walking. I had spotted the Catholic Church across an empty field, and the road curved, and carried me to its parking lot across which I was walking when I felt the pebble in my loafer. Standing on one foot, I removed it, shook out the pebble, put the shoe back on, and walked up the steps, and pulled at the big black handle. But the door would not open. Irritated, feeling denied, I pulled and pushed and when the door moved in its frame, the nave echoed like thunder. I waited, listened, then turned and stumped down the concrete steps through a faint slant of sunlight.

Behind the wheel, I was sorry for the disturbance I had made. In my mind's eye, I could see a thin, white-faced priest come hobbling up the nave to the door. He had seen my retreating form, and, because he had not been on time to greet me, was full of regret. I could see his prickly back retreating, and hear the echo of his tread. And by the time he turned to walk down the right arm of the cruciform, he was the size of a burr.

My car carried me north, back home to Ft. Lauderdale-On-the-Sea, and turned me into a carry-out parking lot. I bought four bottles, one of wine. I would celebrate. I had made a complete confession, without omission and therefore Father Dan Doyle had given me absolution. I felt relieved, as I hadn't in months.

I turned down our street, saw our driveway and front door, and closed one eye, like aiming a gun. Yes, what of it? I hadn't told that priest *everything*, for who can *remember* everything? The priest had walked away from me. I pulled into our driveway and turned off the key. The drapes to our picture window were drawn, to keep out the late afternoon sun. I could imagine Monique and me celebrating, home, safe, where I should be, in the cool shadow. Then I remembered with a shock, Monique was in Montreal, visting her family. Now that I was stronger, and could handle things on my own, she had wanted a break.

I watched an old news clip of Muhammad Ali knocking out George Foreman then went to the bathroom and brushed my teeth. My pajamas were new and crisp. But when Dick Bingold stared back at me from the mirror, my brain bled deafening words into my ears so that I was unable to hear, "Stop now, Dick, before it's too late." Monique's half of the bed a wide emptiness, I lay down on my back and closed my eyes. If I had not been so tired, I would have gotten out of bed and prayed. I had confessed and gotten absolution. A good confession. Not a dozen yards from my window, a dog howled. I dozed and woke to the room shaking in a dark wind. I looked around, sighed, smiled, and dropped back to sleep.

Chapter Eighteen

Scrape With the Mafia

"An elephant is an elephant," the man said, stirring his drink with the handle of a spoon. "Don't give me that stuff that there are two elephants. The only elephant I've ever seen is the only kind there is anywhere."

I was trying to tell one of the last customers at Stan's Lounge that there are two kinds of elephants in the world, the African and the Indian.

"The African elephant is the largest of extant land animals, and the Indian elephant though, smaller, is used in war and as a beast of burden."

I blew smoke rings from my cigar.

"*Now* you tell me. How old am I? I'm fifty-four and what happens? I'm told there are *two* elephants, not one. It's like Christmas. Who would have thought Christmas could be so different?"

"Hap?"

"Yeah?"

"Dick Bingold's O.K. Get me? A good customer."

"Yeah, I get you. You want that I should hike. When you say hike, I hike."

The man pushed back from the bar, stepped back, looked up at me, and said,

"Are you the third kind?"

I smiled down at him.

"The third kind?"

"It's you who told me. There's the African then the Indian then you."

We'd all known Hap around Ft. Lauderedale bars for a long time. "Night, Hap," Stan said, and saw him to the door, then turned the key in the lock, and came back up along the bar. "Have you seen this?" The light shined on silver. Then I saw it was an oblong bottle containing clear liquid.

"I have a friend in the Kentucky hills. This is genuine stuff. The genuine white lightning. Who in the hell is that?" Stan turned and went down the bar to the door, said, "Hey, there, you two. C'on in." The door and keys rattled and people I'd never met before came up along the bar and we were introduced. "Just in time, Nick and Eleanor—my annual celebration with white lightning. And you come along just when needed—experienced drinkers, like my pal, Dick Bingold. He's been drinking here since suppertime."

I looked at Stan and wondered for the second or third time during the evening what Monique had meant when earlier I had left the apartment to inspect our crew at the race track and she had said, "We must talk, Baby. I have to talk." Why was she so distant?

Stan put four short solid glasses on the bar and turned down the light. Our eyes greeted each other as we lifted the glasses, clinked, and threw back our heads and drank it off neat.

"Dick here is full of all kinds of information. Elephants even."

"I love elephants," the woman said. "I collect elephants."

We all laughed and Stan poured a new round.

"Ivory," the woman said, staring down at the drink, but not touching it. "Three hundred, of all sizes."

"*All* sizes," the man said. "Believe me, *all sizes*. When the wife collects elephants, you get used to all sizes. Three hundred?

More like six. If I take one more, Stan, who will drive?"

"I'll drive," Eleanor said. "With one of Stan's white lightnings, I can do anything. With two, nothing. I like you, Dick Bingold. You have a wonderful look about you. A wonderful elephant look, so kind and dreamy. And *expansive.*"

"Right," Stan said. "There's something about Dick Bingold that makes you think he could have done whatever he put his hand to. Might still do it."

We all laughed and the three men downed their drinks and Nick said,

"After two, I don't count. I don't know *how* to count. So count me out. I'll watch."

"Dick?"

I nodded and Stan filled our two short glasses.

"Dick here, has nowhere to go but up. He has the biggest and best security business in Ft. Lauderdale and Broward County. He provides security for the White House. Where does it all end?"

"I seen you at the country club," the woman said. "Matter of fact, I waited on you. Now I remember you. You have four beautiful children."

"Dick Bingold gets around," Stan said and I picked up my glass, titled by head, and drank off the white lighting.

"Oh, no you don't," Stan said, and finished off his.

"I'm outa your league," Nick said. "And we're outa here. The Little Woman has two elephant shows for me to go to."

"Oh, Nick, darling. Oh, Nick. He means *ivory* elephants. Let me tell you a secret, Mr. Bingold." I looked far down or out at her, in the future, as if my whole life had made one big leap into the future. "The secret is, Nick, here, my old fellow, likes elephants well as I do."

We were all standing and Nick was smiling in agreement

and I was smiling and Stan was pouring liquid into a glass. And then Eleanor and Nick were gone and Stan and I were putting back our heads and putting down the bright glasses empty.

"Sickening."

I was where I was but where that was I had no idea at all and the solution seemed to be to lift my head and see but all I saw was a woman's shoe connected with the voice I knew and nothing more. A noise I knew as well as my own name flowed over me and by the time I was able to lift my head I knew that the noise had been a car engine starting up and the sound of tires and a moving car its sound diminishing to a rib across my belly that now I knew was the threshhold to my own front door.

Standing in the hallway of my own apartment I looked back at the closed door and it settled on me that the voice and shoe around a foot had been Monique's and that when both went by, I was face down, half in, and half outside the doorway of my own apartment. And as I walked briskly and straight down the hallway to the bathroom to get a shower and shave and dress in a clean shirt and pants, I put two and two together: It was Sunday and Monique had been on her way to church.

I looked at my face and body in the mirror and I knew I was in good shape. In fact, I had a set a time with Stan for eighteen holes of golf two hours from now and after that I had to show at Christopher's bar to complete a job I had promised. I was one of the best spotters around, work I did with such finesse I was never suspected. Today, I was sure—toward late afternoon—I would pin down exactly the way Christopher's bartender raked his take from the till without leaving a sign.

Behind the wheel, the warm air of Sunday morning whooshing through, I felt a momentary twinge. I was not a falling-down drunk. I seldom, if ever, came to that. I looked out and the sea looked immense and I thought what it might be like to be lost at sea, rollers spreading out in all directions.

The sea was suddenly blotted out by a church and I pulled over to the curb and backdropped by walking people in their Sunday morning neatness stood a man in a black suit and white collar.

"Father," I said, extending my hand.

And when he reached down and took it, he came down on me with all the force of a towering and breaking roller and I withstood it and drove on. It was Father Dan Doyle.

When I walked into the kitchen where Monique, talking into the telephone, stood early evening of that Sunday, I had news for her: at the golf course club house Stan had introduced me to someone who, after a few words, had agreed to buy the services of G-Man Investigation. It would be a big contract and double our income.

"Yes, Mama," Monique said and hung up and turned to me looking lovely and radiant and strange and distant. We kissed carefully hello in the middle of the room. I was missing something and didn't want to disturb something and for once kept my mouth shut. I looked far down or out at her, in the future, as if my whole life had made one big leap into the future.

"Dick," she said. "I'm pregnant."

To all twenty-one employees of G-Man Investigation, I handed out cigars. Monique was in a St. Jean, Quebec hospital, our son, Patrick, at her side. Her gaze when she bent her eyes on him lit up the room, putting me and all else in shadow. I described it now to everyone: how she had wanted him born in her native Canada; how I had flown there with her and, as luck would have it, had been there for his birth. And now in my mind's eye, I saw scenes from the births of my first four children,

Richard and James and Barbara and Catherine. I thanked God for them and I thanked Our Lord for Patrick and Monique.

"Before you know it, your new son will be a little man," said our receptionist Ann. "It was that way with mine. He was right here by me and now he's six. Time flies."

I took longer strides and took on more business and improved my golf game and grew stout but stayed in good shape. Monique and Patrick glowed, at first close at hand, then more distantly, Monique putting up with my refusal to leave Florida and G-Man Investigation and turning all of her life to her little son. We stood in church side by side to have him baptized. I was there and not there, close to Patrick, hearing in the words of the baptism make threads of memories pulling me away, into myself, Mom and Dad, my brother and my sister, to the house of my childhood, then releasing me back into the big world I had built for myself. In one corner of it, lived mother and son, and one day there I stood, leaning forward to watch Patrick blow out the candles on his birthday cake. Six, and one to grow on. And the phone rang.

"Don't answer it," Monique warned.

"It'll only take a second."

And I was gone and back, Patrick smiling up at me.

"It's George Kerns. He's talked her into it and they would like to meet now, this evening—before she backs out—from fear."

"Now? On Patrick's birthday?"

My eyes touched Patrick's eyes, then away, and I said, "It'll only take a second, then I'll be back."

Monique looked at me. She knew better. I was out the door and behind the wheel, torn, but wanting to get at it. At the drugstore, I bought a couple of cigars, and flinched from the news, a newspaper headlining another terrorist bombing.

She gave the paper napkin a final twist and waited. The eyes that pleaded with me out of a pale face were bloodshot. Twist by twist, she had brought her story to a single point: her husband, now doing time, had kidnapped their four-year-old son, Danny, then hidden him with a relative—she thought—in the Ft. Lauderdale area. She wanted him back—and she wanted to leave the U.S for a safe house in Great Britian, she didn't care where

"Will you?" she asked. "Will you take the case?"

Her husband had given her a new house and periodic beatings. Money from his brothers' and his sale of narcotics filled their bank accounts with money and their hearts with gluttony and greed and their heads with madness. He had tried to run over her with his car, and missed. Then she ran, leaving her child behind. There was a field of scattered palms and pines, a dusty road, and a back alley where the next morning she found the homeless shelter. The workers begged her to stay, but she was frantic: what would happen to her little boy? That afternoon, she was back home. Instead of her husband and son, she found the police. They booked her at the local station, put her through an interrogation, then let her go. Small boy? They had known nothing about a small boy.

"How long ago was that?" I asked.

"Five months."

"Why don't you go to court?"

I wanted out. Monique and Patrick were waiting at home.

"A judge—a sympathetic judge—would certainly find in your favor."

I finished off my drink. Her eyes filled with tears and she twisted the napkin in two.

"Court? Me? You've heard my story. A common pick up and without the wit to get out of a bad marriage? Would any judge think I was a fit mother? Or that I was even telling the truth? No, Mr. Bingold. No, you are—you are my only hope."

"Still," I said, then put the idea aside. "Still we would need a court order." But I didn't say it aloud.

She looked down at her fingers and the the napkin's shreds. Monique would—

"Mr. Bingold," she whispered, not looking up. "I'll pay you whatever you want, but *get my son—bring my son home to me.*"

"It's not the money, no, it's that I've got a full plate—I'm— very busy."

All I could see were her fingers crawling among the shreds of paper and the top of her head. It could have been any woman's—one of my daughter's head—and I said through a catch in my throat, "Yes, O.K. I'll do it. I'll take the case." And thought, *This will take me right to the Mafia and away from Monique.*

The next forty-five days were hell. Monique smoldering that I had taken such a case and put our own son in danger, would barely speak to me. It made little difference. I was seldom at home. I let G-Man Investigation run itself. I hung out at strange bars, moseyed into hole-in-the-wall stores that sold fruit or magazines, searched through local records, read old newspapers, combed Organized Crime Bureau dosiers, and talked with other law enforcement acquaintancces, keeping from them the real reasons for my questions. I was certain success depended on my working alone. But, as it turned out, I was wrong.

From the beginning I had hid the boy's mother, Tanya, in a motel where she stayed the whole forty-five days, never stepping outside for even so much as a breath of fresh air. And now I began to fear for Monique's and Patrick's safety. Monique, however, was a step ahead of me. Two weeks into the case, following a lead, I drove to Miami and back, talked with a half dozen people, drank coming and going, ate a hamburger about ten, and arrived at our apartment after midnight.

When I walked in, she was up and dressed. Patrick was asleep, but dressed too. She got right to the point. She had made plane reservations and she and Patrick were leaving tomorrow on a ten-thirty flight to Pittsburgh, from where they would leave for Montreal to stay with her mother.

"I've told you, Dick," she said quietly, "that I could take just so much more of this. These people will stop at nothing. You've put me in danger and worse—worse, you've put our little boy in danger." She paused. "And—you, Dick. I can't go on worrying about you, Dick."

I took a deep breath and tried to stand straight, my eyes searching for the future in Monique's eyes. She must have been doing the same.

"We'll talk—from Montreal," she said. "For now—"

I nodded and said as evenly as possible, "You're right. It's for the best."

By noon the next day, after seeing Monique and Patrick off, I was back at work. I followed up one lead, and staked out an address of Federal Highway that turned out to be a dead end. One after another, tips turned to dust. On a late Wednesday afternoon, I pushed down the handle of the big door to a Catholic church and the door gave and I stepped into the quiet, and stared a long way down the nave at a haze in which hung the Crucifix. I genuflected and made the sign of the cross, and hurried away, hearing between the arched timbers and the marble floor the echo of the banging door. Then minutes later, I was at a bar, carving a steak, having downed a half dozen drinks.

The next day, I got my break. Staking out an address on

Coral Ridge Drive, I pulled my van tight against the curb in the shadow of a row of pines, and put my binoculars to my eyes, wanting to take a close look at a late model car I'd seen when I arrived. I turned the right lens, focused—and saw binoculars looking back at me. Family of the jailed husband? Mafia? Another detective? Who knew?

I put the binoculars on the seat, reached down, put the van in gear, cruised slowly down the street, made a U-turn, and came up alongside.

"Well, Dick," said the guy at the wheel, "what the hell are you doing here?"

"Sam," I said. "What—" He was an Organized Crime Bureau officer I had known for years.

"No," he said. "What are *you* doing?"

And when I told him, he smiled—and I felt like a fool. As part of routine survellience, the OCB knew of just such a kid, but didn't know who his parents or guardians were—and so, of course, didn't know of Tanya. It had been a major error to play it alone. But even now, I had to play my cards close to my chest. I would have to reveal Tanya's whereabouts. But I didn't want anyone to know her destination once she got her boy back. In my breast pocket, I carried two one-way tickets to London's Heathrow airport.

Now it was up to me to persude Tanya to trust the OCB. If we were to get a court order allowing the OCB to pick up the boy, Tanya would have to appear before a judge. I would also have to persuade the OCB to act fast. Tanya had been well enough known by her husband's friends and would be easily recognized in any chance encounter on the street. Black wig and dark glasses made it possible to get her into and out of the courthouse and back to her motel. The OCB got its court order.

Early on a Tuesday morning, Bart, the head of the OCB,

and I in the front seat, Tanya, still wearing her disguise, in the back, we parked on a street lined with palm trees and trash containers already emptied. I had parked my car, with Tanya's luggage in the trunk, in a commuters lot at the entrance to I-75.

I felt uneasy. I was shaved and showered, but I had had little sleep over the past forty-five days, and though I ate well, I had been drinking heavily. I had talked to Monique by phone several times. Her tone of voice was not reassuring. Several times, Patrick had said hello, and only once could I clear my throat enough to reply with anything more than a croak.

Bart gave me a nudge. Two people walked into view. One was a woman, in her thirties, dressed in a plain black dress. The other was a boy. Tanya gave muffled groan.

The OCB had staked the residence several weeks ago, and knew the routine. The woman, who turned out to be the boy's aunt, walked him the several blocks to his baby sitter. She would then go off to errands in the city, not to reappear until she picked him up at noon.

Now we waited. Tanya lifted herself up from her dark corner and strained forward. The woman walked nonchalantly, the boy now and again pulling her forward. They dwindled in size, and even when they gained the second block, we waited. Then, to our surprise, the woman came back up the block. Tanya sank back. But then, after pausing and looking about, the boy's aunt disappeared through the front door of her apartment building.

And still we waited, Tanja quiet, umoving. The clock on the instrument panel clicked. Then, Bart slid the OCB sedan into gear, cruised the two blocks, and drew up to the door of the care-givers house. We watched as Bart walked the twenty yards to the door, stood, waited, then went inside. And once more, we waited. I can guess what Tanya was thinking, but I knew I had one thing on my mind: Had the boy's father gotten wind of our plan and would I end up like so many people in this game, face down in the waters of the Intracoastal Waterway? Once they found out that Dick Bingold was involved, would I ever have a moment's peace?

At last, there was Bart, and, holding to his left hand, his face deadpan, was the boy. Tanya lurched forward, her hand to her mouth. Then we were driving away, the wig snatched from her head, the boy's eyes big and staring and still staring about him as his mother smothered him in kisses.

Fifteen minutes later, we changed from the OCB sedan to my Mercury, and Tanya and her boy and I were on the way to the airport. Bart had honored my request. He hadn't asked where the mother and her boy were headed. As we drove, I handed her the one-way tickets to London. She grabbed my hand and squeezed it hard. A half hour later, I watched them walk down the ramp to board their flight. She took no chances. She didn't turn to wave and I walked back out into a cloudy day.

I drove back into town, stopped at my favorite bar, ordered a big steak and the works, and, after five or six drinks of Scotch, I ordered a bottle of wine and celebrated silently, chewing the steak and french fries, knowing in my heart yet unable to put it into words, that this was it.

"Hey, there. I know you. Darned, if you aren't an interesting cuss. Remember me?"

"Hap," I said, looking up from my fourth or fifth glass of wine.

"Sorry about that, old dude. About the elephants and all. It did surprise me, though, two elephants when I thought there was only one."

"That's O.K."

"Hey, there, Hap," Stan called.

"That's O.K., Stan," I said, and stood.

"You lost weight?" Hap asked, staring up at me.

"Probably," I said, feeling unpleasant. At the cash register, I dug in my pocket for my wallet. But Stan held up his hand.

"On the house, old buddy. On the house. You're a good man, old buddy. A good man."

In the parking lot, under the stars, I felt shrunken and alone. At home, Monique told me over the phone that Patrick was already in bed.

"Good," I said. "He's a good little boy."

"Dick?"

"Yes?"

"Well?"

"Yes," I said, picturing a bottle in the cupboard. "You're right."

"But when?"

"Two weeks. Three weeks. Yes, three weeks. I promise you that within three weeks you and Patrick and I will be out of Ft. Lauderdale for good."

I hung up and I opened the cupboard door.

Chapter Nineteen

Awakening

A long curve that reached into the dense space of snow beyond the car's lights now stretched through the night ahead of me into a dark that every other second was relieved by the glow of a gaurdrail or road sign, the surface now a trackless white, wavering as if it would vanish and I would plunge into the lake that pressed in from my left.

But that wasn't likely. I was full of good food and drink, in control of the car, enough so that even as I watched the road ahead disappear, I pressed down on the accelerator, anxious to get home to Monique and Patrick after a long day on the road.

The bartender, who waited on me at Lake & Wood Bar and Grille, turned out to be the owner and a good Catholic, whose family, I found as we chatted, had only last week cancelled its policy with a large national firm and was looking for coverage that Knights of Columbus insurance might be able to provide.

"Pretty gutsy, starting over, doing something you've never done before," he said, setting down another drink. "And in Vermont, of all places. Take it easy in this wet snow when you head out for…Where did you say you live?"

"Newport."

I had told him about our move from Ft. Lauderdale, our life down there, the business I had run, and about my single interview that had landed me this job selling insurance for Knights of Columbus, the Catholic fraternal organization.

"There's a bad curve out there, along Lake Salem, so just

take it easy," he said when he put my steak and french fries down on the formica top. I was his only customer. He said he had sent his wife home early because the storm meant most folks would head home, even if it was Saturday night. "It's one of those snaking curves that just keep on turning away from you. Know what I mean?"

He took away my plate and before lighting up a cigar and having a brandy, I phoned Monique to tell her where I was and that I would be home by ten-thirty, eleven. Patrick got on the phone and told me to hurry home and I went back to my table to my cigar and brandy.

"It'll be slow going. And don't mind me, I don't close up till I close up. The sign says, 'Open to midnight,' and I stay open till midnight. It's a thing with me. I don't bend the rules. I believe God made the universe in a certain way and the Bible pretty much tells us what way that is." He pulled up his chair. "An evangelist drove his bus into that lake on just such snowy night and lived to go on preaching for another twenty years. My Uncle Dick."

I finished my brandy and blew a long satisfyiing column of smoke to the ceiling. "Would you believe it? That's my name, Dick." We shook hands and said our names. "The disciples were evangelists—they went out and spread the Word of God."

He wiped the table and I stood up. "I never thought of it that way," he said. "You sound like a man of God. Would you like to be an evangelist?" I was pulling on my coat and wrapping my scarf around my neck and following him to the cash register. When he handed me the bill I ran my eye over the amounts after each item and saw I had had seven whiskey drinks and the brandy and that the total price wasn't at all out of line.

"No," I said. "I like my life the way it is—helping people like you with a product everyone needs. And, like you, being good at what I do. And like you, being…Vermont, it seems, you can be closer to…"

He waited for me to finish but I found I had lost track of what I meant to say. He nodded and we said goodnight and I went out the door and after five minutes of brushing the snow off my car, I was on my way.

Now the curve along the lake continued, and I pressed down on the accelerator and chased it and at last picked up in the flicks of snow where it was going and followed it and came out on a straight stretch and I pushed down on the acclerator, felt the fishtail, felt the great and easy care with which I moved the steeringwheel right, in the direction of the skid. I saw the slope of the ditch, the long stretch of field. Then nothing. Snow whacked the windows from all sides. I pressed up on the roof, thinking madly I could save my life in a roll-over.

And then the car stopped. I was inside a tomb, each widow darkened by snow. I pushed open the door and shouldered my way into the night. I looked about, seeing a distant dark row of trees, the silent highway, my own shadowy tracks where the car had skidded then plunged off the road. My heart beat normally. I wasn't afraid. And I thought,

Amazing the way God looks after me.

And I stood still. Quite still. I did not want to dislodge the thought—or did I want to forget it? I turned away from the car, and began trudging up through the snow, thinking, my head bent. Between me and the snow was a bloody gauze, as if my head were swathed in bandages. Still I toiled on toward the road and when I got there, I stopped dead, looked right, then left, and saw the glow of a sign across a boarded front stuck in the center of a Quonset hut. I stared at it, thinking,

I should go that way.

But I wouldn't move. I stood still. What was it I didn't want to forget? Patting my left breast pocket for a cigar, my hand could only feel the lopsided beating of my heart. Would I throw up? I looked down and saw in the night shadow my bedraggled self. And then I caught on: back there I had seen in a stunning flash that *Dick Bingold was a fool and a drunk.*

I leaned over and I was retching and throwing up…

…I was washing my face with handfuls of snow and then I was standing straight and innocent at the side of a snowy road in the middle of winter and I shook myself, dug into my pocket and, acting the part of the smooth alcoholic I had been for most of my life, I popped a mint into my mouth and marched off down the road.

"Working late?"

His head and his upper half had been under a hood, so all that you could see were his narrow buttocks. He was humming. Now, looking at me, he held a pair of needle-nose pliers in his oily right hand. He smelled of used oil and dust and his face was dark and his eyes shined like secrets. You could tell right away he was one of that rare breed you find in odd corners all over America, the self-taught genius mechanic. The engine was his universe and he obeyed its rules.

"Late, right. The guy who owns this mammoth tried to get away with too much and now I charge him triple time to have it ready for its Chicago run at six this morning." He looked me up and down. "Need help?"

"Yeah, off the road," I said, about to add how bad the road was, but kept my mouth shut.

"Let's see what we can do." The hood muffled his voice and then his humming.

I sidled around and looked down at his hands, darting here and there, the pliers flashing as he hummed. I compared Dick Bingold to him and felt sick again.

"Dick Bingold," I said, my name tasting like ashes.

"Chamberlain," he said.

Without a word more he attended to a couple of matters, tossed his head to the passenger seat of his wrecker, ran up the door of the garage, got in beside me. To our left as he braked at the end of his drive we saw the snow-scattered light of a car searching the dark.

"Hello?" Chamberlain said. "A drunk? Or a State Trooper?"

State Trooper, I thought. *I'll tell him the whole truth and nothing but the truth.*

We waited and I changed my mind: *I'll lie*, I thought, and popped another mint.

The car rose up in front of us, the driver hunched over the wheel and peering into the dark.

"Just as well it's no trooper," Chamberlain said. "They complicate things."

We drove to my tracks through the ditch and, humming, he paid out the first few feet of cable from the drum of the winch. I looked both ways. No trooper yet. Pulling the cable after him, Chamberlain walked off into the snow, down into the ditch, and out into the field. As if obstacles were simply the way to get somewhere, Chamberlain kicked aside snow, knelt down, hooked the cable to the chassis ring and in one seamless flow of action was putting his left hand up into his cab. A motor whined, the cable went taut, the car settled and my heart sank: it would take more than Chamberlain to get me on the road again. He lifted his head. There was a louder whine and the car moved. *No way*, I thought. *No way.* But it came on, pushing the snow aside, its weight resisting its backward journey, the dark line of woods beyond the fields sinking, the car rising and growing in size till it stopped, ghostly and driverless. Chamberlain, on his side, unhooked the cable, stood up, went to his cab and the hook clanked snug on the drum.

"Pop the hood?" he ordered politely. "We'll see how much snow you shipped. You're lucky," he said. "I mean blessed. Give it a try. That's it. Let it rest. Not to heavy-footed this time. Now, once more." I could hear his voice and the hood hid him from view but I could see the way he stood, a dark clean half-bent shadow. I could remember the work of his hands. In a moment he was beside me, knelt, reached by my foot, his nose into the floorboard, and pulled.

"There," he said as a mysterious cable popped.

Then the hood went down with a quiet tick! and he nodded, almost bowing, his hands folded.

"There. You'll do fine."

I struggled out from behind the wheel, wanting to vomit. But by the time he had come back from his cab, I had fought it back, looking down at his hand.

"Take this can of oil—you don't seem to have time to look after what most counts—your engine. And this," he said, handing me another small can. "Two things in a car: the engine to start. And the brakes, to stop. I checked your brake fluid. It was almost empty."

I stared down at him, a neat shadow in the failing light. I put out my hand so that he could see the bill.

"No need," he said, putting his palm up to me. "Some day I'll need *your* help."

The engine was still running and I thrust my hand out and grabbed his hand and pumped it up and down and got back in and drove off, the headlights searching along a road without borders over trackless snow. I had left in his palm the fifty dollar bill I had saved for Patrick's birthday.

The dash clock showed three-thirty. I was cold sober and half insane with disgust and grief. My heart thudded as if any minute it would tear itself loose and burst from my mouth. *What's wrong with you, Dick Bingold? This is just another drunken escapade. You've never once been arrested for drunk driving. Not once.* But the lurid light that had blazed in my brain back there in the snow stayed with me. This time, as always, I had escaped the police. But this time I had not escaped myself.

I took my foot off the accelerator. Numbers, muffled and sickening, crossed through the shadows of my brain while in the other direction drifted faces of loved ones, my four older children, Monique, Dad, Patrick. Hanging over them all was Richard Bingold's vast shadow. The numbers added and multiplied themselves and their result emerged, passed by, leaving behind what I couldn't face.

I put a slight pressure on the gas and the car rolled forward. A sleeping village loomed out of the dark. I saw the speedometer rise to thirty-five, knowing that a slow-moving vehicle in the early morning makes police nervous. As the village sank into the dark behind me, the lights of Newport lit the sky.

The night light in the kitchen showed the time from the wall clock and the date from the calendar: 4 a.m., Sunday, February 22, 1987. My two-hundred-fifty pounds weighed on me like five hundred. I was breathing through my nose, my jaw clenched as if wired shut, my lips tight. I could feel the pucker where my tongue had healed after the boat accident.

I looked aimlessly about, my face a mask of dirt and sweat. And then those numbers spilled out on me, one at a time, 2,3,0,0, and my brain put them back together. *Every year for the past thirty-five I had spent twenty-three hundred dollars or more on alcohol.*

Suddenly I craved comfort. I made my way down the hall, past Patrick's room without the strength to look in on him, and put my hand on the knob to the bedroom door. And stood still. *I was drunk and I went off the road.* A half-formed thought went through my brain, something to do with me in my youth and a smile. I pushed open the door and walked across the room to my side of the bed and sat down. I studied my soiled shoes, fumbled with the laces, gave up, then turned slowly, and lay back on the covers, face up, and closed my eyes.

Never in my life had I felt such despair. I didn't want to face Monique, but I wanted her to wake up. Her sudden sigh was a thunderclap, telling me she was now awake. She didn't say a word or budge. Laying next to her, fully dressed in my wet wrinkly clothes I felt for the first time in my life the full weight of shame and self-loathing. My two-hundred-fifty-pound body had withered to fifty. The shame wiped out hope and even the thought of prayer. And then the dark blurred to a dim light and the face of a small child. Me. My face, with Everyman's share of innocence. And I began to sob and as the tears ran down my face, certain dully pressing signs began to assemble themselves in my brain and my brain became a curving screen across which, one at a time, I saw the words,

Dearest Mother, I'm in trouble. I'm out of control. Please understand me—I can't bring my problem before your Son, because if I fail to keep this promise, I could never face Him. But you are my Mother and so I make my promise to You: If you walk with me from now on and never be more than a breath away, I'll never take another drink.

I had finally given up. I was at the end of my rope and knew I had to stop. And I knew that I had been heard by the Blessed Virgin Mary. A circle of silence spread out around me and in that silence I sat up and turned to Monique.

"Are you awake?"

"I've been awake," she said, her tone solemn. She rose up on her elbow and gazed by me, toward the window and we both shifted in the sun's first ray.

"The storm's gone."

"Patrick asked where you were," she said. "I was terribly worried." She stopped and sat up. "I don't know how many times I woke up—and found your side of the bed empty."

"Yes," I said, the widening circle moving through a deeper silence. "I have to talk to you," I said, and then heard my own voice say in the middle of the circle and the hollow of the room, "I'm in trouble. I'm a drunk and I need to get help."

And I began to talk, to tell her every last detail of last night's experience. When I stopped she said,

"Sleep now."

"No," I said, feeling better, stronger, ready to start a new life. "I'll shower and shave and we'll have breakfast. I need to get going."

And Patrick crosssed the bed in a leap, clung to my back, wrestled off to my side and onto my lap.

"Papa, I waited up for you. I fell asleep. But I waited."

The sun lit up the room and lit up the breakfast table and lit up our faces. Patrick listening, I told them, how like a shadow Chamberlain had been, so neat he seemed to wear the vestments of a priest. And I looked across the table and said to Monique,

"I'm sorry," I said as my promise to Mary moved across my brain. "I'm sorry, Patrick."

Monique's eyes filled with tears and so did mine and Patrick reached out and pulled us toward each other.

"I want to change," I said.

Patrick pulled on Monique's arm. "Cornflakes, Mama?"

****

In a ray of sun, just inside a window that showed the fresh

snow of last night's storm, I leafed through the Yellow Pages. I called several numbers, spoke with one or two people, and then settled on Derby Line.

"Shall we go to Mass?" I asked, turning from the telephone.

"Like this?" Monique asked, smiling and pointing to her housecoat.

"Anyway you like," I joked.

Within a half hour, we were out the door and into our car and I was at the wheel, the hood reflecting sunlight as a snowplow went by. The world looked bright and clean and the air sparkling with possibilities. A siren sounded far off.

"Where's the wreck, Papa?" Patrick asked.

"You're riding in it. And with it."

We laughed.

Next to Monique at the rail, I took the Body and Blood of Christ upon my tongue and eased The Host down my throat. I wanted to say, *Dear Lord, I have come home.* But I wasn't bold enough, and so I said, *Thank you, Blessed Virgin Mary.*

And when the three of us walked out of the church, the church seemed to me to be, for the first time since I was a child, a wonderfully weightless vestment all filled with light.

In Derby Line that night, a couple dozen of us sat in folding wood chairs that scraped on nicked and dusty floorboards. The stage was a raised portion of the floor, but each speaker stood down from it, and spoke on his listeners' level. I had kissed Patrick and Monique goodnight, told them that the meeting, at eight, would take maybe an hour-and-a-half, and that I would be back home at ten. And they knew I would.

"When I was in the Military," the man was saying, "they didn't discourage drinking. If you got soused and acted out, why, they just tossed you in the can and put you back to work Monday morning…"

Will I be able to stand up and speak out like this guy?

"…took me to age forty-two at such time that I couldn't stop drinking till they put me somewhere and I always had good jobs and made good money and of course that was part of my denial system."

The man stood there, trim goodlooking, and Irish. And I stood up when he sat down and I went to the stage and stood on it and then stepped down and then I said something that I thought I would never have to say, admit something I thought I would never have to admit.

"Hello. My name is Dick and I am an alcoholic."

Faces gazed up at me out of pool of silence. Inside, I seemed to be breaking up. Cracking up. My life's frozen river. *She said you can do it. She said she will be by your side no more than a breath away even when the storm worse than this breaks over you.*

And I began to talk.

Chapter Twenty

Terror

It's an event that nobody can predict. It strikes you out of the blue. When you are in it, you think you will never recover and when you are out of it, you wonder how you did. In a way, it seems to take care of unfinished business. In another, it seems to prepare you for a deeper spiritual life. For me, it was like speeding toward the end of the tunnel only to smash headlong into a glinting stone that you had mistaken for the light.

I was standing at the kitchen sink, unable to move.

The five years that had flung me into this terrifying moment had raced along on several parallel tracks, family, business, and spiritual. Monique, Patrick and I had settled down in Newport where Patrick entered school. Barbara and Catherine had visited us at our new house on Pine St. and we had all enjoyed visits to Jay Peak and Stowe where, smoking my cigar, I often played chess with Patrick. I got to know Monique's mother and brothers and sisters and they too came for visits. And then we were packing up, and leaving our snug Newport house.

Business had been very good. Knights of Columbus insurance division had made me agent-in-charge in the Syracuse area where we moved several years later. In the meantime, I had worked out the kinks in my invention, the double-loop plastic retraining device, had received a patent, and was searching for investors. I worked hard, was up early, and ran late.

But my spiritual life was another matter. I had thrown myself into AA, attending a meeting almost every day. But compared to my ardent practice of the Twelve Steps, my life in the Faith was bright and hot. I would wake in the morning to pray and go from AA meeting to evening service and from there to a prayer meeting. Monique and Patrick and I went regularly to Sunday Mass and I went regularly to confession. Intense though this was, I was not always certain to be in touch with the Blessed Virgin Mary, often in doubt about the purity of my devotion to God, not clear in mind and heart that my confessions were complete. I often dreamed of the sunlit beaches of Ft. Lauderdale. Too often my will replaced God's.

One event had helped to keep me on course. Monique and Patrick had gone off to visit friends and the house was quiet. It was spring, several months after I had celebrated my first anniversary of sobriety. I had eaten a roast beef sandwich and drank a cup of coffee and was relaxing on the couch, a remote in hand, surfing TV. In the still house, my doubts had come stealing over me. Why couldn't I draw nearer the Blessed Mother? Why did she appear only in the past, at Lourdes or Fatima?

I thrust out and clicked the remote. Certain familiar and at the same time strange sounds and images flooded the room. A spare countryside came into view. Was it California? Fields of grapes and wheat and hot sun. There was village and a two-spired church a voice told us was St. James and then I heard the voices of children tell us they had seen and spoken with the Virgin Mary.

And, as the story unfolded, I sat stunned. Here was an answer to my prayer. In my day and time, visionaries—these children shown here on TV as they had appeared in 1981 when they first saw her blessed face—were speaking with her every day. I leaned forward, took in the name of the village and wrote it down: Medjugorje, Bosnia Herezgovina.

The hour-long documentary went by me in a dream and it

was over. I stared across the room at the the dark face of the TV. Had I turned it off? I hardly knew. I stood in the darkness, alone, afraid, hungry, wishing for more. What had the voice said? That a million or more pilgrims visited the site every year? Why hadn't I known about it? How little I knew of what I needed to know to make myself into a different man, a man who might hope to become a man doing God's will.

At the telephone, I punched the keys for Syracuse area information, got the number of the organization which ought to know about Medjugorje, the Marian Center, dialed, and listened as the answering device gave me the opening and closing hours. I noted them mentally and then began rearranging my week's schedule in order to end up at the Center on Friday. From now on, I vowed, I would ransack every possible source of information about Medjugorje and then I would make the pilgrimage myself. I read books that I purchased or got from the library, bought and listened to audio tapes and videos. I spoke to people and wrote letters. But the more ardently I pursued Medjugorje, the further the possibility of ever, *ever,* going there drew away from me. Insurance sales, Tuff Cuff management, and family took up my time and family expenses the money to get me there. Meanwhile, the very fact of its existence nourished my spiritual life, helped me weather doubts and lapses of will. A strange period of spiritual half-light followed. And then it was I was struck down.

At the kitchen sink, I stood frozen. I held several dishes that I wanted to wash, for I had only minutes ago finished breakfast. While I ate, I read my Bible, marking the passages, thinking about each word, intent to read and understand every verse. Now as I stood at the sink, I could recall the peculiar slant of light, a glint from a spoon, a glow from a plate, the disorderly look of a half-eaten egg. None of it added up. I wasn't sure where I was or what I had meant to do. And then—as if struck with light hard and sharp as ice—nothing.

And I was on the floor. I came to, my hands grabbing my face and head, my body writhing among broken shards of pottery, tears running over my face and the room filled with the sound of my sobbing. My sobs broke into a wail. I thought of my children and former wife and friends and my parents and sister and brother, of Monique and Patrick—of everyone I had ever wronged. I rolled back and forth and cried and cried and could not stop crying and realized with redoubled agony I did not even *want* to stop crying. The remorse was overwhelming. I saw, felt, and relived all the events of years gone by. All of it kept coming and coming at me—places, events, people.

I struggled now to stop crying, but couldn't. It was not to be. Dimly through my sobbing and my tears, I saw that instead of punishment, this was enlightenment, meant to help me. I felt fear, anger, remorse, and sorrow, all within seconds of each other.

Later—I heard a clock tick, a car go by on the road—I pushed myself up against the dishwasher. I crouched there, my face in my palms and the back of my hands on the knobs of my pulled-up knees. I continued to sob, now quietly. Between sobs, I took deep breaths. The intervals between sobs grew longer and at last I stopped altogether.

I pulled my head off my knees and looked about. I was exhausted, the room silent. I sat in that silence for a long long time. Then the silence was broken by a voice crying out, my voice, saying,

"Why? Why? Why did this happen? Why did this happen, dear Jesus? Forgive me! I'm sorry! How can you forgive me?"

All was lost. Why go on living? I listened and heard that clock tick. The future would have to be faced. But what for? I had strayed, all the while pretending that I was near my God, my

Christ, and my Holy Mother. And I was further astray than ever. Tears started up again, in silence, and in silence I stood up, held to the kitchen sink, and stared down into the drain. A flash of light crossed one of my hands and I looked up and out at a tree whose leaves a sudden wind had moved. The April sun was bright and cold and it came to me in a rush that I had got beyond the terror. There was nothing left but to bear up and go on.

Pushing slowly away from the kitchen sink, I walked carefully to the broom closet, pulled out the broom and slowly and carefully swept up the broken dishes. In the dining room I closed the Bible and knelt down by my small crucifix and prayed the rosary, my fingers and palms feeling the warmth of each bead, my brain the warmth of each word, the returning strength from the Blessed Virgin Mary, from the Holy Spirit, from Jesus Christ and from God. And I stood up and walked slowly through the empty rooms to the bathroom to shower and shave. On my way I glanced at the ticking clock, thinking I had lost a whole day. But only an hour had gone by.

Then I was on my way, behind the wheel, heading for a meeting I found to my surprise I hadn't missed. The chief of police of a department in a California city had called to complain that his shipment of Tuff Cuffs had become brittle and I had promised to meet with the head of the company making my device to discuss the problem and see to it the chief got a new shipment.

At lunch I would gather my wits, read new material about Medjugorje and make an appointment to see the man whom I had been told would be able to help me understand what had happend to me, Father Reggis Rodda, a spiritual priest who was always ready and willing to help.

And I would start now saving money to make a pilgrimmage to Medjugorje. Until then, I would pray to God to help me stay on course and calm the doubts that beat on me day and night, making me afraid that I would once again be washed out into the sea of sin.

Chapter Twenty-One

A Vision of Home

Father Zito was with us in the beginning and he was with us to the end. Though I don't remember seeing him when with seventy other pilgrims I stood waiting that spring day in 1993 in the Swissaire lounge, I did see him later, in Rome, and very often at our destination, Medjugorje, Bosnia Herzegovina, where at long last I would meet and speak with the visionaries to whom as children in 1981 Our Blessed Mother had appeared. I would meet them all face-to-face: Vicka, Mirjana, Marija, Ivan, Iavanka, and Jakov.

Ever since I had seen them on TV that day in 1988, I had pursued them in my imagination, in books, tapes, and videos. Now I was full of nervous wonder. What Father Zito was thinking, I can only guess, for he would ask each visionary, "How beautiful is Mary really?" as if he were about to meet her and the visionaries would delight in answering this priest whose earnest love of Mary was so obvious. But it wasn't at all clear why he was he so anxious and urgent about it.

I had said goodbye to Monique and Patrick when our two buses left Syracuse for New York. I had made a half dozen calls on prospective insurance policy customers the week before and had spent Monday phoning potential buyers of Tuff Cuff stock. Every call bombed. Several months before—when my desire to meet the visionaries had overwhelmed me—I had found myself at the same time drawn closer to God, and in a spirit-filled ceremony at the office, I had Jesus enthroned as Tuff Cuff's CEO.

Now as we waited for our flight to be announced, I offered up a prayer, asking once again for a sign from God that I was doing the right thing. Shouldn't other things come first? Patrick was at an age when a boy needs the full attention of his father. Though our marriage was on a firmer footing, Monique and I still felt guilty that we had married outside the church and that I had never gotten an annulment. And the incomplete confession to Father Dan Doyle still cast its shadow. There were money worries. Putting aside a little each day for over a year, I had taken money for the trip that should have been used for business or for family. My business and the sale of insurance were on hold.

Had God given this trip, so self-centered on the surface, his approval? I didn't know. But I accepted the fact that a journey of the spirit is a journey through a dark wood of doubt. Even so, a month before Christmas, the call to go to Medjugorje had reached its peak, and I knew, I must go. I had talked with Our Blessed Mother. Without her I could not have gone; with her, I didn't have a choice.

There were other concerns. The pilgrimage was to last twelve days, five days to visit holy places in Italy, seven to be spent in the valley of Medjogorje. To have seen us in our seats in the huge airplane, we looked like the average tourist group. But each of us harbored an unspoken fear, for we had all watched on TV the ferocity of the war in Bosnia, our destination. No one could guarantee us that once we crossed the Adriatic to Bosnia that we wouldn't be caught up in the hostilities. The religious purpose of the trip gave us some relief, but who knew God's plan?

And then as I settled in my seat, a new worry about an old subject arose. It suddenly seemed to me that I could not complete a trip so crucial to my spiritual life without a new confession, clearing me of the guilt and doubts about my confession with Father Doyle. It was clear I did not deserve the absolution he had given me. Perhaps on this trip I would find a priest to whom I could open the matter and make a full and complete confession. Now it seemed possible, for several seats ahead of me sat Father Albert Shamon, once vicar to Monsignor Fulton J. Sheen. When we arrived in Rome, would he hear me?

In a sudden lurch, the wheels of our monstrous machine slammed the tarmac and we emrged like so many blinking rabbits into the brilliant Mediterranean sun. I was overcome by a flood of Army memories. The next day, we visited St. Peter's Square, lost in a crowd of three-hundred thousand. We watched Pope John Paul II, standing before St. Peter's, lift his hand and bless us all, as Pope Pius XII had done when I stood there in 1957. The power and beauty of it brought tears to my eyes. Later, I saw the spot where I had spoken on the phone with my Army sweetheart, Joan Muhler.

Today, too, Sister Faustina was to be beatified. My heart was full. One thing was lacking. A good confession. Later in the day, I was granted even that, when Father Shamon heard me. And yet …And yet as I walked away from the low stone wall where he had leaned very close, once again I was uneasy.

From Rome, we went to Assisi to pay homage to St. Francis; we bussed to Cascia where the Saint of the Impossible—St. Rita—lay since her death in 1457 incorrupt; in Lorrentto we walked into the Holy House of Nazareth, which first appeared in a field in Yugoslavia in the 4th Century and reappeared here in the 14th, moves made by "angelic mission." We stood awed at the site of the first Eucharistic Miracle, where it had been proved to a Benedictine monk, who doubted the fact of transubstantiation, that the bread and wine does indeed become the blood and flesh of Our Savior.

And then in a twinkling we were racing across the Adriatic

Sea under a wet dome of stars, the hydrofoil's engines lifting the airplane-like craft on skimming fins toward the seaport town of Split. Our hearts in our mouths, we looked out to see the glistening hull of the Italian gunboat that moments before had sent us on our way after examining our passports and other documents to make sure we weren't a Balkan war combatant.

The stir of worried talk had now subsided. Here, near me, a cork popped, then down the line several more were heard. Song soon joined the wine. I let my tenor voice loose. In the shadows of the tiny overhead lamps, smiles and faces came into focus. And I was talking away like an old friend with a family whose spiritual strength and sense of humor shined from their faces, Mary O'Connor and her daughters, Mary and Maureen, from Reading, Massachusetts. Father Tom Foley of Winchester led us in more song. Glimmering on the water and glowing in the sky, lights from Split appeared. It was midnight. Though the newspaper in nearby Dubrovnik the next day carried a headline that we were the first tourist group of any size in the area since the war began, I doubt that the story recorded that we arrived singing.

Now on buses, nobody slept. Five minutes out of Split, engine wheezing and brakes squeaking, we ground to a halt. My neighbor's face glowed red as helmets on heads, carbines on backs, soldiers in a swirl of warning lights checked us out and waved us on. The valley dropped behind, the mountain road mounted upward beneath our tires and, one by one, soldiers at five more checkpoints levelled guns at us, frowned, peered, checked documents, then waved us on.

But when we peaked and began our winding descent, there was a change in mood. Down in the valley, the lights of Medjugorje twinkled. Our buses twisted downward, the black shadow of the mountains rising above, the road reaching ahead into the night's blue velvet and mist. In Split, our buses had looked normal. Now they doubled in size, for as we slipped like a knife in a sheath through the streets of Medjugorje, I could have reached out and touched the face of a sleeping house. And then I took a deep breath: Looming out of the dark, reminding me of all the dreams I had had, the videos I had watched, were the twin spires of St. James Church.

The bus stopped. It was 3 a.m. I was half way back and had to wait in line and I could feel the tension and weariness lift. We had arrived. I stood in the street and not a block away, a rooster crowed. We chuckled at the sound of something so familiar. I looked about, taking in the bobbing heads of people searching for their luggage, the stars leaning down, the fields reaching away into the dark, a morning breeze brushing the fragrance growth of the soil into our nostrils. My heart wouldn't be still. In Italy I had visited the most moving and beautiful—the most awe-inspiring—religious sites in the world. Now Medjugorje, like a powerful lens, lit those sites into a single brilliant flame.

"Dick Bingold?" someone said out of the morning shadows. "Dick?"

I barely knew my name and for the next seven days I didn't have to make a single decision. From that first night on, I stepped into footprints already there, as if they had been put there for me alone. I lived in the glow of discovery, walking blindly into that glow only to find on the other side what I didn't know I was looking for. And so it went, day after day, and night after night

Into bed by four, I was up at eight and at breakfast with the O'Connors by eight-fifteen. By ten, beneath those double spires, I sat in a pew of St. James, one of several hundred reciting in unison the Holy Mass, lead by a priest, Father Philip Pavick, I now saw for the first time. Everything struck me as new and fresh, potent and mystical, so that when he looked down at his pilgrim congregation, he and I exchanged a look of shocked recognition. Or so it seemed.

Ahead of me, on the altar to con-celebrate Mass, I saw Father Zito looking about, his face shining and expectant, as if he were about to witness a miracle—exactly what we all expected, the hours dragging, for we had to wait until three that afternoon to meet with Vicka, one of the visionaries, and hear from her lips the message Our Blessed Mother had given her that very day.

I drifted with others along the road that stretched by fields where women in skirts to their boots picked the large leaves of tobacco plants while others tended grape vines and still others fields of wheat. Snowcapped mountains, the Dinaric Alps, rose in the distant blue haze. Northeast, 180 miles away, lay Belgrade, where many of the husbands and sweethearts of Medjugorje had gone to find work...

...So had these fields lain for centuries, their globe of sky floating us all in the holiness of their immemorial beauty while I ...I searched for something hidden...walking ahead, the road bending to reveal Apparation Hill...and then I put my finger on it and saw clearly what a moment before had been a blur: A stone wall in Rome where Father Albert Shamon had heard my confession, a confession during which I struggled to confess all that was in my heart, and had...I walked on. And stopped. Then I admitted it: Once again, I had failed—failed to make a full and complete confession.

I took a deep breath, and walked on, through the fields that stretched eastward, tilled by settlements of Roman Catholic Croats and Eastern Orthodox Serbs and Bosnian Muslims since the Seventh Century, their diffferences often putting them at each others' throats, their human doubts taking them on the same journey into the Unknown. The valley in which I walked, however, had been Croat hundreds of years, and the people of Medjugorje and the four connecting hamlets, particularly devout.

And then, as if I were coming home, we stepped into the presence of Apparition Hill. *No matter how you come to this hill, it is I who call.* So the visionaries had been told by the Blessed Mother. I could hear her voice, see their images. Yet, I don't know what I expected. That after all these years and tramping pilgrims the path would be smooth? I was wrong. Evidently I expected an easy climb, for I wore a pair of low, hard-soled shoes, chinos, a long-sleeved shirt, and sweater. The hill, after all, is not a mountain.

Like all those who had followed the spiritual journeys of the visionaries, Vicka and Mirjana and Marija and Ivan and Ivanka and Jakov; who had seen the hill in videos; who had listened to the story of their first meeting with Our Lady while she stood on a cloud and little Jakov fell into a thorn bush and emerged uninjured; who had heard the story of their miraculous ascent; who had heard how they ran over the stones without hinderance, carried upward by some unseen force to Our Lady's feet, I wasn't prepared to pick my way over a surface littered with sharp-edged rocks.

But while my clunky feet and weak ankles pushed me step-by-step through the rocky maze my mind was elsewhere. My fingers passing lightly over my beads, I was praying the rosary. And then, as if to make a friend of an enemy, I leaned down and picked up a stone. I stopped climbing and stared down into my palm. There lay colors running softly into and out of each other, from yellow-green to deep purple. I turned it over and looked closer. Its red stain gave birth to fine veins. The stone was the shape of a human heart. Pilgrims passed me right and left and still I stood, a vague thought slowly becoming clear.

I slipped the stone into my pocket and continued to pick my way up the rock-strewn hill. I continued to pray and climb and by the time I had reached the place where the Blessed

Mother had first appeared to four of the visionaries, I had picked up several more stones.

At the top of the hill by the Cross where the visionaries had met so many times with Our Lady, I knelt next to Father Shamon and continued to pray the rosary. And even while praying, I looked down at the stones and with thumb and forefinger, choosing at random, I picked up first one and then another, inspected each and, still praying, put them away in my left pocket, the heart-shaped stone alone in my right. Father Shamon turned. His expression asked, "*What* are you doing?"

I smiled back and said without a second thought, "I'm going to make a rosary."

Father Shamon lowered his head, as if to go on praying. Instead he said, "How do you…?"

I stopped praying, picked up another stone.

"Excuse me, Father?"

"I asked you, How do you make a rosary from a handful of stones?"

"I haven't a clue," I replied, bent down, picked up more stones, brought a white handkerchief from my hip pocket, spread it on my palm, and dropped the stones into the center.

Father Shamon was smiling. Now he joined me, and with light heart, encouraged several women to add to my store, then gave me some of his own. Several minutes later, I leaned down, but didn't pick up a stone. This time I picked up several small branches with thorns. Nobody asked me why.

Together we walked down the mountain and arriving at St. James Church, found Father Zito walking nervously up and down in front of a row of confessionals.

"Wouldn't you know it," he said irritably, "just when you need a priest you can't find one."

Father Zito exchanged stares with Father Shamon, then

said roughly, "*You're* not ready for my confession."

With that, Father Shamon grabbed his wrist and walked him to the wall of St. James where they both sat down and were huddled there when I walked away, on the way to the audience with Vicka. When I saw Father Zito again, he was at small cafe where he sat with four women at a table for lunch.

"Did you get your confession?" I asked, trying to cheer him up.

"Yes," he grumped, "now I can go home."

"Oh, you pain-in-the-neck," said the woman next to him. "You've been wanting to go home ever since you got here."

"Yeah," he said, his sandwich to his mouth. "You're right." And then he glanced at the woman and put the sandwich down, untasted. "Home," he said to himself.

Later, I found that the word had spread. It seemed everybody knew that I was collecting stones. Even though I wanted the rosary to be made from stones only from Apparition Hill, friends—Liz and Tom—gave me one, like the heart of a valentine, that they found among rocks used for road pavement. More stones arrived later. A small plastic bag of them grew to three, then four. To make room in my suitcase, I gave away clothes, a pair of shoes, and my toiletries. I wrapped the stones in towels to keep them quiet, but no customs officer asked why my suitcase was so heavy. On the plane, heading home, I thought how strange, yet how right, it was that Dick Bingold the grown man repeated Dick Bingold the boy, for there was nothing I loved more in those days than collecting and throwing stones.

On the steps to her house in one of the hamlets, stood Vicka. From where we stood, on a lower level, we could see through her beaming smile the traces of cancer she has fought over the years. But as others drew near, she stood patiently.

Restless children clung to parents, older boys darted into the shade. Chased by a little girl, chickens ran into and out of a patch of light. And then we were all silent. Vicka had begun to speak. The sun was bright but Vicka's face was bright in a way the sun can never be.

In the quiet street, there were two voices, Vicka's speaking her native tongue, Croatian, and then the interpreter's, speaking English. I hung on every word, never thinking that I would receive her special attention. Her message was simple: Pray the Rosary, its Joyful, Sorrowful, and Glorious Mysteries; abide with our Lord by receiving him in the Communion; read the Holy Bible daily; fast often; and—I listened carefully—go to confession often. I looked at Vicka, then at the interpreter, who said,

"Love one another as God loves you."

And Vicka fell silent. The interpreter looked her way and she looked back at him, as if to signal that she was about to go back inside. It was then I looked up and asked her to pray over me. She evidently understood my English. Then her eyes caught mine and she smiled and placed her hand on my head with a strong grip—the grip of the Holy Spirit. As she prayed, I trembled, and when I opened my eyes, she smiled at me again and then, as if I had asked a question, she nodded, as if to say,

"Yes."

"Yes?" What had that word meant? That night, unable to sleep, I walked out into the dim streets of Medjugorje, and found myself looking up at the top of Mt. Krizevac where in the twilight I could see the thirty-five-foot high, fourteen-ton cross, "built by the inhabitants of the valley in 1933, to commemorate the nineteen hundredth anniversary of he crucifixion of Jesus Christ, and to consecrate the land below and the fruits of their labor to God." We had climbed up there several times, praying the Stations of the Cross. But tonight I wanted to be up there alone.

I wanted to mull over what had happened to me earlier in the day. To discern its lesson.

At the foot of the huge cross, I knelt down and prayed. When I stood again, I saw the sky to the west fill with lightning, pulse after pulse, each pulse followed by a boom of thunder. I waited, hoping it would stop, wishing I did not need to face the reality. It wasn't lightning at all. Not an act of nature. It was an act of man. The Serbian army was bombing the ancient city of Mostar.

The shelling went on and on, and then rumbled to silence. I pulled a borrowed sweater tight around my neck, nibbled chocolate, and drank from my bottle of water. I had decided to spend the night at the foot of the cross. I wanted to think…to think about what had happened to me this afternoon…in what way it was connected to my spiritual journey… and to be near Jesus as I slept.

…I was sitting in a pew of St. James Church, eight or nine rows back on the left, Father Slavco Barbaric conducting the Eucharistic Adoration. The lovely monstrance, the sunburst shining at the top, stood in place. The consecrated Host—three or four times greater in diameter than the normal Host—was in its compartment for all to see and worship. I stared at it long and hard, for it was the blood and body of Christ. Around me I heard the familiar echo of late-comers finding their seats, the occasional cough, a sneeze, the muffled bomb of a closing door. And then the service was rising and falling sea of song and prayer and long silences. I drifted away from myself and when I came to, I was crying, the tears trickling down my cheeks. The sunburst, the monstrance, the Blessed Sacrament floated in a blur. And I was thinking, *The revealed Word—the Word of God and the blessed objects of the Word—carry the wisdom of eternity, of all men and women everywhere. No wonder it finally hits home, touching springs that are personal and intimate, often forgotten. How grateful I am to you, my Lord God!*

I was in His presence and felt unworthy. I swallowed down a sob, remembering my break down at the kitchen sink. My failed confessions. My life as a ruffian. Song rose about me and echoed in the nave and through my body as if somehow, cell-by-cell, I was being changed. I was ready to go home.

And so was Father Zito. On the Swissaire flight from Zurich to Kennedy International Airport, he fainted and, watched over by nurses Mary and Kathleen, he slipped into a coma. When we landed, he was transferred into a waiting medvac plane and flown to Boston General Hospital, where within a week of the final day of our pilgrimage, he died. Father Zito had gone home.

Chapter Twenty-Two

Stones In the Path of Faith

"Papa?"

I put my hand over the mouthpiece of the phone: "Yes?"

"I wanted you…I wanted to show you something. A question. How…"

"Will it keep?" I whispered. "A phone call. I've got New York on the line."

Patrick's face clouded. He was a big, handsome fourteen-year-old boy.

"Sure, Papa."

And when I went back to my call—another delay in the delivery of two-hundred dollar investment in Tuff Cuff—I prayed.

"Mama," I heard Patrick say to Monique. The wall of the room kept them hidden.

"Mr. Bingold?" The voice from the phone was tiny, far away.

"Help me, God, in this venture," I prayed silently, hearing the voices of my wife and son. "Help me, God, care for them."

"Mr. Bingold?"

For an hour this afternoon, I had sat gazing at the Host on display in the monstrance, what we call in our church the Eucharistic Adoration. I had gone to early morning Mass. I had prayed the Rosary. Early against the dawn, I had whispered, "Good morning sweet Jesus. Good morning my Blessed Virgin."

"Mr. Bingold?"

What was I becoming? Here was my home, on a leafed-out

street in the suburb of a North American city. My wife and son were in the next room. Yet…I had a second home, three-thousand miles away, in the war-torn Balkans, Medjugorje.

"Yes?" I said to the man on the other end of the line, already thinking of something else, a gap in my life. Something missing.

We finished our conversation, the broker and I. But I was no longer thinking about what he had said, or what it was I was missing. My mind was already running on another track. Monique wanted to move back to Vermont with Patrick, to be nearer her family. I needed to increase my income to make the move. This morning, after several phone calls about Tuff Cuff, I met with my insurance salesmen and had to let them know that the number of policies sold this year was five percent under last.

"Dick?"

It was Monique, calling me to supper. A sudden rush of blood to my heart let me know I was letting them both down. In the eyes of the Church, I was living in sin. My marriage to Beth had not been dissolved by annulment or my life with Monique sanctified by the sacrament of Catholic marriage. I knew better. I could not go on this way. The only way was the right way: By annulment and marriage, bring my little family into the circle of God's grace.

As I moved away from the phone, that other thought came back to me, of something missing, a deed done or not done, I didn't know which.

At the table, after saying grace, I silently thanked God for my beautiful wife and my wonderful son. The sun shined on their youth and beauty.

"What did you want to know, Patrick?" I asked after a bite.

"Mama told me," he said, not looking up from his plate.

And I thought, *If I don't take time for Patrick, how can I take time for God?*

When I went to bed that night, I prayed for strength to do both. About to fall asleep, a voice told me, *You are not worthy, Dick Bingold. Your will, not God's, will always come first.*

Toward early morning, I woke, wondering. Where was I? What was I doing? Why was I suddenly afraid, feeling in a flash what I had felt at the kitchen sink, the cold chill of terror? What was missing? What kept limping like a wounded animal through the dark passages of my heart?

I got out of bed, looked out at the dawn, and whispered, "Guide me, Blessed Mother." Then it came clear: Though with the Blessed Virgin Mary at my side, I had stopped drinking and had begun a new life, I had not made a confession that was full and complete. In holding back my worst sins from Father Dan Doyle and Father Albert Shamon, I had committed a sacrilege. I left our bedroom.

At our family prayer stand, I knelt before the crucifix. I asked forgiveness and the strength to make amends. But when I stood up, that voice in my head said, *You can't do it, Dick. You're a man—a man of flesh. Look at yourself in the mirror. You're a handsome guy, a fellow with many years of pleasure ahead. Who are you fooling?*

I knelt back down and prayed long and hard and when I got back up, I felt stronger. It was a good thing, for in the shadow behind my back, my dark doubts crouched, ready to pounce.

I read the black print: Aldi Skegro. Date of birth: 7/3/87. Religion and nationality: Catholic and Croatian. Mother: Nery Skegro. Housewife. Address: Splitska 11, Mostar. Father: Milenko Skegro. Killed 9/24/93. I looked at Aldi who gazed back at me, like any American child, from what might have been his school photo. It had been taken, perhaps, the year in street fighting his father had been shot dead. Aldi's eyes were steady but his lips were not: They seemed to quiver and try to forget.

I read on. I remembered my all-night vigil on the Hill of the Cross. I heard once more the bombs falling on Mostar. I saw the village of Medjugorje in my mind's huddled in sleep, protected by Our Lady.

"Aldi is healthy and lively boy. He likes to play with his friends and watch cartoons," wrote an uknown typist on the application.

Under the heading, *International God-Parenthood for Herceg Bosnian Child,* I signed my name to sponsor Aldi, and made out my first check. For a second time, I read,

"I declare, that with all my actions and the best of my ability, I will influence the intellectual, social, and cultural growth and development of my godchild. I will take an obligation to influence my godchild to be raised in the spirit of peace, justice and mutual respect."

The phone rang and when I put it down I could not believe how cooly I had taken the news that the broker in New York had found the answer to the future of Tuff Cuff: A man who wanted to invest two-hundred thousand dollars. Compared to Our Blessed Mother appearing to visionaries in Medjugorje, what did two-hundred thousand dollars amount to?

I picked up the phone and dialed my son Rich's number and when he answered, I told him about my new godson, from the wrecked world of Medjugorje. There was a very long silence on the other end of the phone. I waited a minute, then I told him why I had called: that the new investment meant that I could carry through on my offer to him—to come to Syracuse to help me market and manage Tuff Cuff. And when he said he would think about it and we had hung up, I walked from the office wondering how soon I could get back to Medjugorje.

And as I drove, I thought, *There's no way I can go back until I have...*I stopped at a red light. And then the idea came to me complete. *There is no way I can go back to Medjugorje until I have built the rosary and then have it approved by the Blessed Mother herself. I will call it the Pilgrim Rosary. It will take Medjugorje to people who can't get to Medjugorje.*

My heart pounding, I put my foot down hard on the accelerator and sped down a country road bright with sunlight.

When I got home, I went immediately to the closet where I had stored the stones. I held a handful of them up to the light.

"What you going to do with them, Papa?" Patrick asked.

"I mean to make a rosary of them—a Pilgrim Rosary."

"How do you do that?"

"I don't know, Patrick. But maybe now it's time I found out."

"Papa?"

But I was down the steps, through the kitchen, and into my garage workshop. There lay the heart-shaped stone, its colors on one side blending softly, from yellow-green to deep purple, and on the other, the red stain forking into delicate red veins. Next to it, as if in challenge, lay the present from my friends, Liz and Tom Harris of Syracuse, the other heart-shaped stone, as if it were made especially for a valentine.

But when I spread all the stones on my workbench, I drew back. The sheer weight and number were like a knife to the heart. Make a rosary of them? No way. And there they lay, blocking my way to God.

"Dad!"

"Patrick!" I said angerily, twisiting around.

"Papa," he said. He was angry too. "I've been calling you— for supper. Mama said come to supper. You didn't answer me. Why didn't you answer me?"

"You're rude, Patrick," I said furiously—and sent a prayer to Mary, and said calmly, "Tell Mama I'll be there in a minute."

Without a word, I heard him leave the garage. The back-door banged. And I was beaten down and alone.

Then I glanced up from the stones to the wall on which I had arranged my tools and saw Dad and felt his presence flow into my hands. And in the next seconds, those hands were at work, Dad in each finger, sorting through the stones, looming over us both, the glowing face Our Lady.

Dick, Dick, I thought. *The stones don't make a wall, they make a road—a road to God.*

At supper, Monique talked about our move to Vermont. After supper, Rich called to tell me he had made up his mind. He would join Tuff Cuff. Later, an old friend whom I had also asked to work with me, called to say O.K. About bedtime, my Knight of Columbus insurance boss called to ask if we could meet first thing in the morning. I agreed. I knew what he wanted, for I had already asked him to replace me as agent-in-charge so that I could go back into the field and deal directly with customers. Doing so, I could continue to sell as many policies as before, and at the same time I could devote more hours to Tuff Cuff.

"I'm going to bed," Monique said.

And I said I wanted to finish a letter to a fellow who dropped by the office. Monique gave me a long look and went off too bed. I finished, and said good night to Patrick, who barely said a word to me. Then I took a hot shower, hoping it would calm me down. But when I lay next to Monique on my side, trying to sleep, all the other worries of the day reduced them-selves to one: The stones of Medjugorje became my a wall and once more blocked my way.

Over the next several days, I prayed for discernment and strength, attended a mass morning and evening, greeted Richard at the airport one day, my friend the next, and sat long hours with both, planning the future of Tuff Cuff. In the meantime, I was on the phone, setting up meetings with people who might buy Knights of Columbus insurance. Monique, as before, found us a house to rent until we settled down. Then we packed half our belongings into a truck, and off we went. I was reading the Bible every day, and, resolving to fast, broke down after seventy-two hours and ate a loaf of bread. My friend told me he was glad to see that I could still laugh at myself.

And then he said, "I'm not sure you're the same Dick Bingold I used to know—the fellow I used to know in those good old days."

On the way to call on an insurance policy prospect, a couple who lived thirty miles east of Syracuse, I thought, *You can't do it, Dick. You can't leave that old Dick Bingold behind.* I pulled into a MacDonald's, ate two hamburgers, drank down two cups of coffee, and drove on, fingering my rosary beads, and prayed the whole, long, complicated rosary, all fifteen decades.

The next week, we moved more of our household belongings to our new home in Northern Vermont, and I returned to Syracuse where I would stay, going to Vermont on the weekends, until the house was sold. Next morning, I met with Rich and my friend, and reviewed a sales plan for Tuff Cuff, attended a Eucharististic Adoration in the afternoon, and then returned to our house alone. I fried two pork chops, heated up frozen french fries, watched the news, phoned Monique and headed for the bedroom. But in midstride, I wheeled, went out the back door and into the garage and turned on the light.

I surveyed the stones, Patrick on my mind, for when I had spoken with him, he had been sullen and uncommunicative, the way a fourteen-year-old can sometimes be, and I was angry—and, angry, I went to work.

Within an hour, I had fixed into my vise two blocks of wood to hold the first stone. I looked along the line and placed the Valentine-shaped one, the gift of Liz and Tom Harris, between the jaws of my vise. But the minute I pressed the spinning drill to its surface, the stone shattered. I was still angry, having forgot why. I picked another stone, and then another and another, and each one flew apart. I turned out the light and went into the house to bed. Once more, the stones rose up like a wall but by the end of morning prayers, I saw the light. There was no way I could make a rosary angry. After breakfast, I asked Our Blessed Mother's help—and her foregiveness—and took out the trash, drove to the office, met with my associates, and returned home late afternoon.

After a snack, I went to the garage, and turned on the light. And then I remembered what Dad had done: To keep it cool, he had drilled metal under water. So that was it: The high heat of the drill had shattered Liz and Tom's stone and all the others.

My pulse beat faster. My eyes lit on the first stone I had picked up on Apparition Hill, of exquiste coloring and heart-shaped, held together, it seemed, by those delicate red veins. It would be the stone which would receive the the blessed image of Our Mother.

The world of Syracuse disappeared.

When I came to, tears were running down my face. The only sound was the whirr of the drill. Through my tears and a half foot of water, I could see my left hand, holding a wood bracket. The whirling point of the bit was sinking deeper and deeper into the red veins. *Stop, Dick, stop!* I could not have stopped, for I was immersed in an intoxicating fragrance.

I blinked and pulled out the drill. I walked out into the cold night of stars. I looked up, and around and down, trying to get my bearings. I dried my eyes with my knuckles. *You're an alcoholic, Dick. You're fooling yourself.* I nodded, and went back to work, expecting to smell nothing but mildew, grease, dust. But when I put the dear stone under water and drilled again, I was once more overwhelmed by the fragrance—and this time, I knew what it was: roses. I walked outside, inhaled the cold air and slapped my face. Was I awake or dreaming? But the second I stepped into the work area, I stepped into the magic ring. At its center was the object at the bottom of the old coffee can, the stone into which I pressed my drill once again. I took another deep breath, expecting nothing. I walked away. I walked back and drilled. And each time I drilled, the stone beneath the water gave off the fragrance of roses.

I wept. I was going mad. Who was I to be given such a gift?

At dawn, I curled up and slept. I woke to drizzling rain. Hair uncombed, and face unshaven and still wearing the soiled kahkis of the magic night, I walked into the garage. My heart sank. The stones and workbench stared at me from the gloom. There was no fragrance. But something else called to me. The Heart Stone from which the odor of roses had come. It was beautiful. With a fine saw, I had cut out of a metal plaque an image of Our Lady's face and shoulders. I glued it to the Heart Stone and sprayed the precious face with 14-carat gold paint.

In a half-moon over her head were twelve holes I had drilled during the night of the roses. Into these, I inserted tiny diamond-like stars (Monique had given me from her jewelry), representing the Twelve Tribes of Israel. Now I laid over the dear face one coat of epoxy after another, letting each dry in turn.

As the epoxy dried, I toiled over the site of the crucifix, a one-inch-thick stone that under the force of my grinder I had made into the shape of the Cross. Hungry and tired, I made one clean cut after another, afraid on each pass the precious stone would shatter. After applying the tenth coat of epoxy to her face on the Heart Stone, I turned back and finished the Cross.

Pulling my light close, I placed before me a thin brass plate. Worn, hungry, and in need of a shower and shave, I went to work with a metal stylus. Hours later, the image of Our Precious Lord began to stand out. With a fine saw, its teeth whirring by his feet and head and arms, I cut him free from the brass plate, only to fix him to the stone cross. With steel wool, I burnished Our Lord so that he shone.

My son, I thought, *my son.*

In my palm, he looked ready to fly. And, strangely, alone and worn out in this old garage, I was suddenly brought closer to Monique, because Our Precious Lord's dear image had been copied from a medal that once belonged to Monique's mother and which she now wore in her mother's memory.

One more obstacle stood in the way: Instead of nails that had to be tiny, I used thorns, taken from the briar bushes on Apparition Hill, as nails for Our Lord's feet and hands. At last I had placed them just so, and applied epoxy. But after five or six coats, the last one refused to dry. I sighed, placed the my new crucifix on a soft cloth. Expecting day, I opened the garage door to night.

On Monday, I was on the road, calling on a half dozen customers. Several evenings during the week, I checked the Crucifix to see if it had dried, in vain. Meanwhile, I stayed at my garage workbench. I drilled the fifty-nine stone "beads" for the rosary, fashioned the links of the chain from extremely thin welding rods, and attached the beads to each other.

Then on Saturday, I was in for another shock. The crucifix had dried at last. But it needed one more coat of epoxy, which I applied, guessing that I faced another long drying period. Instead of turning to another task, however, I decided to speed up the process by blowing my warm breath on it. And when I did so, the crucifix sent back at me a flash of heat, hotter than the sun. And the figure of our Precious Lord on the Cross, dried immediately.

My Pilgrim Rosary was complete but I was undone. That beautiful fragrance—and now this. I walked from the garage in a daze.

Chapter Twenty-Three

A View of the Void

The corkscrew mountian road soared against Ivan's tiny Fiat, his hands on the wheel, the pistol tucked between his belt and belly, the engine straining to carry Bruce Ellavsky, me, and our luggage to the six-thousand-foot summit from which we would see Medjugorje.

At a narrowing of the road, stood soldiers and parked vehicles, blocking our way.

"Another checkpoint, the sixth," I said, wondering if once again Ivan, his papers, and his car would be cleared to cross the mountain. On my lap was a briefcase in which I carried the Pilgrim Rosary. My grip made my knuckles white. I had so much to do in such a short time.

A young man with lieutenant bars on his shoulders leaned down and peered in. He and Ivan spoke Croat to each other. An hour since, we had landed at Split, Croatia's Adriatic port, where just twelve months ago, with a group of pilgrims that included the O'Connors and Father Zito, we had boarded buses for my first trip to Medjogorje. Now I was coming back. Coming back to my second home.

The voices next to me rose and fell. Was something the matter? There seemed to be. I gripped the Pilgrim Rosary tighter. Then Ivan handed the lieutenant a second sheet of paper. The lieutenant grinned—and waved us on our way.

We continued to climb. "Ivan," I suspected was not his real name. I knew he was a native of Croatia, but nothing more. In

Split, in as few words as possible, he had agreed to drive us to Medjugorje, for a price. He was silent most of the way. He didn't explain the second sheet of paper.

"War is bad, bad," he muttered.

The Fiat labored upward, along the corkscrew, a road that ahead and behind was plain white and glaring, as if that strip of road were an opening through which you saw the void of outer space on the other side of a world split in two.

At the summit, the air was clear and sunny. We pulled over and looked down. There lay the holy village, curled in a soft haze, the squared fields of tobacco and wheat reaching between mountains to the base of the Dinaric Alps. I thought I could see the twin spires of St. James Church.

Medjogorje, my heart whispered, *Medjugorje.*

"There it is, Bruce."

"Yes," he said. "Beautiful," he added, the first two words he had spoken in an hour.

I looked back, down toward Split. The trip had taken three hours. I followed the road and the glare, and saw with a jerk of panic my tiny body falling head over heels between two worlds, down that awful void.

For reassurance, I patted the leather top of the case that held the Pilgrim Rosary. I prayed the rosary itself. I repeated my name several times. And I saw in my mind's eye, the list of things to do I had made back in America: take Bruce up Apparition Hill, go to Mostar to meet Sister Janja to see how I could help to restore damaged churches and convents, confess to Father Philip Pavich, and have the Pilgrim Rosary blessed by Father Jozo Zovko, then put into Vicka's hands, the visionary I hoped would get the rosary blesssed by Our Lady. Could I get it all done in such a short time?

"Mostar and all the villages around bombed—but not

Medjugorje," Ivan said, pointing to a mountain that hid the ancient city of Christians and Muslims, Mostar, where bombs dropped the night I spent on the Mountain of the Cross.

"We better get going," I said abruptly. Then, on a hunch, turned to Ivan: "Here's something you might do—drive me to Mostar."

Ivan didn't turn from staring. "When?"

"Tomorrow. Back the same day."

"Good," he said, using the English word.

"Yes," Bruce said absently, staring at the distant blur of the village. "Beautiful," he whispered as the Fiat wound down around the first corkscrew.

"Dick," Bruce said from the back seat.

"Yeah?"

"I feel like I'm leaving an old life behind, going from one world to another. Thanks. Thanks for taking on a perfect stranger."

We made another sharp turn.

"My pleasure," I said, remembering Maureen O'Connor's call, asking me if I minded if Bruce, an old friend of hers, would join me on my second trip to Medjugorje. We had met for the first time, two days ago, at Kennedy International Airport. A Lutheran who only now and again attended church, Bruce, an FBI agent, was divorced and at loose ends. This was the first time I had heard in his voice a bright note.

"You're right," I said. "You're right about two worlds. Just wait till you get there."

And I began telling Bruce the story about the visionaries. How, since childhood, they have seen Our Blessed Mother every day, sometimes on the hill on which in the next several hours Bruce and I would walk. As I talked, I felt a singing in my blood, as if, as I talked, I was discovering this new world all over again.

The way a missionary might. Several times he asked me about the Pilgrim Rosary. I explained that there were two rosaries: the prayer itself, and the beads, which helped memory and the count of litany-like succession of Hail Marys, said with a quiet rhythm, making of the rosary a time of meditation.

We drove on in silence. *A missionary,* I thought. *A missionary? An apostolate?*

Once again, I saw that space between worlds and once again I felt a stab of panic. *You're a salesman, Dick Bingold. But a missionary?* I closed my eyes and saw me falling. And I felt I knew, vaguely, what the falling meant: the image of falling stood for doubt—that could be, if I weren't strong enough, my death.

"Funny thing," I said over my shoulder to Bruce as we went down the mountain through a complex series of twists and turns, "the higher you climb…I mean, the higher a person climbs toward God—the more he feels like a missionary—the more he doubts. And that's what keeps him going."

"*Doubt* keeps him going?"

"The desire to stamp out the last hint of doubt," I said, as if I knew what I was talking about.

And it was then I thought, *Dick Bingold, you sound like a missionary but you're nobody but an average Joe. An average Joe filled with doubt. Full of doubt and unworthy.*

"It was terrifying." Bruce Ellavsky said.

We stood in the dark, below Apparition Hill and the Blue Cross, its color obscured by the night. We were both exhausted, having gone straight to the guest house to check in, wash up, and eat. When I asked anxiously if anyone at the table had seen Father Philip Pavich, the pilgrim next to me said he had heard that he was out of town. And what he said seemed to be confirmed when we attended mass at St. James Church at ten. Father Pavich was absent and my neat, made-in-America list crumpled. Now I realized that though Vicka might yet see to it Our Blessed Mother blessed the Pilgrim Rosary, I could not honestly be its keeper without a full and complete confession to Father Pavich. There were other priests in Medjogorje, but none with whom a trusting bond had so mysteriously sprung up. The thought of returning to America borne down by the guilt of other failed confessions made me ill. My spiritual growth was stalled. Now here was Bruce telling me, that, after our prayers by the Blue Cross on Apparition Hill, he had been terrified.

After mass at ten, we walked the fields until evening, then at twilight, Bruce and I sauntered to the bottom of Apparition Hill. The earth all around us breathed those silences that drop on the eyelids like warm petals the sun has left behind.

We looked about, content to say nothing. Five minutes passed before I whispered, "Bruce?"

"Yes?"

"Would you like to pray the rosary?"

"Am I…I'm not…"

"…not Catholic?" And I said almost in a whisper, "The rosary belongs to everyone…" And saw in my mind's eye, Father Nolan, and heard him say, "And so does Satan."

I tried to smile. My voice seemed small in the large evening.

Stumbling here and there over the stones, we made our way upward, to the Blue Cross, a small grotto where the visionary, Ivan, held prayer meetings. Below us, Medjugorje slept. Down there, when we had walked with a group of pilgrims from St. James Church after mass, one woman, as if musing to herself, had said, "When all is said and done, it's all a mystery." And her friend had added dreamily, "On the shore of the unknown." And as Bruce and I walked away from the village, I wondered out loud, whether that was the secret of the rosary—it was a prayer to the Mystery—the Joyful mysteries of Mary's life and Christ's birth; the Sorrowful mysteries of Christ's agony and death, and the Glorious mysteries of his resurrrection and ascension. It was a centuries-old path of reflection on these powerful themes.

Bruce listened silently, then said, "And Satan?"

"Our shield," I whispered.

"Shield?" he whispered back.

"The rosary prayer is our shield—a shield that protects us from Satan," I said, knowing that nothing was that easy, that the life of the spirit is full of twists and turns and surprises. Where was I heading? Where was Father Pavich? How would I find Vicka? I put my rosary beads around my neck, and Bruce pulled those I had given him from his pocket. He stared down at his palm and the heap of tiny colors in the evening light. He placed the beads around his neck, gingerly, and tried to smile.

"It all seems strange," he said very quietly. "Like another world. A world I wondered about, but never dared enter."

"Shall we pray the rosary?"

"You'll have to show me how," he said simply.

We knelt down and, step-by-step, we prayed. Then I prayed, "I believe in God, the Father Almighty, Creator of heaven and earth, and in Jesus Christ, His only Son, our Lord…" And I thought I felt Bruce relax on those familiar words, his ever since his Lutheran childhood. But when I glanced aside, I saw the whites of his anxious eyes—and continued to pray. And even when we prayed the Lord's Prayer in unison, his voice seemed to tremble. "…and deliver us from evil," we prayed—and stood up.

In the dark and damp of night, we walked back down the mountain, avoiding as many stones as possible. Bruce was silent until we reached the bottom. It was then I asked him, "How did it go, Bruce?" And it was then he said, "It was terrifying."

I stood there in the dark, stunned. Bruce caught my

amazement. But neither one of us spoke, and he began to walk on, and I followed. We walked some distance in silence. I was stumped—and saddened. The trip to Medjugorje that had started out with such promise, was crumbling about me. I seemed unable to help Bruce. I had missed Father Pavich and wondered if I would miss Vicka also.

Then Bruce stopped, and turned to me, and said in a warm and loving voice, "Thank you for taking me with you, Dick. I can't thank you enough. And thank you for letting me pray the rosary with you—for teaching me."

I waited. "Let me put it this way," he went on. "It's stupid—ridiculous—but I'm ashamed to say that all the while we prayed, I heard voices."

"Voices?"

"A voice—a voice saying to me, 'What are you doing here? You don't belong here. *She* will destroy you.'"

In the dark, I could see Bruce's eyes, intent, piercing. He cleared his throat. It seemed he had pulled himself together. Once more, I waited. One thing I knew—and kept it to myself: Bruce had heard the voice of Satan, though it was not likely he knew it.

Now, in the dark of this holy village, three thousand miles from his office in New England, Bruce Ellavsky, the FBI agent, talked to me, not as a pompous official, but like the man he was, of common sense, his tone level, conversational.

"Then at about the end of the prayer, I got hold of myself. I reasoned that the *voice* would be attacking me only if—only if *She* really *was* there. It was then the voice—the voice of Satan—faded away."

In bed at last, I reached out to turn off the light. Then I got out of bed, and got down on my knees. I thanked Our Blessed Mother and Our Lord and my God and the Holy Spirit for the privilege of witnessing a small but mighty miracle.

I turned out the light and smiled. Things were looking up.

Chapter Twenty-Four

The Confession

After a breakfast of ham and eggs and toast and several cups of coffee, Ivan drove Bruce and me through a bright morning some thirty miles from Medjugorje, to the Franciscan monastery where Father Jozo Zovko lived. Afterward, we would drive on to Mostar.

On the drive out, I was anxious that, taking up the time for this trip, I might miss Vicka as I had missed Father Pavich. But it had to be done, for if all else failed, Father Jozo Zovko would have given the Pilgrim Rosary *his* blessing. Even so, I wondered how he would look upon my rosary, whether it was worthy of the blessing of the priest who was the first to believe in and protect the visionaries.

But Father Jozo was not in the monastery. We were told we would find him nearby, at Our Lady of the Assumption Church. We hurried over and on entering we saw Father Jozo speaking to a group of pilgrims. When he looked at us, I saw a face of deep-set eyes wreathed by grave wrinkles and set off by lips on which short flights of smiles took off and landed. We could see why the former Communist government and its agents had respected him: he was nobody's fool. His strength was gentle. Though he had been on his way out, apparently in a hurry, the moment we spoke to him of our mission, he relaxed.

We followed him to the first pew where, after snapping open my black brief case, I spread a red velvet cloth and placed on it the Pilgrim Rosary. I held my breath. Father Jozo stood still, hands folded across his chest. He looked down, as if from a distance, chin up. Then he dropped his hands to his side and lowered his chin. Each stone of the rosary stood in its own pool of light. Our Blessed Mother and Our Lord on the Cross shown. At the bottom of the tall nave, a hand rose, palm out. A voice began to recite a prayer. Father Jozo's hand and voice. I took a deep breath, held my voice steady, and said, "Thank you, Father Jozo." And he turned from the Pilgrim Rosary and blessed us also.

"Did you see Father's eyes?" Bruce asked as we drove away.

"Yes," I said, amazed and happy.

For by the time he had completed his blessing, Father Jozo's eyes had filled up with tears.

Its broken masonary reaching out from each side of the stream to a void at the center, the four-century-old bridge of Mostar stood mute testimony to a broken and divided country. All about us were buildings reduced to rubble, vacant. In the distance a machine gun rattled. Nearby a hammer struck a board to drive home a nail. Now Bruce, Ivan and I were heading out of town, back to Medjugorje.

We had met Sister Janja. Sun and sky shown through the roofs of the church, hospital, orphanage, and her convent. She showed us a children's park converted to a graveyard and windows from which, during a Serb shelling, men and women had jumped to their deaths. We prayed together and climbed back into our car, and crossed the mountain into the valley of Medjugorje, dumb with grief.

I walked rapidly down the narrow street of Medjugorje, the Pilgrim Rosay clutched to my side. The sun was setting. Bruce had gone back to the guest house, and I had gone out in search of Vicka. Our return flight would leave Zagreb tomorrow afternoon. We needed to catch the flight from Split at noon. We would need to leave Medjugorje at dawn. Would I find Vicka in time? Could it be Father Pavich would return this evening?

I reached my destination, and walked through the door of the modest store front. It was the office of Vicka's cousin who ran a small travel business. He stood next to the plate glass window behind a counter. He looked up and greeted me with warmth, in English. And the next instant, I was plunged into gloom. I had asked him if he could speak to Vicka on my behalf and he had said that she had left early morning for a visit to a nearby hamlet. The clock on the wall said four-thirty-five. Two or three cars went by in the road. The cousin turned to look through the plateglass window and turned back to me, a broad smile on his face. How could he smile at a time like this? There was good reason.

"Here she comes now," he said. "You can speak to her yourself."

I rushed into the street and stood by the curb before she even stopped. She was at the wheel of a small car, her solemn face, even then marked with hints of the cancer with which she still struggles. But she smiled up at me. Her cousin stood by my side. They exchanged greetings in Croat and I heard among their words my name and the words, clearly in English, "the Pilgrim Rosary." My heart was in my mouth. I had forgotten to tell her cousin I was leaving at dawn. Was it possible she would present Our Lady the Rosary later today or this evening? Vicka looked down at the wheel, as if thinking, then up, first at her cousin, then at me. And I put into her out-stretched hands, the Pilgrim Rosary. I thanked her time and again, in English, and she looked at me and said, "Yes, yes." She drove off and I thanked the cousin, and then I too went down same street her car had gone. I was heading for St. James Church, wondering if it were possible that inside or at one of the confessionals I might find Father Philip Pavich. I hadn't had the nerve to ask the cousin what he and Vicka had talked about. Was there *any* chance that Our Blessed Mother would appear before Bruce and I had to drive back to Split to catch our flight?

By the time I reached the row of confessionals outside St. James Church, I knew in my heart Vicka would do as I hoped, for I knew that she and the other visionaries were regularly seeing Our Lady during the six-o'clock hour. Had I asked too much? Head bent, I pondered that possibility. I looked up. And there stood Father Pavich.

"I heard that you were looking for me," he said in his clear English, his beautiful smile spreading across his face. "But when I saw you, head bent, staring at the pavement, I wondered if you were still with us."

"I'm here. But when I saw you, I thought you weren't real and so not here at all."

We laughed and walked to the door of the confessional. He went in and I followed, my heart beating hard. The small cell was made of wood, with a wall kneeler and a fold-down seat attached to one side. After months and months of doubt and guilt about my incomplete confession, here I was at last.

"Hello, how are you?" he asked, as if we were perfect stangers.

His face was in shadow. His whole being was surrounded by an aura and I was convinced in an unthinking instant that our auras interlocked. Had all my life tended to this one moment, the rare time that brothers meet? I tried two or three times to swallow, then finally succeeded.

He reached forward and placed a large crucifix on my heart and, with the palm of his left hand on the knuckles of my right, he prayed. I stole a look. Saw the slits of his eyes, his moving lips then in the next second forgot that I had seen a thing. Suddenly his matter-of-fact voice filled the room.

"You better pull that seat down, Richard, because you are going to be here for a while."

His voice was tender, soft, but with an edge of authority. Make no mistake, he was in charge, and let me know it. Instead of fear of his authority though, I felt safe. He would be hard on me, but true, direct, with that talent some priests have—of remaining close at a distance.

He set the agenda. The questions ranged from birth to this hour: parents, childhood, youth, jobs, marriage and children. Though secular, the questions forced me to think spiritually—how had I *behaved* through it all? Then he interrupted himself.

"Now tell me about this confession."

The words hung there, like a thunderclap. I gathered my wits but hedged. I told Father Pavich that I had been carrying the burden of that incomplete confession to Father Dan Doyle for the past fifteen years. He waited and I knew why he waited: I had to get to the point.

"I abused the privilege of the sacrament, Father."

"The sacrament of…?"

"Penance, Father."

"And are you abusing it now?"

I flinched, then leaned forward, for through that tough question came a note of encouragement.

"No, Father. I am contrite, Father." All the busy silences of memory wormed their way through me. I felt like a kid. "I am heartily sorry for my sins and never before…" I stopped. Was I bragging? Exaggerating? And I knew I wasn't. "Never before have I had such a firm purpose of amendment."

"Firm purpose of amendment?"

He kept his distance but his question brought us close: Since childhood, we had recited the catechism of our faith.

"I have changed my life," I recited. "I avoid occasions that lead to sin. I am laboring to change my evil habits."

A long pause.

I struggled to put a thought into words—and did: "I hope I am speaking of the Dick Bingold I know."

From the shadow, was there a muffled chuckle? And then the small wood confessional was filled with the sound of my voice. As my list of sins grew long my face grew red. Sweat dripped from my armpits. I told him things about myself that remain sealed, and that no one, except the priest and I, can ever bring to light.

"How often did you go to Mass?" he broke in on me.

"Off and on—once a month—once every two months."

Silence.

"And now?"

"Regularly. Sometimes twice a day. The Eucharistic Adoration three times a week."

"And how often the meditative summary of the Gospel?"

"The *rosary*," I threw back at him. "Three to six times a day."

"And you made a rosary yourself?"

I sat up; I wanted to take advantage of that question; ask him to see to it that Vicka…I relaxed, ashamed. "Yes, Father."

"And?"

"I've brought it here to present it to…Father Jozo. And—and to Our Blessed Mother." My neck tightened and my heart beat. It would never happen. And Father Pavich said,

"It will," and went on, "You are right about your confession fifteen years ago. You should not have received absolution—but you did. All sins were forgiven you. Your guilty conscience, knowing that your first marriage was still valid in the church and living in a new marriage outside the church needs to be—addressed." He paused, then spoke again. "I believe you when you say you want to make things right—making things right by having your new marriage blessed."

I felt whipped. Slapped. My ears rang. And then softer than the rise of the sun, he placed his hand on the top of my head. And when he said, "You will not leave this confessional without absolution," I cried.

I was running the race with Bobby Lippmier, my feet off the ground, flying, light as the crystal-clear evening air of Medjugorje. I wanted to laugh. A really bad joke came to mind. I sang to myself and then found myself walking and then I was sitting alone, in a pew, in St. James church, praying the penance Father Pavich had given me. I walked out, into the fields, climbed Apparition Hill, and kneeled down at the foot of the Blue Cross. At the bottom, where the path up the hill intersects with the narrow road to the nearby hamlet of Bijakovici, I saw off to my left a single figure in the twilight. I was hungry—very hungry, and I headed away, toward the guest house and a meal. I heard rapid footfalls behind me.

"Mr. Bingold?"

It was Vicka's cousin. My heart leapt into my mouth. Instead of answering, I stared. Was it possible he was saying what he was saying? Yes, it was possible—entirely possible. In fact, his words rushed over me like hollow ice cubes, each clear and each one a hot chill down my spine. Was he taking me to see Vicka? I was sure of it one moment, not so sure the next.

I walked beside the him, matching my step to his, turning when he turned, and stopping at last when he stopped. What did I expect? I looked aside. There was Vicka's small car. In front of me, a closed door, above, a balcony on which Vicka often appeared. The village clock began to strike the hour. I found myself taking in, turning each beat over in my mind, desperately trying to keep count as if my life depended on it. The last beat stood alone, as if it too waited. Then I heard a scuttling, like mice in a wall. Far down a side street, a mother called a child. Had Vicka gone away again?

Now I looked to my side, at her cousin, who was opening the car door. And instead of Vicka climbing out, he pulled from the seat a black briefcase.

That is not the Pilgrim Rosary in his hands, I thought as he crossed back across the pavement to me. He was speaking and I was hearing him, trying to escape from my waking dream. Later, when I thought of the cousin's words, I thought of warm peaches in a golden sun.

"Vicka says to tell you the Gospa—Our Blessed Lady of Medjugorje—has placed the seal of her love and approval on your rosary. She has blessed the rosary and the intention of it becoming a 'pilgrim' rosary."

And when he handed me the Pilgrim Rosary, it passed through the path of the early evening sunlight that bathed its black case in a glow alive as the smile of a newborn child.

I was ready to go home.

Chapter Twenty-Five

Who Will Heal the Healer?

Sunlight threw shadows into the hallway, of trees outside the storey-tall window and of women inside. They were staring at me and I was staring at the frail passenger in the wheelchair. At first, from a distance, the wheelchair seemed filled with a wrinkled pile of clothing. But when the man said to me, speaking with a frail voice from his paper-thin body, "Please—please pray over my wife that she might recover," I saw that the clothes were a woman, bent as if broken, her stringy black hair on a pillow that rested on the arm of the chair. "She's been this way for years," he said, just above a whisper. "Please pray over her."

The two women, whose shadows lay on the marble floor, had turned to stare. Surrounding us in the modern conference center was the hollow roar of many voices.

"I really don't think I should do that," I said. I reached out and touched the man on the shoulder.

Patrick and I had arrived at the Omni Conference Center in Rochester two hours before, set up my display of the Pilgrim Rosary draped around a photo of the Lady of Medjugorje, and a table for pamphlets describing both. This was what I had expected to do: Take the rosary with Our Lady to people who could not get to Medjugorje. I had imagined that the extent of my involvement would be that of a messenger, simply talking to people about the display.

Patrick looked at the women and then at me. They were frowning. We both got their drift: They were waiting to see what

I would do. But what *should* I do? What *ought* I to do?

"Do pray," one woman said quietly.

"Yes, do," said the second woman.

Now I saw that they were frowning, because the sun was in their eyes. In fact, one put her hand to her forehead—and smiled. I recalled the fragrance of roses, the heat from the crucifix. I thought of Our Blessed Mother blessing the Pilgrim Rosary. Of my confession during which I held nothing back. And that stopped me in my tracks: How could I pray over another human being after living the life of a scoundrel? I was falling again, through that void. How could I put the past behind me and go forward into a new life free of doubt? Could I forgive myself? Could God? Would Father Regis Rodda, my priest, my spiritual mentor have an answer?

"Dad?" Patrick whispered. "Everyone's waiting."

One woman moved forward. "I know," she said. "Let's all pray together."

That remark was a release. In several steps I moved in the bright sunlight to the wall, took down the Pilgrim Rosary, and, blinded by the sun myself, leaned down and placed the rosary very carefully over the sick woman's shoulders—and drew back, supporting the rosary with one hand so that it did not weigh on her too heavily.

What should I do next? Through the din of voices I heard a clock ticking. Then I heard the women's voices, reciting in unison, a prayer I'd known since childhood. Almost as if it pushed through a permanent growing wall of doubt, my hand reached out and down, and lay on the woman's head, frail as an egg shell. Now my voice joined the women's. And then it happened.

Beyond the dark of my closed eyes, the sick woman stirred. We all stopped praying. I opened my eyes in time to see her slowly lift her head and look at her husband, then slowly, painfully, sit up straight, reach out her hand and touch his cheek. And smile. He glanced at me, at her, at me again, blinked his eyes, and began to sob.

The cafeteria filled with the din of talk, the clatter of dishes, and the scrape of chairs.

"Want my hamburger, Patrick?"

He looked up, holding his hamburger in mid air. "You sick, Papa?" he asked, concerned. Then: "You're not listening to me, Papa. Didn't you hear what I asked you?"

"Yes, yes," I said, shoving the fear and trembling to the back of mind. "We'll leave for home as soon as the conference is over—about three-thirty or four." The doubt and undeserved joy and the wonder at what had happened—I had put to the back of my mind, but it all came back in a surge. I got up from the table.

I turned at the door. Where was Patrick? Then I saw him and when he caught up with me, he was frowning—and we walked back up to our display. The sun had shifted in the sky and carried away with it the bright light that had filled the hallway. Now the space was filled with the luminous light of the Pilgrim Rosary. Looking up at it, her massive head tilted back, was a woman in a wheelchair.

"Will you pray over her?" the woman pushing the chair asked.

Fearful and confused one moment, joyful and doubtful the next, I searched for a reason not to, and then said, "Yes." And when the Pilgrim Rosary was around her neck, she closed the crucifix in a grip powerful enough to break it. Automatically, against my best judgement, I placed my hand on her head and remembered that Vicka had revealed to us the Lady of Medjugorje's prayer, *I extend to you the blessing of our Lady of*

Medjogorje, and I said that prayer silently now. The woman continued to cry, her tears soaking her blouse. At last, she released her grip on the crucifix, and looked up at me with shining eyes. As the voices sounded in my head, I stood and watched her disappear into the crowd in dumb wonder.

Who do you think you are, praying over people?

And another voice:

But see their happiness.

Was the last, the Devil's?

And still another:

And who are you to doubt? Isn't that the Devil working in you? Isn't that the sin of pride? Yes—and isn't that what you want: the Power?

"Papa? Look what someone left here when we went to lunch."

He pointed to a partly-open, oblong box, made of strong oak wood. I set aside a little of the white tissue paper and the face of Mary looked up at me. By the time another wheelchair arrived, the three-foot-high statue of Our Lady of Medjugorje was standing by our side, the Pilgrim Rosary next to her on display. Where had it come from? I didn't know. In a daze, a dream, I once again put the rosary around a pilgrim's neck, prayed, and the woman in the wheelchair straightened, then said cheerfully, "Thank you, oh, thank you very much," and wheeled herself away.

Lord, what is it that you are telling me? Am I a victim of the Devil? Or am I in God's hands? But why me, O, Lord?

"So that's where My Lady's statue is," said a cheerful voice at my ear.

Patrick must have looked as embarrassed as I did. The woman stood beside me, looking up at Our Lady of Medjugorje and the Pilgrim Rosary on the display next to her..

"I found her in a box—or my son Patrick did," I said, and introduced us both. "I think she looks just great with the rosary like that, don't you?"

"My name is Maureen Flynn," she said, laughing. "I was looking for someone to be a caretaker. Yes, doesn't she?"

And then it occurred to me where I had seen that name before. She was the editor of the magazine she published with her husband, Ted, *Signs and Wonders of Our Times,*" and co-author of the book, *The Thunder of Justice.*

Her cheerful presence helped calm my fear and bewilderment, put off a reckoning. With all that had happened to me, what was I to do? How was I to live? In my confusion, I must have said something about giving the statue back to her, for she said,

"No, that's where she belongs. With you."

****

Driving away from the conference, heading home, Patrick said something about the funny look I had on my face when talking with Maureen Flynn and when I asked if he thought *she* had noticed it, he said, "No, Papa. You were your old cheerful, smiling self—but *I* could see the difference."

Upstairs, in my room alone, I could feel the difference, but I couldn't put my finger on it; it lingered as fear, bordering on dejection, strange for a man of my temperment, of such nervous drive and energy. But there it was. My finger went along the spine of several books, then stopped on the title I was looking for.

"As you know, Father, I do not wish to be a victim of the Devil in any way," I read from one of the letters of Padre Pio who in this century had the stigmata of the Crucified Christ on his flesh. The letter was directed to his spiritual advisor. "And although I am more certain of the reality of those silent voices in my head than I am of my own existence, I am still struggling with myself and protest that I want to believe nothing of all this for the sole reason, my director, you have cast doubt upon it. Am I right or wrong in this?...What am I to do? Am I unwittingly a victim of the Enemy? Enlighten me of this point, for pity's sake..."

I put the book away and went downstairs to my normal life of pleasure and of pain, of family and of business, and had dinner with Monique and Patrick. And the next morning, in the kind of bright sunlight that follows a night of rain, I went about that business, and on the way, dropped Our Lady and the Pilgrim Rosary off at the Marian Center on Taft Rd., Syracuse, where it could be viewed by everyone. And I turned into a stream of traffic, heading for a meeting with a prospective insurance customer I had planned what seemed a very long time ago.

Caught up once more in my normal everyday life, I felt as if I had escaped something; as if I had missed something very important and should turn around and go back and see what it was; something that excited and frightened me; gave me moments of overwhelming joy followed by dejection, bewilderment, and doubt.

By the time next Sunday's mass was celebrated, I felt not quite solidly back in my old rut. That week, I had been to Holy Mass twice and Eucharistic Adorations twice. I prayed the rosary thoughtfully, meditating on each word, like a man caught far out at sea, looking for the the way home. Standing in among the familiar sights and sounds of Sunday mass, however, I felt that once again I had reached the solid shore of my familiar, normal life.

But by Sunday dinner, the fear and doubt had overcome me once again. For chatting just outside the church door after mass, I had met an old friend and her family, Marcia Robinson, a bright attractive businesswoman, and her husband, Mandel, also in business, and their three children, Marcia, Mandel Ray, and

Melinda. We talked in a cheerful, desultory way and then, after a thoughtful pause, she invited me to a prayer service she and the children were going to Tuesday evening.

Prayer service, I thought on my way home, had become a normal part of my of my life and Marcia's invitation would offer me comfort, and new resolve, the aim of such gatherings. And half way through the Tuesday meeting, such seemed to be the case. We had prayed together and I had quieted those fears that the fragrance and the heat of the crucifix and the blessing of the Pilgrim Rosary had excited in me. Besides, I had done with the Pilgrim Rosary what I had set out to do, put it in a Marian Center where it could be seen by everyone.

But then Marcia said, "Dick, do us all a great favor. Pray over us. Pray over each one of us."

I was stunned, taken aback, all but convinced that there was something I could not escape in my life, try as I might. Once more in that daze that afflicts us all when we begin doing something that has no basis in our own wills; when the world seems to turn around us while we stand still, I began to pray, placing my hands on first one and then another member of the family. What was usual seemed pitched to a higher level, each prayer normal in a new reality.

But when I placed my hand on the head of her son, Mandel Ray, even that reality shattered: His head rose upward, against my hands, and I felt myself reaching higher and higher to keep him down. As he rose, my fear and excitement rose also and when I thought he would escape me entirely, I said,

"Amen," and opened my eyes.

The children, even Mandel Ray, were smiling, but their mother was staring at me, as if asking a question. And when I left the meeting, I was once more thrown into a whirl of joy and self-disgust and self-approval and doubt. For I had said to his mother, I've got to talk to you, and she had asked, Why? And I had said, Something very strange has happened, something special for Mandel Ray. And I told her how I had gone up on my toes to hold him down. Had the Holy Spirit entered his body and lifted him up? What did it mean for Mandel Ray? What did it mean for Dick Bingold?

That night, alone in my bed, Patrick and Monique two hundred miles away in our newly-rented house, I prayed to Our Blessed Mother for help. Afterward, I lay on my side, staring into the dark: Did that really happen? Am I going crazy? Where am I going?

I sat up in bed, and turned on the light. I read from Padre Pio's letters. As he had asked, I asked now, Am I in the hands of the Enemy? If not, why should a man like me receive such gifts? I turned out the light. Such heavy heavy gifts? By morning, I knew what I had to do: I must find a spiritual advisor. I knew who it would be: the charismatic priest, Father Regis Rodda. And I would see him under circumstances I could never have imagined.

Fr. Jozo speaks to Richard about his rosary thru interpreter Anka (Apr. 1994)

Fr. Jozo comes to tears as he blesses Richard and the Pilgrim Rosary (Apr. 1994)

Monique, Richard and Visionary Vicka with the
Pilgrim Rosary (Dec. 1999)

Visionary Vicka (Note the beam of brilliant light
passing through her from behind to front)

Richard, praying over school children
(Ocotlan, Mexico, Feb. 1999)

Fr. Jozo, praying over priests
(Siroke Brige Monastery, April 1998)

Maureen O'Conor "catching" for Richard
(Pittsburgh Marian Conf. 1994)

Richard, praying over Sisters at St. Bernadetts, 1996

"The Rose" offered to the Blessed Mother during Vicka's public apparation, 1995

Richard prays before Statue of Mary at the Blue Cross, Medjugorje, 1997

Christina Gallaher, Irish Mystic/Stagmatist
examines Pilgrim Rosary with Richard, 1998

Medjugorje Visionary, Mirjana with Richard, 1997

Richard with Fr. Svetozar "Svet" Kraljevic, O.F.M.

Joe "Mac" McLaughlin, Richard's friend, Medjugorje, 1999

Richard and Dragon Kosina

Ivanka Kosina (Dragon's wife)

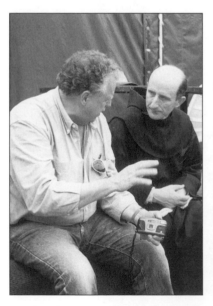

Richard and Fr. Svetozar (Svet)

*Good Sisters of Mothers Village
(Croatian Franciscans)*

The Vasilj Tunin Family
(My Medjucorje Family)

More family (friends) in Medjugorje

Mostar: City ruins

*Mostar: Graves in
children's park*

*"War survivors", Richard's friends Jasmir, Ines, Marinko, Nenadic
1996, Mostar*

*The Mandel Robinson Family (l to r) Mandel Ray, Melinda,
Mandel, Sr., Marcia & Melissa (above)*

*Aldi (top), (l to r): Daniela, Nery (Aldi's mother) and Lara
& my daughter, Barbara (top rt.) Mostar, 1995*

Chapter Twenty-Six

Witness to the Dark Side

Each time I dropped in on Father Regis Rodda, he was absent, and when he was there, I found later, I was out of town. He went one way, I went the other. When I called him, on the way out in the morning, his line was busy. And when he called me, he left a message on my answering machine.

Meanwhile, I sold insurance and Tuff Cuff, working with my son Rich and my old friend. I attended mass and Eucharistic Adoration and sat afterward and prayed to God a new and ageless prayer: *Don't do this to me, Lord. Let this cup pass.* For every time I smelled roses or saw at the left of the altar, Our Blessed Mother holding Our Lord and Our Lord holding the world, my spirit fled away and toward them, tangled in feelings of sin and righteousness, pride and humilty, hope and doubt. On the surface, I was cool and collected. Under my skin, I was more confused than when at age eight I first saw Mary: Now the sphere of my world had expanded beyond my understanding. I dangled like a tightrope acrobat in a maze of tangled wire and rope of pride, humilty, fear, disgust, joy and doubt. I knew and didn't know my direction. Nothing seemed sure except that nothing was sure. And finally, when I called on Father Rodda, he was standing in his office, his hand out.

I had barely sat down to talk, when I was getting up and walking out. My mouth had been ready to pour out all my heart. But I had completed only a sentence or two, when Father Rodda said,

"Dick, I've got an idea. If you agree. We're holding a Marian service the last day of July it would be great favor if you would attend. It will be held in a tent, in Wetzel Park."

As I drove away, the words hit me strangely. A park? A tent? And the words brought home to me something that had been in the air and a fact since Vatican II: the new fervor in our Catholic Faith for evangelism. Who might such evangelists be? Where did they come from? Were they lay people like myself?

No, Dick. Your life is full enough. Evangelism—an apostolate —is not for you. You are still what you've always been—an unworthy man of the world.

I pressed down on the accelerator. My car sped ahead, through shadows cast by a row of sycamore trees, and onto a sunlit interstate. In the distance was a dark row of clouds. Soon my wipers were flicking rapidly on high. I ran through rain to the door of two insurance customers I had promised to call on. They broke out donuts and coffee and we chatted and I was on my way again. By the time I reached Syracuse, the sun shone.

I saw the sign, "Weltzel Park" too late, and drove on by to the next block, turned left and then left again, went down two blocks, missed the correct turn, then found the street that took me back to the main street, found the sign, and turned in. Belted into the back seat, rode the statue of Our Blessed Mother.

From my parked car, holding the black case of the Pilgrim Rosary close by my side, I saw the picnic tables, the big tent billowing in the breeze, the blue waters of the lake beyond, and the pale dome of sky holding off eternity. Beneath it, tiny figures moved about, all members of the Central New York Marian Society, and all Medjugorje pilgrims. The sun was at about three o'clock. A siren wailed, a truck driver slammed into a new gear. But the fragrance of new-cut grass and the summer heaviness of the trees muffled those sounds, as if they had rolled up against our little island and then had fallen back. And when I spotted Father Regis Rodda, I felt safe.

But when I shook his hand and saw his smile, all my confusion and doubt came rolling back. His eyes seemed to say he had something up his sleeve. Why, when I wanted so desperately to talk to him, had he lead me to action? To this conference? These weeks of turmoil made me search for one solid place to land. But every time I put my foot down, I sank deeper.

Almost every folding wood chair placed in rows beneath the billowing canvas of the tent were taken. I sat half way back, agitated and peaceful by turns, the traditions of the mass a comfort and a mystery, the words of Father Rodda loaded with double meanings—or no meaning at all. It was as if I were alllergic to everything I heard, felt, or thought. I was breathless and smiling and praying and hoping for the best. In any case, the minute Father Rodda said my name, I was standing up, listening. He had asked me to show everyone the Pilgrim Rosary. Tell everyone how it had been made.

Now, the Pilgrim Rosary held in my hands, I stood before people who knew Medjugorje as well or better than I did and our common experience gave me increased confidence. As I talked about the making of the rosary, they knew the very hill on which its stones had been found. I drifted into technical details, how with three-thirty seconds-of-an-inch-thick welding wire I had connected stone to stone.

I stopped and looked out at the congregation. Who but Dick Bingold cared for such detail? And I told myself,

Dick, you are hiding something—hiding behind those details—hiding, like we all do, behind your acts.

And then, suddenly, I came out in the open, out of the closet.

"I'm a drunk," I said flatly to a hushed audience. "I am an alcoholic who has destroyed his family. You can't imagine the heartache I put upon my wife and my family and my friends. Can you imagine a man my size coming home in the middle of the night and finding a bicycle on the front lawn in the rain and going into a rage and pulling off my belt and whacking the bottom of two young boys?"

The sides of the tent flapped, a siren wailed.

"I remember going to my oldest boy's room one night when he was about twelve. I had called him up because of something he had done. And I knew he was going to lie to me because he was frightened and, like a coward that I was, I waited for the moment I could strike him right across the face. And with all my might, I let my hand go and struck him on the cheek and drove him across the room and he went down like a wet towel."

I stopped, looked out, got my bearings, and went on.

"I was in shock by what I had done. And I stood there and he got up and in tears and wailing he came back across the room and stood in front of me, and he looked up at his dad, and I remember the look in his eyes, as if to say, 'What are you going to do to me now, Dad?'"

I was breathing hard and fighting back the tears and I said to the faithful in a loud voice, "Well, shame on me and shame on any dad that lifts a hand to face of a child or spouse, or any member of a family that is supposed to love one another. Shame on me."

The large silence of the tent something out at me from each face. I looked from one side to another, as if I meant to escape. There was as ripple of movement. Father Rodda stood up, walked up to me, and put his arm around my shoulders. Richard, he told the silent congregation, would pray after mass with anyone who wished to come forward. I took my seat.

The mass went on. And when it was over, people began to get up and file out. Father Rodda motioned me to come to the front of the tent and as I took that very long walk there, I heard people leaving and wondered if anyone would be left to pray over. My back still to the milling congregation, I took the Pilgrim Rosary in my hands and turned around and faced a line of fifty or more people. Father Rodda had disappeared.

I watched the first person in line, a burly man of sixty or so, drift toward me. He stopped. *Do something, Dick. You're unworthy, of course, but do something.* And I reached out and did what I had seen priests do since I was a child. On this broad wrinkled forehead, I made the sign of the cross and on his grizzled head of hair, I placed the palm of my hand. *Now, Dick.* And it came to me, the blessing from Our Lady of Medjugorje and, moving my lips, I pronounced it silently. The line dwindled. And it was then I saw Father Rodda. He was standing in line also.

"Really, Father," I whispered. "You should be praying over me." I pulled back. He frowned.

"No," he said out loud. "It's O.K. You pray over *me*."

And without one more thought, I reached out and made the sign of the cross on the forehead of a priest. And then I plumped my hand down upon his head and he smiled and I said the blessing and when I was leaving, bewildered, excited and yet feeling I had come a long way and still had a long way to go; feeling that if I were on the wrong path I would sometime soon or in the future be on the right path, I shook Father Rodda's hand.

"That was a long talk we had—back there in your office."

"Wasn't it though?"

When I drove away, my confusion whirled more tightly around my head, in more familiar arcs, lines that though barely seen, had for the moment at least, a more distinct look than ever before.

Back home, in my empty house, I baked a potato and fried two pork chops and watched the evening news. Later I read the Bible, and the words, *I knew you in the womb.*And I thought, *The Lord in Heaven knew our names and where we would be in the eternal scheme from the very beginning. It is* his *plan.*

But when I was falling asleep, I started awake, saying, *Lord, save me from hell.* And I dropped off to sleep, thinking I knew something the Lord didn't. And I was just too tired to figure out what that was our how it could be. All I could feel was that I had been picked up in the talons of a wild bird and dumped here, without directions or answers. But then in the middle of the night, I woke with a jerk, and sat straight up in bed, saying before I had even collected my thoughts,

"If this is what I think it is, don't do it to me, Lord. Find somebody else. I'm not strong enough to take this. I want no part of it."

Chapter Twenty-Seven

Stepping Over the Line

The long curve of the narrow black macadam road went on turning away from me, the lake beyond the guardrail sparkling, the moss on the bare rock cliffside shining as I turned the wheel hard in that direction, away from the lake that was suddenly replaced by an open field that I headed for and just in time avoided

I was back on the road, having gotten off the interstate at the wrong place and now driving back to it so that I could keep on my way to the suburb in the Boston area, Woburn, where Maureen O'Connor had invited me to bring the Pilgrim Rosary. At a rest stop, I had made two phone calls, one about Tuff Cuff and the other about Knights of Columbus insurance, and then had gotten back on the road, heading into a rack of clouds that promised rain. I could not stop thinking the thoughts that had been on my lips when I woke up several nights since,

"If this is what I think it is, don't do it to me, Lord. Find somebody else. I'm not strong enough to take this. I want no part of it."

But now, no matter how I looked at it, I knew I was like the man who had put one foot over a line drawn in the sand and was afraid to put the other foot over and thereby tell the world that he had made up his mind to fight. In my case, though, both feet on the other side of the line would mean that I had committed myself fully to God. I had given, what they call in my faith, my *fiat: Let it be done.*

The windshield wrinkled with a splatter of rain. I turned

on the wipers and shot on by a semi and trailer, on the rear door of which was the sign, *We Are the Best! No Job Too Small, No Job Too Big.* And I drove on, angry, thinking, *You don't even have one foot over the line, Dick. You're still your same old ambitious self.* But when I drove off into the busy streets, through Woburn to Reading, where the O'Connors' house sat on a street shaded by trees, I was singing another tune, unable to forget the woman, paralyzed, all twisted over in her chair, who had risen under my touch and prayer and I prayed, *Please, Lord, guide me. Give me a sign, Lord, that these things that are happening to me are part of your plan, not the Devil's.*

But even when I stood in the front room of the O'Connor's house, grandchildren coming and going, a sister with a new baby smiling at my side, it did not occurr to me that anytime soon I would cross that line. That without deciding anything, I would work at my own faith, and when it came to correcting my own bad habits, I would keep on trying hard. I would show the congregation at the O'Connor's church, St. Joseph's, the Pilgrim Rosary and statue and then head home to my job and family.

Everything would be the same: phone calls and meetings and the rise of stone into the shadows of faith at the peak of the nave and the flicker of votive candles and the echoes of the voices of priests. And whenever anybody asked for the Pilgrim Rosary, I would take it and pray with anyone who was in pain. The image of my tiny figure falling between two worlds receded, like the memory of a candle gone out. I would remain on this side of the line. I would get what a scoundrel deserved. And then I thought, *Dick, the annulment.* And turned away.

****

The Saturday Vigil Mass was drawing to a close. The big doors of St. Joseph's Church framed the lingering of an evening of summer falling on the streets and trees of a former

Massachusetts mill town. The light shown on the heads and shoulders of the communicants, a few in the doorway, a scattering down the aisle. And I wanted to call to them, *Come back. Give me another chance.*

It was then a feeling that had been forming at the back of my mind, came in the dim air in front of me into focus. People sat or stood or now turned away, unsure, dreamy, cheerful, as if in a state of euphoria. Earlier, I had spoken to several masses about the Pilgrim Rosary, had prayed over dozens of communicants, but had not witnessed to my past sins, unsure, as if suddenly I had forgotten the steps to a familiar dance. And now, as people drifted away, I had to face it: little had come of it. Yet...Here in the air as people turned away, was this strange euphoria.

Was it my doing? It was true, that for the first time since I had begun praying over people, I had added to the blessing of Our Lady of Medjugorje, a silent prayer to the Holy Spirit to enter into the heart of the person on whose head I placed my hands. Had that brought about this mood? *Don't, Richard. Don't believe for a minute you are blessed with such...*I looked far down the aisle, at the summer evening that now outlined the head and shoulders of a woman who sat as if built into the last pew... *power.* The word stung and I flinched.

The church emptied, and still the woman sat.

"Patty, come, let Dick put the rosary around you and the baby.

It was the voice of Sacristan Bill Mulrenan. But the woman didn't budge. We both waited. She stirred, stood up, and came toward us, a baby sucking a bottle in her arms. Bill bowed away, saying from the side of his mouth, "My daughter," and there before me stood the mother and her child. Moments ago, the church had been emptying. Now it was full. And I reached out and placed both my hands on the bowed head of the mother. A car or two foamed by in the street. The baby, sound asleep, made the kind of sucking noise that tells you the bottle is almost empty. I closed my eyes.

"I extend you the blessing of the Lady of Medjugorje."

My voice was too low to have reached further than the dim hollow between our faces. I saw the lids of her closed eyes. Bill stood nearby. And when I called silently on the Holy Spirit to enter her soul, I lurched forward and grabbed her baby, for at that instant Patty swayed backward and fell to the floor.

Holding the baby, I kneeled at her side while Bill stood over her, saying in an urgent, low voice, "Patty? Patty?" Her face sunk in deep repose, her eyes closed, a feather of a smile wafted across her lips. Then she drew in a quick rush of air that sounded less like a breath than a sob. Her eyes opened, cast about, filled with tears, and her mournful sobbing began in earnest.

"What…" she tried—but the sobs cut her short.

"What have you done to me?" she brought out at last.

An answer leaped to my tongue. I hestitated, then dared to say, "I didn't do anything to you, but I…" hesitated again, then said, "But I know who did." And as Bill leaned down to help her up, he shot a meaninful glance at me and I nodded.

Still holding the baby, I sat on one side, Bill on the other side of his daughter who now between sobs asked, "What happened to me?" as if she hadn't heard me. Then: "Oh, my baby," she said, looking aside, her eyes clouded, her hands in her lap. "I'm scared. I'm very scared." She looked up through her tears, seeking help, first from me and then from her father.

"Nothing," I said. "You've done nothing." I looked at Bill, then back at his daughter, avoiding the thought, then leaning back into it, knowing that she needed reassurance, and I said, my tone covering my doubt, "You are fortunate." I hesitated. Then I said it, "You've been visited by the Holy Spirit." There was a long white tick of dead silence. My heart stopped. Bill leaned down and whispered a word of comfort.

"You put the rosary beads around me," she began, wiped her tears, and went on. "I thought it would be nice for us both to receive a blessing. When she began to fuss, I put the bottle in her mouth and then we came up. I closed my eyes as you put your hand on my head and forehead. Suddenly, I felt a surge of warmth that seemed to extend from the inside of my chest, out to my fingertips." She was smiling, now, though her voice was strained. "I was floating back and felt totally at peace with a sense of complete calmness. It was the most beautiful feeling that I ever experienced. The most beautiful," she repeated, her smile brilliant.

She looked up through a fresh fall of tears and smiled. The baby stirred in my arms and she reached out and drew in her arms, in a way that only women have, that fits the body of a baby exactly. The sucking noise started up again and I saw now that the bottle wasn't empty at all. It was full to the brim. And the baby had slept through it all.

The next day, Monday, I joined a handful of devoted parishioners who say the rosary every morning before the Mass and then meet in the basement for refreshments. On the way down, I met the Devil coming up, sniggering, sneering. *So you think you're someone, do you, Dick Bingold?* And he went on his way and I on mine, to a small wood chair on which I sat and chomped a jelly donut and drank a cup of coffee. When, ducking my head, I had walked into a roomfull of women, the chatting died, then revived as I sat down. I had a second cup of coffee, then went about my business. Evening devotions were to begin at five. I was to meet the O'Connors at one for lunch. Afterward, I would nap and then shower, and be ready for the service.

It was well-planned, events timed to the minute. Father Alexis Mulrenan, a Franciscan priest from New Jersey, would help his brother, Father Donnie Mulrenan, who was regularly invited to St. Joseph's by its pastor, Father LaBlanc, to help with these three-day weekend masses. The Mulrenan name was no coincidence, for the Mulrenan brothers were Bill Mulrenan's cousins. Each priest had his place.

There was to be three hours of Eucharistic Adoration and a unified prayer offering to Our Blessed Savior, Jesus Christ. We were to begin with readings from Father Gobbi in which he tells of the messages he received from Our Lady. All this would be followed by the rosary, the communicants all sharing in, and saying, the mysteries, decades, and closing prayers. Time was set aside for meditation and for Father Alexis so hear confession. The Pilgrim Rosary hung on its display panel beside the hand-carved statue of Our Blessed Mother adorned with roses.

There were worries, however. Empty pews. Monday was "Monday Night Football," or any other sport that, as the seasons change, takes its place. At about five, only a few people had arrived, but by five-thirty, parishioners edged over to make room, and by six, late arrivals stood along the side and back walls.

I sat in the fourth or fifth pew on the left side, just one row ahead of Maureen O'Connor. The packed church overwhelmed me. Had word gotten around about Patty? My heart thudded and my face burned. I had no notes, no idea of what I would do or say. Without moving from my seat, I prayed with all the force I could command, for God to be present. I prayed to the Holy Spirit to fill my mind and heart with the right words. I prayed to the Blessed Mother to be with me in shame and defeat or gratitude and victory.

Evening devotions began, and went on smoothly. But sometime during the second hour, Maureen leaned forward again.

"Dick," she whispered, "why don't you go up and ask Father Mulrenan to let you pray over some people with the rosary—the *Pilgrim Rosary*," she emphasized.

I felt the full force of the packed church on my shoulders. Was I ready? Would I ever be ready?

I turned my head to the side slightly, and whispered from the corner of my mouth, "I don't think so—the Eucharist is exposed," and turned to gaze at the Eucharist in the sparkling monstrance. But Maureen leaned forward again, tapped me on the shoulder, and put her lips next to my ear, "Do it, Dick. Please."

I turned back and once more faced the shining monstrance and the Eucharist, my eye skirting Father Mulrenan, kneeling in the front pew. *During Eucharistic Adoration?* But Maureen's, "Do it!" was too heavy, too much of a dare, stinging my pride, bringing to a boil by my hunger always to be fastest and first. And without deciding, I stood up and edged my way to the end of my pew, walked around to the first pew, and knelt down.

"Father?" I whispered. "Would it be all right to pray with the Pilgrim Rosary over a few people?"

I waited by Father Mulrenan's bowed head. If he said, Yes, would he be breaking some rule, and be to blame? If he said, No, would I be blamed for asking, be belittled? I held my breath. Father Mulrenan's position didn't change when he whispered,

"I think it would. Go ahead."

I got to my feet, borne up by everything I was and had been, pushed down by doubt, by the fear of failure, by a streak of light through a varnish of desks and floor and wet pants and a marching nun in a schoolroom that still held the stain of my shame.

*Do it, Dick. Do it. You can do it, Dick, because it's not you, Dick...*And when my feet felt their way to the statue of Our Sacred Heart, my knees bent me down and I prayed to Our Lord for help...*not you, Dick. It's the Holy Spirit working through you, Dick.*

And I stood, hot, bothered, on the edge of tears. I lifted the Pilgrim Rosary from the display next to the statue of Our Lady of Medjugorje and fought off a fresh barrage of doubt. *How can you be sure, Dick? Has the Holy Spirit spoken to you directly?*

I faced the congregation and found that the congregation had turned to stone. In the air of the nave above heads and shoulders my voice sounded pleasant, Irish and, in a house of worship, out of placce.

"I will pray over anyone who wishes to come forward," I said, holding out the Pilgrim Rosary.

And I waited an eternity's silver chill. No one moved. A small woman to my left patted away a yawn. Did she, like me, believe I was committing sacrilege? I waited. Then one man stood up. And it was as if his rising had torn open a fabric, thin and electric, that had been pulled tight over everyone.

One by one, first from one pew on one side and then another pew on the other, people crowded into the main aisle. Father Mulrenan looked up, frowning. I was cut, embarrassed, feeling that this well-planned, sacred service had gone smash.

"Please wait," I said in that friendly, story-telling voice of mine, "wait—and I'll..." And I hestitated, having never thought or said out loud such a thing before—and I went on, "...and I'll pray over...I'll stay until midnight, if need be."

But it did no good; I had got what I wanted, and didn't want it: those in the aisle crowded forward. A man stood before me, looked up, smiled. "I better hold my wife," he said. "She goes out in the spirit." I reached forward, made the sign of the cross, and saw him sway, stagger back. Behind him, Bill Mulrenan appeared, signalling two other people to come forward as catchers. They were just in time, for both man and wife went out like lights.

I was shocked, trembling, hoping against hope that the man and wife, now stretched out on their backs on the floor, were the end of it, and order could be restored. I looked to Father Mulrenan for help. A bright wavering had replaced his frown.

"What should I do?" I pleaded in a whisper.

"Go ahead, don't stop," he shot back.

I took a deep breath and prayed to God that I was doing his work and not the Devil's and that Our Blessed Mother would lift my doubt and tell me something new, about myself, about the world of the spirit in which so much was hidden. And I put my hand out on heads and the Pilgrim Rosary around shoulders and brought to each person the Blessing of Our Lady and asked the Holy Spirit to enter each person's life and more catchers came forward. A wave of dark brightness kept coming and coming at me and moving up and toward me and pouring over and through me as the catchers stepped around the prostrate forms, caught others slain in the spirit, and eased them down to the floor.

Suddenly in the hubbub, I came to. My body trembled, my breath came short, and my spirit cried out for help. *Help me, Lord, if this must be done, to do it right.* Something turned me around, made my feet move, and pushed me to my knees before the altar. The Eucharist and the crucifix loomed. I searched for exactly the right prayer, in vain. But what was in the back of my mind, now came forward and, tears in my eyes, the knuckles of my folded hands white, I whispered,

"*Dear Lord, if this is what you want from me, you have my Fiat. Let your will be done.*" I had placed both feet over the line.

I stood up, blessed myself and, still shaking and wanting to cry or shout, I turned around and found the disorder I hoped would go away: Faithfull stood in the pews and in the aisle, carried on whispered converations and stared about. I looked down and met Father Mulrenan's gaze; he frowned—and I made one more plea. But to no avail. The parishioners pressed forward in a steady stream. I placed the rosary on shoulders, bent near, to hear whispered intentions for which prayer was needed, signed foreheads with a cross, placed my hand on heads, and prayed. When those who had fallen got up, their places, in a row of a dozen or more bodies, were immediately filled.

Then I saw the door of the confessional open and the frowning face of Father Alexis Mulrenan appear. He glanced up at me and then down at the people on the floor, then up at those who had turned to stare at him. I had just finished a prayer over a young couple who had not fallen and was about to ask the middle-aged man behind them to wait. But it wasn't necessary. He had turned away to find the cause of the sudden silence. And with dozens of other communicants returning to their pews, he returned to his, and I to mine. Maureen smiled and gave a quick nod. I had her approval but did I have mine? God's?

Bewildered, I asked myself what I had done. By what right had I declared my *fiat* and made such a disturbance? *No, Dick, there is something you don't understand.* I took a deep breath, closed my eyes, and asked the Lord to guide me. And then I saw what stared me in the face: I had given myself to God but had gotten no sign from him in return. I opened my eyes and looked for a sign. There was none. But behind me, stood a line of people that reached the length of two aisles. And once more, I put the Pilgrim Rosary and my prayers and the blessing of the Lady of

Medjugorje to work. A long time later, Bill Murenan whispered into my ear, "It's past midnight, Dick."

At one-thirty in the morning, we sat in Mary O'Connor's kitchen, sipped hot chocolate, chatted about the day, and nibbled pieces of candy. From across the table, Maureen looked at me. Nobody said a word about the crowded aisles, the Eucharistic Adoration. The number of people who had fallen, slain in the spirit. There was no need to. No longer in the past, twenty blocks away at St. Joseph's Church, the service was here and now, in the O'Connor's kitchen, the shuffling, the talk, the chaos, the way, as one body, we had all had been surprised by joy. When we stood up to say goodnight, I was smiling and when I climbed into bed I was still smiling. I was content in spirit.

Chapter Twenty-Eight

Riding High–Again

"Could you say a quick prayer over me? I have to catch a bus home."

The woman smiled and glanced over my shoulder at the escalator. I smiled too. In fact, I had smiled ever since I had put my other foot over the line. My life and service now belonged to God. A wave had carried me to him and even to this hour my virtues sparkled on its crest.

Suspecting I needed guidance (a shadow the size of my hand hovered over me), I had sat down with my pastor, Father Ronald Bill, in his study in Sacred Heart Church. And I had opened my heart to him, telling him of those who had been slain in the spirit and of my declaration to God. He listened, didn't give me advice, didn't accuse me of pride. Then he had asked,

"What are you going to do now?"

"I've been invited to a *regional* Marian Conference," I said. "In Pittsburgh." I flinched from the importance I gave the word "regional."

"Good," he had said. "Are you going?"

"Yes," I said without a second thought.

The woman's plump body filled out her pink blouse, a neat ruffle brushed her chin and against her bosom she clutched a disorderly bunch of pamphlets. For sure, she had been to every one of the fifty or so displays at the Marian Conference. The pink skin of her forehead was lined with shining beads of sweat.

She exchanged a smile with Maureen O'Connor. When I

had decided to attend this conference, I had asked Maureen to meet me in Pittsburgh to assist me in setting up the display of the statue of the Lady of Medjugorje and the Pilgrim Rosary.

"I must hurry," the woman said. "Will you?"

"Of course," I said.

Clutching her pamphlets, she drew near. The movement and talk of hundreds of people filled the metallic light of the vast conference hall with an echoing din. Around her neck I placed the Pilgrim Rosary, made the sign of the cross on her forehead, and placed my right hand on her head. But I had barely begun to pray, when she fell backward. Maureen rushed to catch her, then lowered her to the floor. For the next ten minutes she lay with her eyes closed, her hands clutching her crosscrossed pamphlets, not a finger changed.

She stirred, looked about, and said, "Oh, dear."

We helped her up and I said, "I think you missed your bus."

"Oh, my goodness. My bus. Oh, yes, my bus. *That* has never happened to me before."

Maureen helped her straighten up her pamphlets, she thanked us, and hurried off. But the event had not gone unnoticed. Over the next three hours, I prayed over first one and then another person, the line stretching down the hallway, mothers and fathers with their children, men and women and nuns and many rested in the spirit.

When the afternoon drew to a close—when you could hear the echo of a single door closing or a voice calling—I kneeled at the Adoration Room altar alone. That shadow that had been the size of a hand, had got bigger. Was it the step I refused to take: To petition the Church for an annulment? Maureen asked me what had happened to my smile.

"Not a thing," I said and gave her broad smile to prove it.

But still, it seemed, something was not quite right.

I met with Rich and my friend about Tuff Cuff. I sold insurance. I went to mass every day, prayed morning and night, prayed the rosary regularly, tried to read and answer my pile of correspondence, and attended the prayer group my friend, Barbara Stiles, started. Evening news every weeknight and a three-hundred-mile roundtrip every weekend to see Monique and Patrick in our new house in Vermont made time fly.

But my new spiritual life seemed to bring time to a stop. Instead of riding a carpet of hope I sat still under a cloud of distrust. Every day, without a miss, a blinking red light lit up my answering machine, or I was there to catch one more call from someone who wanted to talk to me about the Lady of Medjugorje or the Pilgrim Rosary and what dates I had open. And when Sister Augustine invited me to the Dominican Monastery, I accepted: that a nun would ask *me* to pray over *her* made me proud. I drove over the next day beneath an overcast sky in heavy traffic and, with Our Lady and the Pilgrim Rosary, walked through the convent door. But suddenly I ducked, slowed my steps and, for whole seconds, gazed stealthily around.

"Here I am, Richard."

It was the voice of Sister Augustine followed by her solemn habit and her cowl and, moving inside that small world as if it were a separate human being, her face. I liked "Richard" and would remember it.

"Sister," I said, relishing the title.

We talked about the last time we had met, and then she surprised me. She told me she had been to Medjugorje and had walked up Apparition Hill and prayed at the Grotto of the Blue Cross. Her eyes shown, she began to say something, then stopped. What wasn't she telling me? I followed her glance and saw two stooped figures, in dark habits, moving toward us in dim light then through a beam of sun.

"The Pilgrim Rosary and Our Lady of Medjugorje are here with Richard," she said in a loud, cheerful voice.

Sister Augustine introduced the two nuns and the young postulant who was their aide. I took and held both hands of first one and then the other and held their hands and said something about the weather and outdoors and wished somehow I could bring the color of leaves and sun to them for they were blind.

We followed Sister Augustine into a small chapel where, on the first step, I stood Our Lady's statue and placed the Pilgrim Rosary around her neck. Without help, the blind sisters moved forward gracefully, their hands in soft slow flight till they touched a stone of the rosary. Having landed, the fingers felt one stone and then another, lingered on the figure of Mary, discovered the crucifix, and trailed from there to the ruffles on Our Lady's attire. In a shadowy life of their own, the hands reached her face, and paused. Then, the tips of their fingers their eyes, the blind nuns saw the beautiful nose, the eyes, the lips and the chin.

Sister Augustine whispered, "They're the reason I asked you to come, Richard. They asked me if you would pray over them with the Pilgrim Rosary,"

I did. And when they were led away and I had asked Sister Augustine whether she would like me to do the same for her, she looked up at me, her face alive with a listening look, as if she were suddenly somewhere else.

"Yes," she said. "But Richard, let me tell you about Medjugorje."

And she told me that when she walked down Apparition Hill and had almost reached the bottom, something forced her to turn around, and look up: There, in a brilliant light and smiling at her, stood Our Blessed Mother. She motioned to Sister Augustine and pointed to herself and nodded, as if to say, "Yes, it is me."

Sister Augustine put out her hand and rested it on my arm. "A sinner like me, Richard. A sinner like me."

"You, Sister? Oh, no." I didn't want to believe it.

"Yes, Richard. Oh, yes."

Inside the convent, a bell chimed and died.

"Now, Sister?"

"Oh, yes, Richard."

I arranged the Pilgrim Rosary on her shoulders. I made the sign of the cross, put my hand on her head, and began to pray. Then I felt it: Her head had made a slow circular movement, had stopped, had started up again and now went around in wider and wider circles. I was worried. I did not want to break in on her spirit's journey but I did not dare let her go down. Then I bent over this tiny figure of a faithful nun whose head reached barely above my belt, and asked,

"Sister—Sister Augustine—are you all right?"

I gazed into the cowl at the blind, fluttering eyelids that at that moment came wide awake, as if a young girl had lit there and now looked out surprised.

"Oh yes, Richard." Her voice was strong and sweet.

"Where are you?" I asked, testing her.

And she smiled and said, "Somewhere between here and heaven."

Driving away from the convent, I stopped for a second to gaze across the lake. It was like looking into my future: The sun was bright and the air clear and over the glassy surface of the lake you could see a long distance. By the time I reached home, I was ready to tackle that pile of correspondence but before I could start, I had to answer old calls and check on new. One of those was from the organizer of a Marian conference in Endicott and she seemed worried. Putting that aside, I phoned Clare Vallmer of Vernon to tell her I would attend the prayer meeting at her house tomorrow. I made several other calls, made notes on the calendar, then settled down to the letters.

"We had a very special guest at our church, Dick Bingold, with his Pilgrim Rosary and Blessed Mother statue," wrote Michele Hyde of Bridgeport, N.Y. "He left his Blessed Mother card. I took it home and placed it on my china cabinet. My oldest daughter Michele had five tumors. I was with her when she was told it was cancer and she would need surgery. Within an hour after my call to him, Richard was there."

"When Dick came into my home, I felt a very warm feeling from him," wrote her daughter, Georgette Zak. "He told me the story about himself and put the rosary around my shoulders and told me I had nothing to worry about—the Blessed Mother was with me. A few days later, I had my nine-hours of surgery. I know that Dick coming to my home to bless me is what helped me through it all. I truly believe Our Blessed Mother is in all of us."

"It was your words, not mine, that gave the family hope," wrote a woman who had given a tape of mine to the parents whose son was ill.

"We very much appreciate Richard's sacrifice of giving himself, his time, his energy for the Lord to bring these graces and blessings to us," my old friend, Julios Arteuga, wrote from Tulsa.

I stopped and thought, *Dick, this is not your work. This is the Holy Spirit working through you.* I looked up. What had I thought just then? I couldn't remember—and read on.

"You have touched so many people's lives, including mine and my daughter's, Donna. I am rebuilding my life one brick at a time. I think of myself as a house being gutted and rebuilt....You are doing a wonderful job of bringing us all closer to our Lord and his Mother," wrote Carol, whom I had prayed over several months ago.

Another letter: "Having had a husband, grandfather, brother and several friends as alcoholics, I know somewhat where you are coming from. You are such an inspiration for all of us."

I read on: "It takes great courage to do what you do, by sharing your story. You really helped to strengthen my faith in myself. Thank you for everything. Keep your wonderful sense of humor."

I turned away, then back, when the letter from Rev. Thomas D. Homa, pastor of Our Lady of Fatima Church in Bensalem, Pennysylvania caught my eye.

"Besides your moving talk after Mass, I'll always remember your dedication in praying over every person in the church for hours and imposing on them the Pilgrim Rosary. The power of this exercise is attested to by all the people who stood in line for hours to receive this special blessing."

I sat back and closed my eyes. A thought crossed my mind I could not put my finger on. Then I set to work, answering letters and filling out lists and making plans for the future. In the next hour, I was on the road for Vernon, New York and three hours later, I headed home, having prayed over twenty people. Two children and eight adults had fallen, slain in the spirit.

Then, the next morning, when I had attended to insurance and Tuff Cuff matters, I called the office of the Marian conference in Endicott. When the organizer came on the line, there was an embarrassed silence. Then there was a flurry of flattery: How much she admired me and how worthy she thought my prayers and the Pilgrim Rosary and the statue of Our Lady of Medjugorje were. Then apologies. And then the clincher: She asked me *not* to attend.

In the old days, I might have been cool and aggressive, made her explain, asked to speak with her boss. Today, I recited several verses of the rosary, hung up, and mulled things over.

Medjugorje, under the study of a board of Balkan bishops, was not an apparition site approved by the Catholic Church. Nor had it been disapproved. For certain, the Marian board had not acted unanimously. Now my old instincts welled up. Around them, other thoughts whirled. I made several calls and got my answer. One Marian board member, Father John Mijckalous of St. Joseph's Church, Binghamton, had cautioned against my appearance with the Pilgrim Rosary and the statue of Our Lady of Medjugorje. Satisfied—cooling off—I sat back. Instead of staring into the yard and the leaves and sunlight, I looked into the house, into shadows. Why should I be disturbed by a single setback? I stood one with God. Then that dark cloud hovered over my mind and grew bigger.

That evening, I fried a couple of porkchops, watched the news while I ate, prayed long and hard and went to bed early. Tomorrow I would speak to parishioners at Sacred Heart Church, members of my own congregation.

As the hour of the service approached, the pews of the church looked empty. But by the time the ring of the bell stopped, I faced some eighty people. I told my stories, about my life and about the Pilgrim Rosary and the statue of Our Lady. I prayed over almost everybody and went home exhausted. Once again, I read letters, made plans, and prayed. I felt the oppression of failure. A few of my fellow parishioners had whispered their pains and intentions into my ear but not a single person had fallen, slain in the spirit. Though I knew God hears and answers all prayers, I felt a pang of fear, as if I had failed.

Prayer and a good night's sleep restored me. At breakfast, I read the Bible, and afterward, more letters, and tried to answer as many as I could. "I was baptized in the spirit through your ministry," a young woman wrote to me. "I was baptized by the heart with my own tears." And I read, "You are a very blessed instrument of the Lord." I put the letters away and got ready for my trip to Maine where Charlene Parsons, whom I had met at the Marian Conference in Pittsburg, would meet me. I felt cheered up and ready for battle. I pushed out my mind a vague but important thought and thanked God for my special talents and got ready for the trip to Maine.

****

Charlene met me at the airport and drove me to Bar Harbor, to Rick and Denise Daugherty's sunny front room where four or five people held coffee cups and chatted. I ate several donuts and drank coffee and waited—a half-dozen more people, local Catholics, were expected. But by the time I said my first words, the room had filled, some people having driven fifty miles, a number of non-Catholics among them. A Protestant woman felt a tingling when she touched the statue of Our Lady and when I prayed over each person, the Pilgrim Rosary on shoulders, she and fifteen others went out in the spirit.

In the afternoon, I spoke and prayed with members of St. Joseph's Rosary Society, held healing services there, and the next day, at St. Vincent's Church in Buxport. Afterward, Tina and Bob York invited me to their house where I testified and we prayed the rosary together.

Among the guests was a young girl, Kendra, who had been in a terrible auto accident last year. We had barely begun our meal of soup and sandwiches, when Bob complained of pains in his lower back and thirty minutes later Tina phoned from the hospital that doctors had diagnosed kidney stones.

With several others, I stayed at Yorks', for Kendra's parents had asked me to pray over her. Since the accident, she had lived in a slanted chair designed to help her inflate her lungs properly. I was told she was totally paralyzed. I put the Pilgrim Rosary around her neck and several minutes had passed when a sudden movement made me open my eyes. Kendra had grabbed the rosary's crucifix and wouldn't let go. I continued to pray, hoping to calm her, and on my "amen" she opened her hand. Now I placed the statue of Our Lady close to her and in her line of sight—I thought Our Lady would give her joy and that a light in her eye would show it. And it did. But she surprised us all: In a valiant struggle to kiss the face of t he Blessed Mother, Kendra moved her lips. Her parents were stunned, overjoyed, and asked me to pray for Bob. And when Bob came home an hour later, he told us he, too, had been praying to God, not to lift his own pain, but Kendra's. In a ring of silence, we all stared at each other, dumbfounded.

Chapter Twenty-Nine

Nosedive–a Second Time

When I got back to our empty house, I phoned Vermont, talked a few minutes with Monique and Patrick, hung up, confirmed the flight for Tulsa, and drove to the airport at the crack of dawn the next day. My old friend, Julios Autega, picked me up and, after a grueling Marian weekend schedule during which I visited hospitals, churches and a school, I flew back to Syracuse to face the music. I would overcome my fear to face my past and fill out the application for the annulment of my first marriage.

After the agony of years, I had made up my mind in a moment. The weekend in the Tulsa area had been a success. Many had been slain in the spirit. And when Julio and his wife put me on the plane, they told me how many had been inspired by my talk. From the jet window, I looked down at the Mississippi River, the houses scattered along its bank, the squares of farmland beyond, and the thousands of toylike houses in villages and cities and it struck me how tiny and frail we humans are and how much we need Christ's help to survive and I asked myself what I had left undone which, done, would help me carry out Christ's work on earth and the answer was to make Monique's and my bond right with God by an annulment and a marriage in the Catholic Church.

But when I drove away from the airport, I was borne down by that other cloud. What was the matter? I had given my fiat; I had turned my life over to God and I seemed to have the talent to do the work He wanted done: To touch lives, to comfort, to encourage, and to take into my body and soul the pain of others. What more did I need?

As I drove, the sun went down. I flicked on my lights, made all the right turns, and was soon back home. I made two phone calls, one to Monique and Patrick, the other to Father Ronald Bill. He picked up the phone right away.

"Working late, Father."

"Hey, Dick. How was Tulsa?"

"Very fine," I said, and thought, *Was it?*

Once over the pleasantries, I told him why I had called: I wanted to apply to the church for an annulment and would he be my procurator, the person to guide and counsel me and help me prepare to present my case to the Tribunal? He would. We set the time for our session, tomorrow at three. About to hang up, he said,

"Dick?"

"Yes, Father?"

"Just remember…" He paused, then went on, "In answering the annulment questions, you may slowly—very slowly—come to realize who it is you most need to forgive…" He stopped talking.

I listened—and knew why I feared an annulment.

"Yourself," Father Bill said.

I waited and listened.

"And Dick…"

"Yes, Father?"

"Don't lose your sense of humor."

I went to bed early and slept the whole night through.

****

Though Father Bill and I met the next afternoon, Tuff Cuff, insurance sales, church, and my apostolate took up so much of my time, I didn't sit down and face the probing annulment questions till three weeks later. And even then, I set them aside to read more letters, this time from the students of the school I visited on my trip to Tulsa, St. Peter's, across the line, in Joplin, Missouri.

"Dear Richard," one reads. "Thank you so much for coming the other day. It really touched my heart. The rosary was so beautiful and the blessing was so neat because I felt like I was going to pass out. That is called something like, Receiving the Holy Spirit. Right? The rest of the day I really tried to be nice to everybody and it worked. Usually I'm not nice, but your blessing and talks really made me think about Mary and God and their love. Godbless, Natalie."

Stacked in neat piles, letters covered the table. I picked up another.

"…When you blessed me I smelled roses and I thought I was going to faint. P.S. could you pray for me and my family— my great aunt has just died. She was 66. God Bless you, Shannon."

These young lives. I can see their faces, looking up at me from their pews in St. Peter's Church, teenagers in a crowd. Now, as I read, they become single and individual, each a child of God. A boy writes in very large letters,

"I think it is amazing the way you turned your life around. I wondered to myself if my life would get like that or even if I did would I be able to overcome it. When you blessed me with the rosary, I almost shuddered and fell down."

And another: "You have given me good advice on how to control my life if I drink or do drugs. I could majorly alter my life. Nicholas."

Salrina wrote: "I have never felt so peaceful in my life when you were praying. And when everyone was looking at the Mary statue, it looked like she was crying. My friends and I said a Hail Mary and I was about to cry, I don't know why."

I stared into space, lost in the mystery of our temporary human life. But in the next instant, I flinched from a sharp clear feeling of…What? I could not turn away. Then I caught the drift of what had been bothering me, what hid behind the cloud. But only the drift, for the words had no sooner flown through my head, than they vanished: Ever since I had given my fiat, I had been driven by thoughts of pride and success. Overcome by them. And they had covered up doubt and fear, replaced the humility that would have put God at the center of my life instead of me at the center of His.

I looked out at a sky of late afternoon, heard the distant roar of traffic, the sound of one boy calling another, their voices wavering on the air, as if one hesitated to call until the other answered, each anticipating the other's answer with apprehension, their voices packing the air with nervousness and doubt. I prayed, "With our sins we dressed Jesus in a purple cloak and mocked Him—we hit Him—we spat on Him—and we slapped Him.

"Because of our evil thoughts and sentiments, we made a crown of thorns and pressed it into His head—Yes, because of our sins we crowned Him with thorns—But He, instead, crowns us with glory. Mother most pure, pray for us and help us to obtain the grace of Purity of Heart and Mind. I humbly pray for the virtue of Humility."

#

In the slant of the late afternoon light, I drew the questionnaire to me, and took up a ballpoint pen. I hesitated, my mind off on another thought. But the moment the thought came clear—the danger of pride—I turned back to the annulment questions.

Following instructions, I printed my answers. A boy, I worked fast, to get the job done. An adult, I did the same, the letters leaning forward, the answers short and to the point, my heart heavy.

"Immediately attracted. She was shy and pleasant to talk to, very beautiiful," I printed in response to questions about how I had met my first wife, Elizabeth Fiala. And where: At a church dance.

It was fullsteam ahead now; eighteen more pages lay ahead.

"Was a poor student—always struggled with school work—got along well with my classmates—never did homework without crying—my mother had no patience—would smack me or pull my hair.

"Devoted to my father—loved both—feared my mother's discipline. She actually hung a cat-o-nine-tails in the closet for smacking us. Brother deceased (3 1/2 years older)—early on knew he was a homosexual. Sister (living) younger by 4 years, separated from her own family. Mom spoiled her. Father, warm and understanding—would do anything for my mom. I molded myself after him. I grew up as a result of my U.S. Army career. Started drinking at that time."

Was there any marital problems between your parents?

"Looking back now, yes. My brother's homosexuality destroyed them. They couldn't accept it. Both had traces of bigotry, passed on to the three of us. Dad not so much as Mom. When they married, Mom was still a virgin for 2 or 3 years. Dad was very patient."

Did you consider your home life to be a happy life?

"At the time, I guess so. Looking back, No. I was called a 'cry baby.' Very sensitive."

Describe the religious background of your family.

"Mom and Dad Mass on Sunday. Sometimes novenas. I was

an altar boy. Not any spirituality in the family."

To what extent did you practice your religion?

"Loved being an altar boy—obeyed God's laws until I went into the Service."

In general, what were your activities after leaving school?

"After high school, went into the U.S. Army. Became a sergeant—went to Germany. Upon discharge met Elizabeth Fiala—never dated another woman—had one fling in the Army."

Prior to your marriage, did you ever drink?

"Yes—for years. No drugs. No police record."

Did you experience any signs of nervousness, tension, etc.?

"I was insecure when I was young hated fighting, arguing, etc. Insecurity stayed with me in some form most of my life. In interior emotions (tensions, nervousness) always present."

Please describe in detail the problems that arose in this married life…

"The excitement of being together and having a relationship was wonderful. We were sexually active and I never realized how strong a drive I had—began to see women were attracted to me and me to them. Up to that time I had only one time had sex, in Europe, as a soldier. After seven years of marriage I became distracted and was unfaithful on many occasions. My alcohol fueled the desire."

I stopped writing and looked up. Twilight. I swallowed and hurried on, flinching from the pain.

"I was irrational and in denial about myself. Not one friend ever approached me about it. I spent money like crazy. I lost my job, lost 2 businesses in a few short years. I felt invulnerable. Had at least seven major auto accidents during those years. Drove my wife away from me. It took years later to look at myself and ask Our Lord's help to save me. Finally spirituality entered my life. I had been living a lie too long.

"I think looking back on my life I would have to say my lack of self esteem was clearly the single factor in building a false image around myself and trying to live it. I completely lost sight of reality and coupled with alcohol addiction it left me going nowhere. My need to be loved, my insecurity, all stemmed from my lack of self esteem. Or the reverse."

And then I put down: "I remember growing into the type of man I disliked—the 'Bully,' the 'Liar,' the 'Cheat.' Lord knows, I interiorlly hated who I was. As a young man I prayed on my knees every night and when I went into the Army it left me—I did attend the Sacraments but I was drifting away."

I looked up into the depths of a dark and empty house. In the pool of light of the table lamp lay the completed questionnaire and next to it, the stack of letters from the children of Joplin. Seven o'clock. Stiff and exhausted after the four-hour stint, I pushed my chair back and stretched my legs. I had done what I had set out to do; the annulment process was underway. I stood up, elated. Now I needed Father Bill's signature and his cover letter to the Tribunal. I smiled. And then I felt my smile— and sat back down. A face and name: No smile, modest: Father Swizdore. The black robe of a Franciscan. A healer.

I found his name, punched in the numbers and he picked up his phone. His voice was the man I remembered: simple and down-to-earth. I hung up. No show of being too busy: I could see him tomorrow, any time in the morning, because he had a funeral in the afternoon. In the morning I drove west, away from the sunrise, stopped for a breakfast of bacon and eggs toast and coffee at eight, and reached Auburn, at the head of Oswego Lake, at nine.

Father Swizdore. My heart aches. Two years after our visit, and a long illness, God called him home. Now he opened his door and I peered into a face neither ugly or handsome but one you might call pasty until you saw that the glow came from *behind* his wrinkles, from the man he was. Not tall and a little too thin to be healthy, he had the mind and heart of an elder, the combination that turns experience into lessons.

And with a true elder's grace, he ushered me in. We took chairs in a room on the fourth white wall of which hung a small crucifix. Instead of a direct look, he eased his face sideways, presenting his left ear, and took me in with a sidelong glance.

"I need your help, Father," I began humbly—and then took off—and filled that left ear with my exploits. The healings, the number of people slain in the spirit, the letters…And I stopped—and began another tack, telling him of my sudden return of doubt, my feelings of unworthiness. Still I did not get to the point.

The left ear and Father Swizdore's silence waited and gave me nowhere to go but the truth: Dick Bingold was the center of the universe, not God. I had fallen prey to pride and on its heels came doubt, not doubt in God's existence, but doubt that he had heard me and that I was doing his work.

Father Swizdore's face pivoted slowly toward me as the fire of skepticism about me died down. Still, I held back: There was something more I wanted to say. But he had asked a question.

"Yes, Father?"

"I asked whether your doubt was honest. Honest doubt."

"Honest doubt," I repeated, pretending I didn't get his drift. He nodded. I sat back and he sat still.

"No," I said with more confidence than I felt. "No, Father, I'm sure of it. I don't doubt to hide my pride. I *doubt*. I gave my fiat but how do I know it has been accepted?"

"By your works?"

I didn't want to hear that and I said nothing and then he began to talk: About the Holy Trinity, and especially about the power of the Holy Spirit and how God in three persons worked as one. He asked me when and what I prayed; he tested my commitment—wanted to know, I think, the depth of my sincerity. Did I fast? Prayer and fasting are needful for clear discernment. What did it mean that the crown of thorns was pressed into Our Lord's head?

"Humility," I said boldly, shocked that I should have made that prayer only twenty-four hours ago.

Father Swizdore looked at me and asked me again why I ought to fast and I nodded, hoping I got his drift, feeling again how those rods long ago had been drilled into my skull. A bell tolled. It was eleven o'clock. We had talked for two hours. I could hold it back no longer.

"Father," I said. "You've helped me with my pride...I've cooled off," I joked and we both laughed. Then I said what I had wanted to say but was afraid to say because it would not meet with his approval, I had no idea why.

"I keep looking for a sign that I'm doing God's work—an unmistakable sign." I stopped. He stared at me and I saw that I had not asked for his approval at all. "And unmistakable sign," I repeated like a dunce, wondering what I was missing.

Father Swizdore lowered his head, stared at his threadbare carpet, lifted his head and, looking at me straight on, told me to keep a journal in order to reflect events as they occurred. He prayed over me and then in a small quiet gesture that admitted me into his sacred brotherhood of healers, he handed me a small bottle of holy oil, to be used for blessing others.

At the door, he told me to call him whenever the need arose. I took his thin hand into mine and shook it carefully. I drove eastward, the sun bright and my face grave. Who was I to believe I had joined Father Swizdore's brotherhood? Would I ever become as humble as he was? The answer, I told myself, lay in some sure sign from God. Ahead of me, the interstate changed from two lanes into three, and I moved to the outside, into the fast lane. I watched as the speedometer climbed to seventy-five and thought,

What did he mean? What did he mean—when he stared down at that threadbare carpet?

And Padre Pio came to mind and I drove on, faster, trying to get away from something.

Chapter Thirty

The Chase

March in Northern New York can blow the color of shattered slate across the cold sky of late afternoon and hurry the already fading light into a black night. I got home about six on just such an evening, warmed up a TV-dinner, ate, watched the news, and climbed into bed at nine in order to be on my way again at the crack of dawn.

Before falling asleep, I phoned Father Swizdore to ask him how he was feeling, and got a busy signal, then read a page or two from Padre Pio's letters, my drowsy eyes half shut. I woke to a ringing phone. The voice of my friend Erin calling about her friend Helen reached out of the hollow dark. She said Helen's husband Mark had called moments ago to tell her that Helen's battle with cancer was over. "Come quick," he said. "She won't last the weekend." I gave Erin what comfort I could and offered to keep Erin constantly in prayer.

I turned out the light and settled down and quietly listened to my own thoughts. A window framed dark trees that swayed in the wind. Tuff Cuff and insurance sales and the threat of snow worried me and the success of my ministry made my heart pound.

I turned my back on the window. "Success?" Padre Pio's warning slipped into my mind: "As you know, Father, I do not wish to be a victim of the Devil in any way." I turned back to the window and the trees and wind and the dark. Might the unmistakable sign be the Devil's? Who was to say? Only God. The wind cuffed the house and made the sour note of a mouthharp between the window and the sill. I shivered and settled down to sleep and jumped out of bed before the alarm rang.

Erin's words rang in my ears. I had many weeks before, at Eric's pleading, gone to see Helen at her home in Burlington, Vermont. I set up the Pilgrim Rosary and placed the statue of Our Blessed Mother alongside. After I explained in detail the meaning of the Blessed Mother in our lives, I put the rosary first around Mark and then Helen, praying over each in turn. Helen is an agnostic, Erin had told me when she asked me to make the call, and Mark is an atheist.

As I prayed over Helen, she sat in a wing chair, shrunken, her robe snug about her neck, a bandana over her head. I won't soon forget Helen's eyes: Their plea to hold the world still. Their plea for time to figure things out. How their pain beat upon my prayer like hot rain through sun's shadow.

I showered, shaved, and hit the road by seven. Two calls to Knights of Columbus insurance prospects, a long conversation with Rich about Tuff Cuff behind me, I stayed the weekend with Monique and Patrick and when I walked into the house in Syracuse Monday at dark, I heard the phone ringing. Helen died yesterday, Erin told me from the other end of the line, her words a picture of a human being's last moments on earth—her final hours with Helen.

"I sat by her bed. 'Helen, it's Erin. I'm here for you,' I whispered. Helen lay motionless, eyes wide open and focused ahead.

"'Helen?' I asked.

"This time, Helen turned her wide gazing eyes on me, her tiny forefinger to her lips, "Shh," she whispered. "She's here."

"Who's here?" I asked.

"The Blessed Mother," she whispered and pointed to the

foot of her bed. "The Blessed Mother has been here all morning— waiting for me."

"I couldn't speak. I got into Helen's bed and held her in my arms and after a while we dozed and suddenly I was awake— Helen had poked me in the ribs."

"What, Helen?" I asked, alarmed. 'What is it? What can I do for you?'

"Look! She's leaving!," she whispered excitedly, pointing to the foot of the bed. 'The Blessed Mother is leaving.'" Erin watched Helen's eyes follow the Virgin Mary upwards.

Erin's voice faded away and I waited.

"She—she died a short time later, Dick, and do you know what I believe? I believe she knew the Blessed Mother had come to take her away," Erin said.

I waited again. I didn't want to ask about Helen's eyes. But Erin said, "Her eyes, Dick—her eyes had such a look of peace."

And later that night I wrote in my journal: "Helen, Erin's dear friend, made peace with God through his Blessed Mother."

The March wind pounced on the house and shook windows and I saw out the back door the rush of flinty clouds. And far above the clouds, Helen's earthly life had been mended by the pull of God's eternity. Decay and death had taken wings. To my right, stood the garage where long ago I had smelled the roses and had made the Pilgrim Rosary. I had come a long way. Tomorrow, before the sun was up, I would be on the road again. I would map out my talk and prayers at St. Barbara's Catholic Church, Winchester, Massachusetts, where Father Vince Malone had invited me for a Marian evening and healing service. I would phone two Knights of Columbus insurance prospects and Rich about his brilliant plan for marketing Tuff Cuff.

I closed the door on the night but not the dark of my mind. Keep going like this, I told myself, and you can claim the prize.

Half way down the hall, I stopped, and thought, *Prize? I meant sign.* And I went off to bed.

The March clouds, clean as ice, raced across the brow of a long climb but I looked too late to slow down and I was urged to the shoulder of the interstate by a blinking light and low siren wail. The young trooper noted that the radar had clocked me at eighty and he had also noted on his way from his cruiser the crumpled hat decorated with Immigration and Nationalization Service insignia. "Keep it down," he said, pocketing the pad. I drove on, toward a rack of dirtier clouds that scudded the black prickles of leafless trees. You never could tell about March. You most always could about the law enforcement brotherhood. The fact that for a long time now I had been an INS officer gladdened my heart.

The bright March day closed to a night of chill. But inside St. Barbara's Church, candles on the altar burned in the warmth of the organ's low notes that seemed to give life to Our Blessed Mother's white and gray vestments and an inner fire to the stones of the Pilgrim Rosary. *Is this you, Dick Bingold?* I took my place to the left of the pulpit and began my witness. The choir balcony hung black above the crowded daubs of bright faces. *Tonight?* I asked in spite of myself. *Will it be tonight?* And I began.

By late afternoon the next day, I put the key into the lock of my front door and went inside, straight to our small home altar and prayed. At the St. Barbara's Church service, Father Swizdore's illness was brought to my attention, and I now asked God to be with him. And I asked God to give me strength to imitate Father Swizdore and Padre Pio. Still elated by the service, I prayed for humility and when I had finished praying, I stood up and walked to my office. *You're doing well...*I sat down at my desk and, according to Father Swizdore's instructions, prepared to write in my journal. But before pen had touched paper, the sentence completed itself, *You're doing well, Dick. You're a O.K. You're doing fine. The sign will come. You'll see.* And I wrote.

"After I testified at St. Barbara, it seemed everyone stayed to be prayed over with the Pilgrim Rosary, perhaps two hundred. Among them were two sisters, Pat and Ginny G. They were crying and shared with me the fact that they were manic-depressives, and so was their younger brother. Their drunken father went into rages and beat them and now they were both married to men who abused them, one verbally, the other physically. Ginny had just been released from the hospital where she had been taken after a suicide attempt.

"Pat and Ginny asked me not to pray for them but rather for their girl friend, Susan, who was dying of cancer. She had been in remission and had come out of it. They didn't give her much time. As I always do, I prayed for the sisters who wanted to be proxy for their friend. I thought about their act of love for their friend and asked the Holy Spirit to descend into all their hearts and heal them if it was in accordance with the will of God. The sisters returned to their seats.

"When we were closing up, Father Malone came to me. 'Please go and talk to those two women,' he said, nodding toward the last pew. 'They are crying and very upset.' I walked back and found that the two women were Pat and Ginny. I asked whether they could make it home O.K. They then related to me their terrible lives, Prozac, depression, family problems.

"Have you ever asked Our Lord to remove your depression? I asked them. They looked at me like I was crazy and I said, Come with me, let's go ask him. And I brought them to the altar and said, Kneel here and ask Our Mother and Our Lord for his mercy—to remove your illness from you. Pray from the bottom of your heart. When I was putting away Our Lady of Medjugorje and the Pilgrim Rosary, I heard Pat and Ginny G. talking to Our Lord and when we closed up, Pat said to me she and her sister felt God's healing love." Then I added a note: "Don't forget Jamie Sweeney!"

What was that! I flung down my pen down and wheeled. Nobody. Nothing. The wind bumped the house and sanded the windowpanes with granules of icy rain. I shivered and went to bed.

****

The next morning, I woke with fever and chills and took aspirin and drank juice and went back to bed and slept. About noon, a burning sensation in my stomach woke me and when I put my hand there, I felt a swelling. A list of meetings I had set up, I cancelled and went back to sleep. When I woke late in the afternoon, I felt better, but because my stomach still hurt, I made an appointment to see my doctor the next day. I guessed that an old hernia had acted up and that a bout of flu had caused the chills.

My doctor agreed and, to prepare for surgery to repair the hernia, he sent me on to another doctor who, after tests, asked if I had ever had a heart attack. I told him never but that a boat accident seventeen years ago had broken ribs the splinters of which might have damaged my heart. I showed the accident's other memorials: the chewed-up tongue, pointed to locations of the cracked scapula and collar bone, broken left arm, and the dents left by rods that helped cement jawbones that had been broken in nine places. And for good measure, I bragged about scars from my eleven auto accidents.

"You're a survivor," he said, wrote on a pad, and ripped off the sheet that sent me on to Dr. Bill Berkery for a stress test that I passed with flying colors. But with a warning: The thickness of my heart muscles could have only one cause: a great deal of stress, for which he prescribed a small pill to be taken once a day, in the morning. And although the hernia operation was a snap, I found myself back in Dr. Bill Berkery's office several weeks later.

Because on my first visit he had told me about his little boy, Matthew, I had given Dr. Bill Berkery and each of his nurses the calling-card-size photo of Our Lady of Medjugorje holding the

Pilgrim Rosary. A rare lung disease had, since his birth, kept Matthew on a liquid diet and on respirators twenty-four hours a day. And now we made arrangements for Dr. Bill Berkery, his wife, Darcy, and Matthew to attend our prayer group the moment he felt up to it. Proud that I had been able to offer comfort, I went home and waited.

The flinty March skies softened to the foregiving fleece of April. I paid a staggering car repair bill, stayed on the road, met with Rich and my friend to try to come to grips with dwindling Tuff Cuff sales, walked into and out of a dozen homes, selling insurance, attended mass and several Eucharistic Adorations a week, scheduled a half dozen Pilgrim Rosary sessions at as many points on the compass, smoothed the wrinkles in my plans for the next trip to Medjugorje—this time with twenty pilgrims—and awaited the Office of the Bishop of Syracuse to grant me permission to speak in Catholic parishes and looked forward to the day I would receive a letter signed by the bishop himself, the Most Rev. James M. Moynihan, and see for myself his signature with the Cross, it was said, he always placed in the loop of the "J."

In the meantime, I cleared away a block of time to talk face-to-face with Father John Mijckalous, the Binghamton priest who last year had blocked my appearance at a Marian conference. I phoned him and, on my way to another parish for a talk and prayers, I stopped off at St. Joseph's Catholic Church, Binghamton, for a meeting.

I walked in on him when he was preparing for mass and, after introductions, we walked to the right, by the first pew where something caught my eye—I wasn't sure what—and out a side door and into his study. From behind his desk, he looked at me cautiously and, with a smile, I got to the point of my visit: had he cautioned against my appearance at last year's Marian conference?

An honest man, Father Mijckaolous didn't duck. Yes, he said, he had.

Why?

He wanted me to know his objection wasn't personal. On the contrary, it was rooted in his belief that only those apparition sites, like Lourdes or Fatima, approved by the Holy See and the Pope were free of the abuse of blaspheme. He listed several arguments from theology and noted that my ministry took life from a statue of Our Lady of Medjugorje, the place where visionaries say they see the Blessed Mother, the place where I had picked stones to create the Pilgrim Rosary—and it had not been approved by the Pope.

"Are you a theologian, Father?"

He paused. "No, I'm not," he said with emphasis.

"Neither am I," I said and sat up straight and smiled. "But I believe that good works disprove blaspheme—good fruit can't come from bad roots."

I looked at Father Mijckalous and saw my own doubts reflected in him. My own guilt. My own—pride. The Devil could not bring million-and-a-half people a year to Medjugorje, could he? Why couldn't he? What if…What if he had brought me? Why then couldn't he bring millions?

I felt defenseless and grasped at a shadow, thinking: *What did you see near the first pew when you walked out here with Father Mjckaolous?* And then it came clear.

"I saw that you have a statue of Our Lady of Medjugorje, Father."

He looked at me—then nodded.

"Have you visited Medjugorje?" I asked.

"Yes," he said. A moment of silence, then: "That's my *personal* statue."

I waited for him to tell me more but when his silence lasted too long, I stood up and we said goodbye, between us the shimmer of a shared feeling that both of us had learned something. Most of the way back to Syracuse, I broke the speed limit. Once, at very high speed, the grating light of the racing guardrail broke in on me like guilt and I remembered what Father Bill had said: How crucial it is for men to forgive—wives, sweethearts, parents—and themselves.

At a roadside cafe of wood painted red and a neon light hung crooked, I noted the young man at the bar, paid the three-sixty and carried the Coke and juicy hamburger, garnished with tomato and lettuce and onions and green peppers, to a booth whose seatbacks had been rubbed smooth by a half century of vanished generations. The sandwich fell apart each time I began to chew until at last I got it right and finished it off with even orderly bites, drinking the Coke meanwhile. At the counter I asked and paid for a Coke to take with me.

"I'm not guilty and I'm not proud," the young man at the bar said. From the looks of it, he had had one too many—Johnny Walker Black on ice. "The only thing I am, is—wanna know what I am? Well, do you?"

"Sure," I said.

"Doubtful," he said. "And that makes me proud and guilty. To tell y'the truth, I'm guilty as hell and guilt, m'friend is nuttin' but pride. And listen—ever occur t'you that we all live by signs and don't know what's behind them? Ever that happen to you?"

"Don't mind Jimmy," the gaunt woman behind the counter said. "My sister's boy—a philosopher. Went to Harvard and plays the banjo and has hives and makes honey."

"My aunt," Jimmy said with a wink and another drink.

It was midnight when I got home and punched in the key of my answering machine. Dr. Bill Berkery asked me to call him back and Ginny G. said she must talk to me as soon as possible. But I was not to call her; she would call me. I smiled into the dark and sighed.

Our prayer group, assembled once more in Barbara Stiles' third-floor walk-up in Syracuse, heard footfall on the stairs. I opened the door in time to see Darcy's spring-like profile, her eyes turned to watch Dr. Bill, Matthew in his arms, ascend the last step. Father and son looked straight at me, their faces shuttering into and out of each other's, the man's radiance filling the Christ-like suffering in the boy's face and that suffering in turn printing themselves on the man's

The group's heart and mind went out to the mother and father and little boy in a rush. Your average baseball cap would have covered little Matthew to his tiny shoulders. I placed the Pilgrim Rosary in a loose ring about his sparkling eyes and began to pray. My silence made room for a second prayer and the second, a third, a rise and a fall, like the limbs and arms of one body. When the family was about to leave, I prayed over them all, but when we watched them by the door—then saw them off, down the stairs—I knew what each of us was thinking: Would the mercy of God descend on this life of this little boy? Would the Holy Spirit come to little Matthew's rescue? We said goodnight to each other and went our several ways into our private lives.

I put the phone to my ear. "You probably don't remember me," said a woman's voice. "I'm Ginny, one of the two sisters you prayed over at St. Barbara's. I have a wonderful story to tell you. My sister Pat and I haven't experienced a moment of depression since that night. I'm off Prozac and Pat is almost off hers. We have had the most peaceful Christmas of our lives—our husbands went back to the sacraments—we are so happy.

"But that's not why I called you," she said. A cloud settled in the room. Was she calling to tell me about bad news? I turned on a light. "Well, remember my girl friend, Susan, we prayed for? Well, we called her the next morning to tell her what a wonderful evening we experienced. Did I tell you that Susan couldn't be at St. Barbara's that night because she was bleeding so bad her husband wouldn't let her out of the house?

"She asked what time was it that we prayed for her—we said it was around seven and she stated that around that time she felt different—better—and she went to check on herself and she wasn't bleeding and Mr. Bingold— she called me yesterday and told me she had been back to Boston General several times and they cannot find one trace of leukemia! Mr. Bingold?"

"Yes?"

"You there?"

"I'm here."

"Praise Jesus!" I said.

"Oh, yes, praise Jesus!"

"Surely the Holy Spirit because of the love of you and Pat for Susan saw to it that all of you were healed," I said, and went on in a room floating in April sunlight, "what gifts flow from Jesus to those who trust in him."

"Thank you, Mr. Bingold. Oh, thank you, Mr. Bingold."

"Ginny," I said. "God bless."

Toward the end of April, Bruce Ellavsky called from Boston to ask if he could see me: he wanted to talk. Back in March, at St. Barbara's Church, I had prayed with a woman who had asked me to pray over her nephew, Jamie Sweeney, in a coma at the Veteran's Rehab Center in Boston since a car accident last year. And so Bruce and I met at the Center.

When I asked about Jamie, the nurse let her head sway

darkly. "Spastic paralysis," she murmured.

The hallway—echoing with the squeak of thick-soled nurse shoes—shined with well-run chill.

I took the Pilgrim Rosary from its black case and approached the bed. The lids of Jamie's eyes fluttered, his hands twitched, his bone-thin arms and elbows flicked to and from his frail body, his feet jerked.

"Jamie," I said in a subdued voice, "my name is Dick Bingold and this is my friend, Bruce Ellavsky."

I leaned down. The invasion of rippling twitches sped on. The young nurse looked on, mute, skeptical. Bead-by-bead, I placed the Pilgrim Rosary on the pillow above Jamie's head and then across his chest. Bruce and I exchanged a glance: had we seen a sudden calm? My thumb left the sign of the cross on skin thin as the membrane inside an eggshell and then my hand just barely touched the pitching head. I closed my eyes and Bruce and I began to pray and Jamie's head jerked and his body shuddered and we prayed and I thought I felt the head slow but wasn't sure and so went on with the prayer until, once again, I seemed to feel a change in the head's rhythm and this time it was for real: it was motionless. I opened my eyes and looked down at Jamie: he lay there in a peaceful doze.

The nurse, seeing us to the door, popped to the surface of her skepticism, shook her head, raised her eyebrows, and nodded.

Bruce and I said goodbye in the parking lot of a Burger King where, over coffee, hamburger, and french fries, we talked about Medjugorje and then about how much better he felt after praying with me—and just talking.

"Hey," he said. "That nurse—you made a believer of her."

We laughed.

"Where to now?" he asked.

"Who knows?" I said.

He chuckled. "No, I mean, now—today."

I told him I would swing by Moodus, Connecticut to see my spiritual mentor and guide, Father Bill McCarthy, then head back to Syracuse.

"*You* need a spiritual guide?" he asked, turning away from me to edge into the driver's seat. He looked up at me over his elbow.

"*Everybody* needs a spiritual guide," I said, then added, not meaning to, "and an unmistakable sign."

"Unmistakable sign?"

"A definite sign that you're doing God's will—doing God's work."

Bruce pulled his elbow in and turned on the engine then put his elbow out again and said, "You mean like today—with Jamie."

And back on the interstate, heading for Moodus, I wondered if Bruce didn't have a point.

I phoned Monique and Patrick from a pay station north of Springfield, Massachusetts and got back to Syracuse after midnight. From the battlefields around Medjugorje the late news over the car radio had brought ominous warnings of dark streams of the dispossessed, arrests, mass graves and killings.

Toward morning, I fell into a deep troubled sleep. Once I woke out of a dream that God had given me that unmistakable sign.

But the next time I became aware of myself, I lay paralyzed, spread-eagle, only half awake, amazed: I could not move a muscle, not even the fingers at the end of my outstretched arms. But then, when I came fully awake, I discovered that an outside force held me prisoner: A massive, glutinous pillar of pressure, as if I lay at the bottom of a cylinder beneath a piston's downward thrust.

I wasn't afraid. I fought back. I planned every move. Inch-by-inch, I dragged my hands to my hips. Then, ticking off the seconds, I tightened each muscle one by one and when the time came, I pushed with my hands, twisted my hips, and rolled out from under. When I hit the floor, I didn't hear the thud and when I stood up, I felt no pain.

As I shaved and showered and dressed, I prayed the rosary, and when I sat behind the wheel, on my way to a Tuff Cuff meeting, I wondered out loud, baffled and astonished—and shamed: I should have expected the nightmare; should have known I still plodded about in the dark wood; should have known conversion stood for a beginning, not an end.

When I got to the office, Rich greeted me with bad news: Sales of Tuff Cuff had dipped and a shipment had been been rejected. Tense and gloomy, our meeting ended in a stalemate: Though I kept my cool, we couldn't agree on how to proceed. And when the phone rang, Rich handed it to me but the line went dead. "I couldn't catch the woman's name," Rich said. We agreed to meet in a couple of days to decide where to go from here. For now, I had three home calls to make for Knights of Columbus Insurance. And as I went out the door, I wondered: Who had called me on the phone? Was the nightmare a punishment or a warning?

All the insurance calls turned to ashes. At a dingy restaurant on a side street near a shopping mall with half the stores empty, I ate a hot roast beef sandwich drenched in hot gravey, a piece of lemon meringue pie with two cups of coffee and drove home through pouring rain. The house cried out with the absence of Monique and Patrick and on the answering machine the message from the realtor told me a prospective buyer had declined our offer. Sid, of Sid and Mary, the couple I had called on to sell insurance, told me they had decided not to buy a policy at this time.

Then, just about bedtime, the phone rang, Dr. Bill Berkery on the line. He said Darcy had tried to call me at my office this afternoon but had been cut off. For himself, he wanted to tell me that Matthew had shown extraordinary improvement. I strode about, the phone to my ear. Now Darcy came on the line.

She was laughing. Just eight hours ago, she had phoned a friend she was to meet the next day, and in the course of the conversation, she mentioned that she had only then put the finishing touches on the evening meal—spaghetti and meatballs. Behind her in his highchair, Matthew sat quietly but the moment she put down the phone, he shouted a word she couldn't make out. She turned round.

"What did you say, Matthew?"

And with all the breath and voice he could muster, he shouted the first word he had ever uttered:

"Meatball!"

"And Dick," Darcy said over the phone, "I put a meatball on his plate, broke it up with a fork and Matthew *ate* the first solid food of his life!"

The next day, when I drove to the post office with a stack of correspondence to do with my next trip to Medjugorje, I laughed.

Now there's God's unmistakable sign—meatballs.

Chapter Thirty-One

Baptism

The bus gears ground rubber-clad wheels heavily against the concrete that climbed yard-by-yard to the peak from which we could look far down through a film of blue haze and see the double spires of St. James Church. Bloody torrents of the dispossessed and mass killings flooded the valleys round about Medjugorje but Medjugorje itself lay living and untouched, a-shine in Mary's glory.

Beside me in the car sat my daughter, Barbara. For a very long time, I had wanted her to inhale the area's health and holiness and had pleaded with her to go with me. It had given me the chance I wanted, to talk—to tell her how sorry I was for the kind of father I had been and help her look at the pain she felt because of it. No matter, when all is said and done, children are certainly one of God's greatest blessings.

But now, as the car crawled up the mountainside, I regretted I had invited her, for who had not heard how many times during the Balkan wars pilots had mistaken cars like ours for the enemy and strafed them with machine-gun fire. And I worried about my new godson, Aldi Skegro, and whether he might this moment lie dead beneath Mostar rubble.

I prayed the rosary and chewed old themes. Here I was, taking my daughter to an apparition site when I myself had never seen Mary or received from her or Jesus Christ a clear unmistakable sign even though the path I had taken the past several years lay strewn with hints. I had been converted—

brought back to my faith—and yet in what way had I changed? Had I, since then, experienced one full day of peace? Had my appetites died away? The only thing certain in life was God's plan. But who could fathom it? I passionately wanted to trust God but would I be waylaid by some dark destiny? A...I pushed the idea down—it surfaced, sank, surfaced once more: Would I— I turned away, came back to it: *would I die a martyr?*

Yet...hadn't I got everything I wanted?

On my desk back home lay the letter I had prayed for and worked for, from Most Rev. James M. Moynihan, the cross, sure enough, in the "J's" loop of his signature. "I grant [Richard Bingold] permission to speak in your diocese/parish as it pertains to his testimony of conversion leading him back to the practice of his Catholic faith."

The car labored toward the peak. You could smell the engine's heat.

And the Bishop's second letter. My heart thudded. Father Bill McCarthy's large kind face came into my mind's eye. At a weekend healing service at My Father's House in Moodus, Connecticut, he had asked me to testify and, with the Pilgrim Rosary, to pray over all who came forward. A woman, held by two men, whispered to me that her name was Linda and that she had meneires disease. Though I didn't know what it was, I placed by hands over her ears, not on her head, and prayed. She rested in the spirit and when she woke she was helped to her seat.

Several months later, a caller from his office informed me that Bishop Moynihan wished to see me. After a cordial greeting, he indicated a letter from, he said, a Mrs. Stapleton of Cheshire, Connecticut. At his request, I had brought along the Pilgrim Rosary and when he had questioned me closely about it and my ministry, he handed me the letter.

Breathless, I read that the writer suffered from meneires, a disease of the inner ear and then in the last paragraph the lines, *"I drove to the retreat at My Father's House…and I heard Richard Bingold speak. I was deeply moved and felt in my heart that he should pray over me with the Pilgrim Rosary of Medjugoje. I was completely healed of all spinning and today I am functioning normally.*

The signature jumped out at me: *Linda* Stapleton.

"I am sure that your recent healing of Meneires Disease has been a gift from God," Bishop Moynihan had written in reply. Now *his* words leaped out at me: *I know Richard Bingold and know him to be a very faithful and practicing Catholic, deeply devoted to Our Blessed Mother and the healings that she has brought about in his own life. Consequently, like yourself, I believe that he is truly God's instrument…"*

The engine strained, coughed, and eased the toiling car over the peak into the sunlight. Below us, the rack of clouds that shadowed the valleys of Medjugorje and Mostar now and again drifted open to display a miniature strip of field or roof of house or the gleaming spires of St. James Church. *Doesn't the sacrament of the Holy Eucharist unite you with Christ?* We began our descent. The sudden question wiped the smile from my face. Its correlate had hit home: If I need more than the Holy Eucharist to signal God's approval, then I'm infected by pride. Gas fumes? A faint stench wormed its way through the car.

In the small restaurant, not far from Vicka's house, we drank coffee and ate our favorite Medjugorje dishes. The sun shone through a window. Several people went by in the street. Beyond them, I could see the road that lay through the fields and into the mountains over which we had driven.

Next to Barbara and I, sat Lara Klepec. From the start, she and her family and I had become close friends, bonds that you know in your heart will last a lifetime. Our interpreter, Lara had made this pilgrimmage the smoothest ever, waiting as she did on my every word to relate it to Aldi and his mom.

Now Lara Klepec's lips moved and I caught in the blast of voices her words. "Dear little one." I leaned closer. I knew she meant my new godson, eight-year-old Aldi Skegro. Yesterday afternoon, we had crossed the mountain into Mostar and met Aldi and his mother, Nery. She showed us new repairs to the apartment, spoke to Barbara and me through Lara, and smiled darkly. Aldi stayed close. He laughed when I told him I wanted to try on his jacket; his eyes still had the steady look of his photo and his lips its suggestion of a quiver. Hardly twenty-four months had gone by since, in nearby street fighting, Aldi's dad and Nery's husband, Milenko, had been killed by a mortar shell. When we said goodbye I took Aldi's small hand in mine to make a seal, to make him know that he had a friend—a godfather—for life.

Now from the small restaurant's talk and clatter, we walked toward the twin spires of St. James Church for an hour of Eucharistic Adoration. Being suddenly outdoors made us look up, out and around. The old village and the ancient fields and the sunlit wave of the distant mountain burst on us bright, new, and high. And though we walked into the shadow of the nave and sat down in our pews, the sunburst of the monstrance around the Host carried us beyond the fields and peaks to those dark mysteries of hope and grace. Would it all forever be so beyond me? Out of my reach? Beyond my understanding? Envy? How could I envy Vicka? But I did. And tears flowed down my cheeks.

On our last night at Medjugorje, I said goodnight to Barbara and went to my room, said my prayers, and climbed into bed. Through an open window, I heard the dying hum of a village settling down to sleep. But I was keyed up by our early departure—we had to be up at two to be off on the bus to Split where we would board our flight to Zagreb—and sleep was out of the question.

I got up and went out. I would climb Apparition Hill to the Little Grotto of the Blue Cross to pray one more rosary. As I toiled upward slowly, stepping thoughtfully to avoid the stones, misty stars and moist breezes settled like the world's first summer on my heart. Then village lights winked out, one by one and turned houses into blocks of black shadow and misty stars into bright beacons.

I struck a match to several candles and kneeled and stated my intention, to pray for humility, and raised my right hand to my forehead to begin the sign of the cross—and stopped. What was that! I shook my head and listened. The mountains to the north released peals of thunder, then the night settled in again. And I began to pray again and again whatever it was came humming out of the dark. Then I made it out. A voice calling…

"Richard," it seemed to say in the syllables of a breeze. "Richard."

I jumped up. Was Barbara playing a joke on me? I peered here and there and saw and heard nothing. A call to her died in my throat. My heart raced. I was afraid. From the mountain, came another roll of thunder. I waited, took a candle, shaded it with my hand and peered over its feeble flame into the dark.

"Barbara?" I called out dismally. "If that's you, it's not funny. Come out—now."

Nothing. No reply. No Barbara.

I took a deep breath, uttered a Hail Mary, and tried to calm myself—but to no effect—and walked out of the candlelight into the shadows and listened again and tried to remember my mother's voice when she called me "Richard" and in the flow of memory I saw bother John and sister Irene and an avenue of trees bent down by a soundless storm and the kick of a noiseless rifle and broken glass shining silently into the dusk—and then I remembered—and then turned back, walked into the light of guttering candles, and kneeled and prayed the rosary, all fifteen decades of it.

Then I was walking among the stones down the mountain without heeding my steps. How many times as a boy had I wished to call myself "Richard" and how many times, since my life began fresh in that snowy Vermont field, had I wished to do the same? And now I had done it. A priest had baptized me "Richard" at the font. Now, out of the God's plan from which all things come, I had stepped into the name meant for me. I had completed a lap on that ever-widening arc. A noose of joy pulled eternity tight. I wanted to sing.

Chapter Thirty-Two

World of Promise?

The sun's bright eye watched our flight from Zagreb to Frankfurt and from there almost to New York, but we didn't see Kennedy International Airport until clouds trailed upward and we downward across a metal gleam of sea and the mist and spit flying from the flick of runway lights.

Barbara and I had talked all the way, exchanging remarks and reliving the week's gifts. As we ate our airline dinners, Barbara said,

"One thing is certain, I'll always call you 'Dad.'"

We both laughed at me calling her name out of the dark. And she pressed my hand and smiled when I told her that when I got back to Vermont, I would ask Monique to marry me—in a Catholic ceremony—and that I had kept the approval of my annulment secret to surprise her. The event on the mountain still made my heart sing. But when the jet stopped and we unbuckled our seatbelts, I faced reality. When I got back to Syracuse, I would have to close the Tuff Cuff office and take over sales and promotion from my friend and Rich. Though all three of us knew it had to be done, it was left up to me to do it.

The drive north up the interstate out of New York City seemed to take hours and hours, over a road clogged with cars and dismally slick with rain. West of Albany, I stopped to eat and, back on the road, realized I hadn't smiled or tipped the waitress. I ticked off the rosary and the miles together and when south of Troy I saw the clouds break and the sun shine, I woke to a murmur in my brain. Though I couldn't for the life of me clear it up, it was something to the effect that my change of name had drastically changed my life, in ways only God in his wisdom and good time would reveal.

I drove on and watched the exit signs and the names of towns and the signs for sharp curves and the signs that told me the speed limits and then I gazed far out along a concrete and grass divider that stretched far beyond any sign that I could see, into an indefinite blue.

It was three in the afternoon when I walked into our office in Syracuse and my old friend and Rich greeted me with their own plan. They were uneasy and looked gloomily about. But it wasn't long until the three of us were smiling: Their plan matched mine exactly, for their reasoning had taken them to the same destination. The Tuff Cuff double-loop wrist restraint would never be a big item and its sale and marketing could be handled by one person—me. That evening we celebrated our decision at a restaurant with steak, french fries, and wine for Rich and my old friend. We shook hands and went our separate ways.

Toward morning, I woke up lying on my right side and sensed someone's presence in my room. I turned over slowly and saw between the foot of my bed and the bedroom door, the true presence of Our Lord and Savior, Jesus Christ Himself.

He stood at a slight angle to me, his arms outstretched, his eyes tilted back, evidently looking up. On the surface of the ceiling a gold light shone. When he lowered his face slightly, I saw that he wore a crown of thorns that, like fishhooks, pierced his skin in two places, where the thorns went in and where they came out. His bloodshot eyes shone from a face beaten and black and blue. His Adam's apple was very pronounced and so were his cheekbones which were high on his face. Dark blood caked his hair.

He wore a crimson-colored, exquisite robe, like a king would wear, with big bell sleeves, now pulled back from his wrists and exposing the wounds in his hands. Behind each hand shined a golden sun whose rays pierced the wounds and sent misty shafts of gold upward.

Now I saw that his robe opened full length to reveal a creamy white tunic, open at the neck and embroidered by tiny flowers.

He stood motionless and seemed to look at the golden light above his head. He did not look at me or speak to me. I struggled up and now sat frozen, unable to move. I just watched.

At last I heard myself say, "I want to hold you. Please don't leave."

From where I lay, I could not see his feet. Behind his Precious Head a larger sun shone and I knew God stood there.

****

My beautiful partner of nineteen years, Monique, and my handsome son of sixteen years, Patrick, stood each side of me. Before us, prayer book in hand, stood Rev. Ronald Bill, my priest and spiritual guide. No stretch limo or hundred-foot yacht waited outside Sacred Heart Church, Cicero, New York. There would be a simple meal and a gathering of close friends, among them, Margaret Reith, who now stood by as witness.

For Monique and I were about to hear our names spoken in the marriage rites of the Roman Catholic Church. We were to be united by one of the seven sacraments of our faith, Matrimony, of which St. Thomas Aquinas wrote, *The indivisibility of Matrimony shows forth the indivisible union of Christ and his church.* I had both come back home.

I had all but lifted from my shoulders one of those terrible burdens of life: closing an office in which you've spent many years of your life, a painful process for pack-rats like me. However, I had thrown away enough for two trips to the dump. Now I had to pack my car, head for a talk and prayer meeting and, at long last, drive to Vermont and home.

I had already talked to Monique and Patrick by phone and, impatient to be gone, I yanked one of my posters from the trunk—and jerked back, a sharp pain jabbing my eye.

In the bathroom mirror I saw the cause: a splinter of wood from the sign had torn the cornea. I washed it out, finished my packing, and hoped for the best. But the next morning, I found that the eye had become bloodshot and infected and decided to go to outpatient unit of a hospital nearby, even though I had no medical insurance.

But distracted by preparations for the trip, I kept putting it off, until about five, when going out the door, I heard the phone ring and found Margaret Reith on the other end, asking me to attend the Mass for Anointing of the Sick at St. Steven's, a Polish Catholic church where the rail at the altar still remains. I told her about the eye, and she agreed to take me to outpatient after the service. The eye throbbed.

The pastor, Father Gleba, and another Polish priest stood before a packed church and when he called on us to come to the altar rail for the anointing of the sick, I made my way in the glimmering light, guided by my one good eye. I kneeled and waited and prayed and when the priest blessed my forehead I asked God to remove all the crazy thoughts that come into my head every day and when he blessed the palms of my hands, I asked God to allow me to continue to do his work on earth—I would ask no more than that—no more than the life he had given me—no more than the morning of golden light. No more.

Back in the pew, I kneeled and prayed then looked about the lovely church, filled shoulder-to-shoulder by people of all walks of life, the votive candles flickering, the statue of Our Blessed Mother glowing in her robes and the golden lights of the altar shining about Our Savior on the Cross. How beautiful and sad, how temporary yet eternal and I saw Dad and Mom and my sister and brother beside me and my five children and my dear Monique and a dark feeling of unworthiness and waste overcame me. Tears from my good eye and tears from my injured eye flowed down my face. Instead of being beneath the water, I stood this side of it, on the ever-shifting, changing, burgeoning land of faith.

Richard, I thought, *you can't do that.*

And I answered, *Oh, but I can.*

And I prayed: *Would you, God, heal my eye for me now as an unmistakable sign that I am doing your will and that you hear my prayers.*

And I said, *Lord, I'm not afraid of the pain. I can deal with it.*

And I said, *Should you heal my eye right now, I would know you hear me.*

And I heard a *ping!* like a tuning fork and felt a pressure ever so soft, like a finger on the lid and I said under my breath,

"Jesus, I trust in you," and to myself,

"If you trust in God, open your eyes."

I did—and I immediately realized that the eye had been healed. I rolled the eye in my socket, trying to discern some pain—any pain. I laughed out loud then whispered to Margaret,

"Look at my eye."

She glanced at it, then away, then back again.

"Richard," she said. "What happened?"

Outside, on a street corner of cars and people and fresh night wind, I told Margaret Reith what I had said to God, she looked at me critically, said,

"I can't believe you challenged God like that."

For once, I had nothing to say. But after Margaret and I had said goodnight and I had driven for several hours, heading for Vermont and home, I braked just in time to miss a deer, standing, his face toward me, frozen in place by my headlights.

And I drove on, thinking, *How bright and blinding the light in the eyes, the deer unable to leap or flee—robbed of God's grace. How dark, lost.*

Sometime later, at the sign of a single light hung over white clapboard and *EATS* painted across a sheet glass, I pulled over for a cup of coffee. But when I stepped into a smallish room of empty booths, a counter with white napkins—everything immaculate—it was empty. I called out, walked back through the kitchen, and out on a narrow lawn bordering a wide dark lake.

I looked out. A number of small boats bobbed about, pulling at their moorings, their chains creaking in the dark.

How dark, I thought.

"Whatcha doin' out here, friend?"

I staggered around groggily. How I needed sleep.

"Looking for a cup of coffee."

"Out here?

"No, in there."

"Well, come on in there then. None out here."

We walked back through the immaculate kitchen into the immaculate room of booths and white napkins. I waited. The man—thin and gaunt and gentle—brewed a fresh pot and handed me a white cup and we sat down and drank coffee together.

"How many boats you got?"

"Boats?"

"Out back."

He looked at me. "Those are cows."

I began to wake up. "Then that's not a lake?"

"Good thing I'm here to serve y'coffee, wouldn't y'say? Nope, nobody's goin' to drown in that lake."

We had a second cup of coffee.

"Usual for y'to cross the line like that? Go where yer not supposed to?"

I stood up, still groggy. He leaned against his counter, spreadeagle.

"I couldn't find anyone here," I said. "I was in a bad way, so I went looking."

He wore a scraggily pointed beard. "I'll always remember you thinkin' it a lake. I've always wanted to set sail. Step out. Step across. You're a good sort."

We said goodnight and I set off again, behind headlights that reached not very far into the dark. And I thought how it had been, when I began my journey to God. How it had been.

Bleak and dark, frought with danger and evil, and yet, though my destiny was dark, God, in His wisdom, guided me to the light of love on the hillside of Medjugorje where I discovered through Our Blessed Mother the true meaning of love.

Ahead of me on the narrow road, red warning lights blinked.

The true meaning of love of God and my fellowman and, yes, the necessity to love oneself. For...

I braked in time to miss a small truck turning on a road that ran between two trees that framed the twinkle of lights on a broad lake. Printed on the back of the truck were the words, *Mirror and Windshield Doctor.*

I stepped on the accelerator and my thoughts ran on,

...For only in loving oneself can one avoid the self-destructiveness born of self-contempt. And only in loving oneself, despite his imperfections, can one accept the imperfections of others.

And I drove on and on, a strange feeling building.

I lay in the doorway, a drunk, and Monique walked around me, disgusted.

In a state of perdition, headed for hell, I sank beneath the waves.

In a state of grace, I kneeled at the cross on Medjugorje's holy hill.

And the feeling grew. My hands gripped the steering wheel. Hands of healing.

Hands doubled to fists, now open to healing.

A feeling of joy.

Who needs signs in a world full of promise? Full of God? I would be home pretty soon. Home with those I love. To a life of service. My life of healing had begun.